The Definitive
FIREBIRD &
TRANS AM

Facts, Figures and Features of Pontiac's
Legendary Firebirds & Trans Ams

GUIDE 1967–1969

Rocky Rotella

CarTech®

CarTech®, Inc.
838 Lake Street South
Forest Lake, MN 55025
Phone: 651-277-1200 or 800-551-4754
Fax: 651-277-1203
www.cartechbooks.com

Edit by Bob Wilson
Layout by Monica Seiberlich

ISBN 978-1-61325-149-2
Item No. CT530

Library of Congress Cataloging-in-Publication Data

Names: Rotella, Rocky, author.
Title: The definitive Firebird and Trans Am guide 1967-1969 / Rocky Rotella.
Description: Forest Lake, MN : CarTech, [2016] | Includes index.
Identifiers: LCCN 2016003429 | ISBN 9781613251492
Subjects: LCSH: Firebird automobile–History. | Muscle cars–United States–History.
Classification: LCC TL215.F57 R68 2016 | DDC 629.222/2–dc23
LC record available at https://lccn.loc.gov/2016003429

Written, edited, and designed in the U.S.A.
Printed in China
10 9 8 7 6 5 4 3 2 1

Front Cover: *After posting stellar sales volume in 1968, Pontiac had positioned the 1969 Firebird as a rising star in a field of hot-running late-1960s performance cars. To maintain exclusivity, a handful of special-order exterior colors were limited to the Firebird line. Code-72 Carousel Red (an eye-popping shade of orange most commonly associated with the 1969 GTO Judge) was among those finishes at model year startup.*

Front Flap: *The 1967 Firebird used the same body shell as Chevrolet's Camaro. Although the silhouettes were quite similar, Pontiac used specific front and rear treatments and well as unique exterior styling cues to create a four-seat sports car that exuded Pontiac identity and looked very much unlike a Camaro from this angle.*

End Papers: *Although Firebird details leaked out and a general press release was distributed in January 1967, the first opportunity most consumers had to view Pontiac's newest model was in the division's display at the Chicago Auto Show, which began February 25, 1967. (Photo Courtesy Chicago Auto Show)*

Frontispiece: *The UB5 Hood-mounted Tachometer was a popular option with performance enthusiasts and its availability continued for 1968, but not without a few modifications. Most likely to comply with FMVSS number-205, housing height and length was reduced by .75 inch, which made it less obtrusive from the driver's seat.*

Title Page: *The Firebird H.O. was a hot package that combined small-cube V-8 performance with exciting styling. It included a 326-ci V-8 with 4-barrel carburetor rated at 285 hp, dual exhaust, and distinctive side striping. This particular example is equipped with N95 Wire Wheel Discs, which was an extra-cost option at all levels.*

Contents Page: *Although the concept was somewhat radical for the times, Pontiac envisioned the 1969 Trans Am as a better seller than the 697 units it produced that model year. We mustn't forget that it was a very late-year addition to the model lineup. That the package wasn't eligible for competition directly from the factory certainly didn't help. (Photo Courtesy Larry Delay)*

Back Cover Photos

Top: *Revered as a performance leader among its peers, Pontiac was at the top of its game during the mid-1960s. GTO sales peaked in 1966 and developmental work was underway to create a second Pontiac super car to complement it. The 1967 GTO hit the ground running, and when the 1967 Firebird was introduced mid–model year, it simply reinforced Pontiac's image as GM's performance division. Many Pontiac purists consider the 1967 Firebird a venerable classic. It's easy to understand why with beautiful examples like this. (Photo Courtesy of Tom DeMauro)*

Bottom: *A rear air spoiler that spanned the width of the body and blue accents went a long way in visually separating the 1969 Trans Am from other Firebirds that model year. The Trans Am's appearance was DeLorean's attempt at creating a hip, customized Pontiac to compete with Shelby's successful efforts with Ford's Mustang. Pontiac developed the entire appearance package and sent the prototype Firebird to the designers at GM Styling for finishing. The team in Pontiac Studio had to pull away from 1970 Firebird development to complete it.*

OVERSEAS DISTRIBUTION BY:

PGUK
63 Hatton Garden
London EC1N 8LE, England
Phone: 020 7061 1980 • Fax: 020 7242 3725
www.pguk.co.uk

Renniks Publications Ltd.
3/37-39 Green Street
Banksmeadow, NSW 2109, Australia
Phone: 2 9695 7055 • Fax: 2 9695 7355
www.renniks.com

CONTENTS

DEDICATION

To my wife, Jennifer, my daughter, Sofia, and my son, Rocco. Thank you for
the support and understanding of the commitment required to complete a
project such as this. I know it took a while, but you have allowed me to fulfill a dream.

FOREWORD *by Joe Oldham, Author of* Muscle Car Confidential

In 1981, I wrote *Supertuning Your Firebird Trans Am.* It did well, went through three printings, and I made a buck. Twenty-one years later, I was editor-in-chief of *Popular Mechanics* magazine in New York City.

It was there that I received a letter from a guy named Rocky Rotella asking if I was the same Joe Oldham who used to write about muscle cars for car magazines back in the day, and did I write *Supertuning Your Firebird Trans Am?* And, if I were the same Joe Oldham, would I know where to get a copy of that book, as it was long out of print?

I was a bit surprised by the letter, not having thought of that book for many years. And I was flattered that someone still sought it. As it happened, I still had a few copies left at home. That night, I found one of them, signed it, and mailed it off the next day, no charge.

A few days later, I received another letter from Rocky, thanking me profusely for the book and telling me that he had been a fan of my work, had read all my articles, especially those about Pontiacs, and hoped one day to write magazine articles and books about cars.

Today, Rocky Rotella is one of the most successful automotive writers in the country. He has contributed articles to *High-Performance Pontiac, Smoke Signals, Hemmings Muscle Machines, Hot Rod,* and many other magazines. His book, *How to Rebuild Pontiac V-8s,* was a huge success and now, his new book, *The Definitive Firebird Guide: 1967–1969,* sets new standards for a single-marque title.

Rocky had a great story to work with. Pontiac's F-Body Firebird began life as a second-class cousin to Chevy's Camaro but went on to establish its own place at the table by becoming America's premiere high-performance car in the 1970s, and an American cultural icon. Rocky combines this history with a plethora of technical material, factory service bulletins, production numbers, assembly line anomalies, and obscure year-to-year details never before revealed. In many ways, this is the Firebird book I wish I had written in 1981.

Following Pontiac's demise as a car company several years ago, it's more important than ever to preserve this information, not only for Firebird owners (I own two myself), but for Pontiac hobbyists, enthusiasts, and all automotive historians. As always, you're in good hands with Rocky.

ACKNOWLEDGMENTS

Every author must rely on others for assistance when writing a book and this project was no exception. Many friends, hobbyists, and professionals have assisted me during the completion of this book and I want to take a moment to acknowledge them.

I must first recognize two organizations and those responsible for their operation. By allowing me access to their libraries of rare and unusual Pontiac documents, which complemented those of my own literature collection, their contributions played a significant role in accurately writing this book.

Christo Datini is lead archivist at General Motors' Heritage Center in Warren, Michigan. I got to know Christo while writing for *High Performance Pontiac* magazine. Whenever I needed the Heritage Center for assistance with a story, Christo always took the time to research my request and often replied with detailed information and/or an interesting document on the subject. When Christo learned of my Firebird book project, he graciously offered me the opportunity to access GM's private historical library. I accepted and spent two days perusing the entire Pontiac file; I photographed and/or photocopied nearly 2,000 individual documents. Not only did I locate unknown model details, I also discovered a plethora of first-generation Firebird production figures that I can share with hobbyists for the very first time. Thank you, Christo, and your team at GM's Heritage Center.

The Pontiac-Oakland Museum and Resource Center (POMARC) located in Pontiac, Illinois, has been another immense asset. Curator Tim Dye and his wife, Penny, allowed me to spend several unabated hours in the museum's library on two different occasions where I pored over the reference materials Tim has gathered over the years. During my time there I photographed or scanned more than 3,000 documents he has collected or has received from former Pontiac employees. Thank you, Tim and Penny.

I also want to point out some individuals who deserve credit for their assistance. Sincerest thanks go to Tom DeMauro, Don Keefe, and Christopher Phillip, whom I worked for and/or with at *High Performance Pontiac* magazine over the years. These guys are devout Firebird enthusiasts who have dedicated their lives to furthering the Pontiac hobby through accurate and professional journalism. They allowed me the use of several Firebird-related photos for the book. Guys, I sincerely appreciate your support. And I want to again say thanks to Tom DeMauro who, while editor at *High Performance Pontiac,* gave me a chance to write professionally for the first time in 2003. He helped me hone my skills and it's resulted in more than 200 articles for various well-known titles so far, and now this, my third published book.

I need to thank the Midwest Firebirds club, its president, Ken Pitcher, and its members for gathering together one Saturday morning and allowing me to photograph several of their first-generation Firebirds in the Chicago area. Thanks to Rob Lozins for allowing me to photograph his wonderful collection of very rare and highly desirable Pontiacs and his pal, Moe Neuburger, for prepping them and spending the day shuffling cars around for me. I also need to thank Pontiac hobbyist and Firebird enthusiast David Belz for his assistance and contributions.

Jim Mattison at PHS Automotive Services not only deserves credit for his assistance with the book, but also for his contributions to the Pontiac hobby. If you attempt to document the factory-installed options your first- or second-generation Firebird was originally equipped with, Jim can provide you with a copy of the particular vehicle's billing history card or dealer invoice, depending on the model year. That information can help you accurately distinguish between factory-issued items and dealer- or owner-added equipment. Not only will it give you an understanding about a particular Firebird's originality, it could also save you from purchasing one that has been converted or misrepresented by someone at some point in its life. Examples of these documents are included in the chapters that follow and you can learn more about Jim's services and his current pricing at phs-online.com.

In addition to all those previously mentioned, I also want to credit a number of individuals who have provided content for this book. I sincerely apologize in advance to anyone I inadvertently leave out and can assure you it was in no way intentional. Those who were instrumental in helping me complete the project are listed below in alphabetical order.

Herb Adams, Dick Boneske, Steve Bothwell, Merlyn Boyden, Harry Bradley, Tommy Lee Byrd, Christo Datini, Jarod Tim Dye, Craig Ehrlich, Jarod Elsberry, Tom Fischer, Mitch Frumkin, Preston Grant, Dave Hall, Jim Hand, Tom Hand, Dan Hardin, Kurt Harrington, Ben Harrison, Ron Hill, Frank Johengen, Larry Kinsel, Lance Kramer, Bill Krause, Michael Lamm, Bob Luyckx, Berdie Martin, Mac McKellar, Jim Mino, Gregg Peterson, Bill Porter, Beverly Reedy, Curt Richards, Nunzi Romano, Cliff Ruggles, Rick Salzillo, Steve Schappaugh, Tom Schreitmueller, Stu Shuster, Fred Simmonds, John Wilkins, Bob Wilson, Gene Winfield, and Jeff Young.

PREFACE

Thank you for purchasing *The Definitive Firebird & Trans Am Guide: 1967–1969*. If you're reading this book then you, too, must be a dedicated Firebird fanatic seeking to further your knowledge about Pontiac's first-generation F-car. If you're like me, you've probably enjoyed reading virtually every Firebird book that has been published over the years. Although the Firebird story has been written time and again, I have striven greatly to add unique content to this book, and I think you'll find that it's quite unlike others before it.

I love Pontiac's F-car. I was born in 1976 during the middle of the second-generation era and lived and breathed Trans Ams like so many Americans during the 1970s and 1980s. When I became of driving age in the early 1990s, I bought my own (a 1976 Trans Am) and can vividly recall the excitement surrounding the introduction of the new-for-1993 fourth-generation Firebird as well as the aggressive 1998 restyle that included LS1 power. I was so enamored with the last Firebirds that I ordered one (a 2001 equipped with the optional WS6 Ram Air and Handling package) in July 2000 and took delivery that September. I still own both today.

My love for Firebirds, and really all things Pontiac, started at a young age. My grandfather and father bought and regularly drove performance-oriented Pontiacs during the 1960s and 1970s, and I learned the inner workings of the Pontiac V-8 and how to maintain it in a very short time. My father drove second-generation Firebirds exclusively during my youth and kept all of his yearly Pontiac brochures, Firebird books, and magazine articles readily available in the house. I read and re-read them, admiring the beautiful body styling and exciting history.

I have to admit, however, I really wasn't overly fond of Pontiac's first-generation Firebird at first. Looking back, it was likely due to the simple fact that I grew up in and around second-generation Firebirds. As I became more involved in the Pontiac hobby and my interests expanded, I grew increasingly fond of them. So much so that in recent years I was intimately involved with the restoration and maintenance of my cousin's 1967 Firebird. I can understand and appreciate the nuances of the first-generation cars from an operational standpoint.

I became intrigued by Pontiac history and the information contained in the sales and service materials that the division sent to its representatives. Some of these resources were commonly available to the dealership network, while others were internal memos that were never intended for distribution. No matter the case, I have collected these materials for decades. I have picked them up piecemeal at local swap meets and dealership auctions, national conventions, various publications and online sources including eBay, and through the generosity of fellow literature collectors and hobbyists like you. My

I have always enjoyed Firebirds of all generations and have a sincere appreciation of the complexity of the history surrounding Pontiac's first-generation F-car. Imagine the excitement of being able to purchase a 1968 Firebird convertible like this beautiful example when new. It's equipped with the optional 400 Ram Air engine and a 4-speed transmission and retains its original, factory-applied Solar Red finish. It shows just 19,000 miles on its odometer.

Authoring this book not only gave me the chance to photograph some unbelievably rare and desirable Firebirds, I was also able to spend a significant amount of time experiencing the massiveness of some Pontiac collections located in the Chicago area. I was amazed at the generosity Firebird owners were willing to extend simply so I could photograph their prized Pontiac.

collection grew exponentially each year and the information it contained led me to write for *High Performance Pontiac* magazine.

My father had subscribed to *High Performance Pontiac* since the publication premiered as *Thunder Am* during the late 1970s. He maintained his subscription until SourceInterlink discontinued it and eleven additional titles in May 2014. I read every issue cover to cover countless times growing up and never dreamed that I would be qualified to write an article for it. I was floored when I met *High Performance Pontiac*'s editor, Tom DeMauro, at the Pontiac Southern Nationals in Dallas in 2002 and he asked me if I'd consider writing for his magazine. I explained that beyond what I learned in typical high school and college English courses, I had no formal writing training or experience, and wasn't very good with photography.

Tom was willing to teach and I was willing to learn. Because of him I became a published author in 2003. I was so enthused about sharing information that I literally couldn't wait to finish one article and move on to the next. The result was more than 150 different freelance bylines in *High Performance Pontiac*. In 11 years I wrote historical, technical, and feature articles for it, and had the pleasure of interviewing many of Pontiac's greatest designers and engineers.

From *High Performance Pontiac* came other opportunities. Magazine work included *Hot Rod, Car Craft, Hemmings' Motor News, Hemmings' Muscle Machines*, and POCI's *Smoke Signals*. I also had the opportunity to write two books for CarTech on Pontiac V-8 engine building. Then the chance came to author this book. CarTech and I agreed upon a time frame and work began at a feverish pace.

The Super Duty 421 engine and midsize GTO catapulted Pontiac's image into that of a premier performance manufacturer during the 1960s. Jim Wangers, who worked for MacManus, John & Adams (Pontiac's advertising agency) created some of the most iconic automotive advertisements of all time. One of the most controversial was that of a 1968 GTO stopped at a turnabout on Detroit's infamous Woodward Avenue that seemed to suggest the GTO as a predator stalking its next victim. General Motors quickly pulled the ad to prevent its association with street racing. Even today, hobbyists attempt to re-create this scene with their own Pontiacs on Woodward Avenue. This 1968 Firebird looks right at home. (Photo Courtesy David Belz)

INTRODUCTION

This book was originally intended to span the 1967–1981 model years and was supposed to be completed in 2014. As the project progressed, however, it became apparent that 14 model years were just too many to cram into a single book, and the timeline that I agreed to simply wasn't enough to produce work that met my own stringent expectations. CarTech decided that it was best to split the title into two books: one from 1967 to 1969 for first-generation Firebirds and the second from 1970 to 1981 for second-generation Firebirds. It was a natural break.

I felt I had an above-average knowledge of Pontiac's first-generation F-car and its history, but after diving into the two-year research project that resulted in the 1967–1969 book and actually speaking with those remaining individuals who had worked at Pontiac or GM Styling on the F-car project, I realized that the first-generation Firebirds were much more exciting than I had ever thought. It resulted in an even greater appreciation for them. Authoring this book has given me the chance to explore the uniqueness of each model year. All of this is exactly what makes projects like this so enjoyable for me!

In the pages that follow, I hope to provide you with an understanding of what made Pontiac a top-performing player at the top of its game during the early 1960s. Throughout Chapter 1, I share the hows and whys of the canceled developmental projects and reasons for the Firebird's existence. I try to convey Pontiac's sense of frustration after being handed Chevrolet's Camaro for 1967 and then given little lead time and few resources to create its own sporty four-passenger F-car. I also want to show the company's determined charge to create a vehicle that was undeniably Pontiac.

In Chapters 2 through 4, I discuss the 1967 Firebird and its direct relation to the Camaro, how Pontiac injected a sense of individuality for 1968, and how well it really separated from Camaro in 1969. Chapter 5 contains a detailed look at the Trans Am.

One point I hope you're able to take away from *The Definitive Firebird and Trans Am Guide 1967–1969* is that John DeLorean was absolutely the right person for the right auto maker at the right time. I don't think you'll find anyone to oppose the argument that he was a maverick. He had the gift of being a true marketing genius who was not only in tune with the hipsters, but also knew how to market Pontiac's performance image to consumers of all ages. He was confident enough to force those ideas into production vehicles, and that simply drove the division's sales through the roof. If there was ever a perfect storm, it was Pontiac during the 1960s. I enjoy hearing that story from older Pontiac employees and hobbyists who lived it. Being able to retell that story and excite younger hobbyists about the Pontiac family is what drives me!

I find that whenever I get into a project, I always want to know "why." Although I welcome discussing topics with very knowledgeable hobbyists and find it quite enjoyable, when writing I always prefer to document points with materials issued by Pontiac. Rarely have I found the information refutable. My literature collection has proven to be a great asset for that. During this project I had the distinct pleasure of visiting the private libraries at General Motors' Heritage Center in Warren, Michigan, and the Pontiac-Oakland Museum and Research Center (POMARC) in Pontiac, Illinois. I added thousands of digital copies of rare and unique Pontiac documents from those collections to my own cache. Others shared copies of materials they'd collected. I've compiled much of this literature into the following pages.

General Motors maintains many of its historic assets in a facility known as the Heritage Center. Located very near GM's Technical Center in Warren, Michigan, the Heritage Center is home to a large number of significant GM concept, prototype, and/or production vehicles and engines. Researchers sit in an office area where row upon row of large, sliding book shelves contain the corporation's paper history. I was invited to view the entire library while researching this book. I bring some of it to you for the very first time.

The Heritage Center museum is generally closed to the public, but it is available for group tours and functions. You may wonder what Pontiacs are displayed at General Motors' Heritage Center. The collection contains an array of vehicles that Pontiac maintained and campaigned at events during its existence as a division of GM. Those displayed at the Heritage Center are among the most iconic models that set Pontiac apart from its peers. In addition to what you see here, a number of other Pontiacs are stored offsite and are periodically rotated in to update the display.

The Pontiac-Oakland Museum and Resource Center (POMARC) in Pontiac, Illinois, is dedicated to generating interest in the Pontiac hobby. Several Pontiacs can be found on display in the museum's showroom areas on any given day. The elaborate displays and its vehicles are frequently changed. Visiting the museum is a must for any Pontiac enthusiast. POMARC hosts various Pontiac car shows each year, so there's more than one excuse to go.

This panoramic photo reveals the expansive library housed in the Pontiac-Oakland Museum and Resource Center (POMARC) located just off Route 66 in Pontiac, Illinois. The museum is open to the public, but access to the library is generally closed. Arrangements can be made with POMARC operators to gain access for project research (by appointment only). I was able to spend several hours in the POMARC library researching materials for this book and was amazed at the interesting information I found.

Although no one will ever have all the answers and there may be some inadvertent mistakes in this book, I've tried to be as thorough as possible in answering the "whys" using the resources available to me. I invested a considerable amount of time verifying the accuracy of the material here. I tried very hard to source facts directly from Pontiac-printed documentation. Although you may question the veracity of a particular fact or figure, you can rest assured that unless the source it was gleaned from was incorrect, the material can generally be backed by a hard copy once distributed by Pontiac. The production numbers are as accurate as those I could find from General Motors or other known, reliable sources. If you find something in error or have a document that you'd like to share, please contact me through CarTech Books. I would love to hear from you.

I tried being as finicky as possible when selecting the Firebirds I photographed for this book. In the months I spent finishing it, I traveled many miles to shoot some while others happened to be at major Pontiac events that

I attended. I'm keenly aware that many other very qualified Firebirds are out there, you may even own one or more, but regrettably, the time and funds just didn't allow me to get to them all. I am, however, confident that you'll be pleased with the overall quality of those I chose for this book. Not every car is absolutely perfect, but I felt that the particular Firebird chosen suitably illustrated my intent.

I should point out that while selecting the Firebirds I was very conscientious about originality and came to allow only one major concession, tires. Like many Pontiac purists, I prefer the look of original tires over modern radials, but quickly came to the realization that photographing only those with original (or reproductions of originals such as those from cokertire.com or kelseytire.com) tires was an unrealistic expectation. A few very-low-mile cars retained their original tires and some wore vintage replacements that were commonly available when the car was regularly driven years ago. I found most others riding on modern radials. Knowing that reproduction tires are costly and can compromise ride and handling

when compared to a modern radial, especially if the owner drives his Firebird regularly, I decided that I had no issue with a modern radial so long as it's correctly sized for the model year. Wheel covers and/or styled wheels had to be correct for the model and model year, however.

If you're new to the Pontiac hobby, there are many great clubs that can help you become acquainted with other owners and provide excellent monthly publications or newsletters. The Pontiac-Oakland Club International (poci.org) has nearly 10,000 members and hosts an annual national convention at various locations throughout the country. Its monthly *Smoke Signals* magazine is unmatched. The National Trans Am and Firebird club (firebirdtaclub. com) is an excellent national Firebird-only resource, and there are many regional Pontiac clubs, including Dallas Area Pontiac Association (dapa.org) and Midwest Firebirds (midwestfirebirds.org), just to name a couple. Many others can be found with a simple Internet search or through their Facebook pages, and there are countless web-based clubs and forums that you can join for free.

Published resources have become harder to find in recent years. *High Performance Pontiac* magazine was unexpectedly dropped when SourceInterlink reorganized in May 2014 and became The Enthusiast Network (TEN).

Although some titles such as *Hot Rod* and *Car Craft* print an occasional Pontiac story, the dedicated Pontiac magazine in that group went away. A new independent start-up publication has recently surfaced. *Poncho Perfection* is author Don Keefe's latest venture and it has the potential to pick up where *High Performance Pontiac* left off. You can learn more about it at ponchoperfection.com.

Although this book isn't about Firebird or Trans Am restorations, I understand the need for quality replacement components to keep your vehicle on the road. I have found Ames Performance (amesperf.com) and Year One (yearone.com) among the very best. It's also my understanding that Classic Industries (classicindustries. com) is working to bring new, high-quality Firebird body panels to market. If you need engine parts, Butler Performance (butlerperformance.com) or SD Performance (sdperformance.com) are my first choices.

My ultimate goal was to provide each reader, no matter how experienced or knowledgeable, with something they didn't know before about Pontiac's 1967–1969 Firebird. I'm confident that virtually every reader will be able to take away something fresh. I sincerely hope it exceeds your expectations and sets a new standard for first-generation F-car fans.

CHAPTER ONE

DEVELOPMENT

Although the last Firebird to roll off the assembly line was produced in 2002, Pontiac's F-car remains among the most exhilarating vehicles on the road today. Created by a division that built an image of strong performance dating back to the 1950s, the Firebird was almost predestined to become a market trendsetter that others would seek to copy.

From the horsepower wars of the 1960s to the bleak days of the late 1970s and 1980s when engines were stran-gled with anti-smog equipment, consumers relished the fact that no matter the year, the Firebird was instinctively perched atop the performance car food chain. Pontiac engineering continually conjured up ways to inject leading-edge technology into its vehicles. Most agree that not once during its 35-year production run was the four-passenger sports car any less thrilling to drive as it was styled.

With its performance heritage and iconic body styling that makes its silhouette immediately recognizable,

Pontiac introduced its Firebird in 1967 and it was greeted with significant media attention and strong consumer sales. With performance enhancements and iconic styling of the generations that followed, it went on to become an American super car in the 1970s. It remained a staple of Americana until its discontinuance in 2002. Firebirds of all generations retain a strong hobbyist following.

it's easy to understand how the Firebird became a symbol of American culture. Despite Firebird's close relation to Chevrolet's Camaro, since its introduction in 1967, Pontiac went to great lengths to give its pony car an identity that was unique. The result captivated America's youth market when new Firebirds were still being produced. It continues today as hobbyists and collectors seek to partake in the same excitement that the Firebird created during the 1960s and 1970s. But let's look back before there even was an F-car platform.

History

The divisions of the General Motors Corporation (GM) during the 1950s were industry trendsetters. Not only were Buick, Cadillac, Chevrolet, Oldsmobile, and Pontiac rivals that competed to develop uniquely attractive vehicles with new innovations, they were organizational brethren whose inter-corporation relationship allowed them to collectively share many technological revelations. The result was a highly skilled team of players fully prepared to take on the likes of Ford and Chrysler in an intensely competitive market. What they masterfully churned out continues to fuel the dreams of hobbyists of all ages today.

During the infancy of the performance era, Chevrolet was first to offer a two-passenger sports car with the 1953 release of the Corvette. Powered by Chevrolet's popular 6-cylinder engine, and typical of the European racer market it was intended to compete in, Corvette lacked any real comfort features in its first few years. That limited its success with American buyers.

It was only natural for Chevrolet to offer its new-for-1955 V-8 in the Corvette as well. It was at that point that the two-seater launched its journey into becoming the corporation's performance flagship model. It continues to be a halo vehicle and receives an extreme amount of resources to support that image. To date, it has been GM's only V-8–powered two-passenger sports car. And as you'll learn, that was much to Pontiac's chagrin.

The concept of a small four-passenger sports car had been discussed by many of GM's divisions since the late 1950s. GM Styling even modeled numerous examples in advance studios, but corporate interest was low. That, unfortunately, prevented further development of any concept. Pontiac created the two-door Grand Prix for 1962, and the Buick-exclusive Riviera soon followed. Both cars offered personal luxury with powerful engine options, but neither midsize model catered to the average buyer's budget.

Based on the success of early 1960s personal-luxury vehicles, the divisions fought even harder going into the mid-1960s for a small, sporty four-passenger coupe with a reasonable base price. Many felt an affordable, sporty small car equipped with a V-8 would be as popular with performance enthusiasts as a 6-cylinder would be with secretaries. Chevrolet even displayed its Super Nova (of which the Camaro is a direct descendent) at the 1964 New York International Auto Show, but corporate leaders maintained their stance of showing little interest in making it, or any sporty four-passenger job, a production vehicle. Until April 17, 1964, that is.

That's when Ford introduced its new Mustang at the World's Fair in New York, and it forever changed the direction of the Pontiac. General Motors didn't take Mustang too seriously at first and felt the redesigned Corvair II would be the corporation's combatant. Mustang's lower $2,300 base price and optional V-8 power allowed it to overshadow the Corvair, however. It also offered much greater versatility and a gamut of optional equipment that made it appealing to men and women alike.

"I didn't find the first Mustang's styling very exciting," said GM designer Ron Hill, who headed Chevrolet Studio at the time, "but it appealed to a very broad market base and that made it very successful. The corporation looked to the Corvair Monza as its Mustang fighter but the concepts didn't compare. They even installed an aluminum V-8 into the back of a Corvair II as an

During the early 1950s, General Motors allowed its divisional styling departments to create concept vehicles for its Autorama (and later Motorama) displays. One of Pontiac's first entries was the 1954 Bonneville Special. Boasting fiberglass construction, some considered it Pontiac's take on Chevrolet's new Corvette. No matter the interpretation, it certainly was the precursor to the two-seat sports car the division longed for. This particular example is one of two hand-built examples and is privately owned.

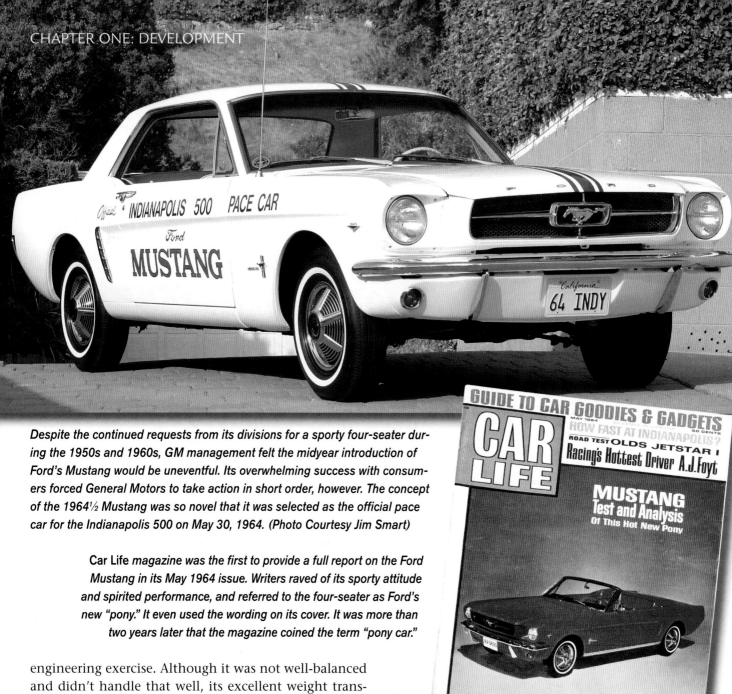

Despite the continued requests from its divisions for a sporty four-seater during the 1950s and 1960s, GM management felt the midyear introduction of Ford's Mustang would be uneventful. Its overwhelming success with consumers forced General Motors to take action in short order, however. The concept of the 1964½ Mustang was so novel that it was selected as the official pace car for the Indianapolis 500 on May 30, 1964. (Photo Courtesy Jim Smart)

Car Life magazine was the first to provide a full report on the Ford Mustang in its May 1964 issue. Writers raved of its sporty attitude and spirited performance, and referred to the four-seater as Ford's new "pony." It even used the wording on its cover. It was more than two years later that the magazine coined the term "pony car."

engineering exercise. Although it was not well-balanced and didn't handle that well, its excellent weight transfer allowed it to accelerate unbelievably well. General Motors realized it needed a vehicle that was comparable to the Mustang."

The 1964 Mustang was a smashing success with consumers and sold more than 120,000 units in the few months that remained of the 1964 model year. With its launch, Ford effectively created an entirely new four-passenger sports car segment that *Car Life* eventually termed the "pony car" market. Although it referred to the Mustang as "Ford's new pony" in its May 1964 issue, "pony car" was coined in *Car Life*'s October 1966 issue when the Camaro and Cougar were introduced. *Car Life* decreed that it would refer to vehicles aimed at that growing market segment as "pony cars" not only because of the equine-named Ford, but because "pony" implied some-

thing small and nimble and the definition accurately described the vehicles of this sporty class.

Mustang's overwhelming success, which included nearly 560,000 units in 1965 and more than 607,000 in 1966, spawned many competitors as the 1960s progressed, and Pontiac's Firebird was one. But Pontiac's F-car didn't come without a series of struggles and disappointments. It was actually the result of a corporate project the division was forced to take on. Without some background on the division and Firebird's journey from concept to production, the story can be rather confusing, however.

Changes Within Pontiac

The Pontiac Motor Division of General Motors evolved from the Oakland Division. The Pontiac was introduced in 1926 as a lower-price complement to the Oakland. Viewed as an excellent value for the consumer dollar, within a few short years, the Pontiac became so much more popular than the Oakland that the Oakland was discontinued and the division was renamed Pontiac.

Competition was tough during the 1950s and overhead valve and V-8 technology were hot marketing topics. Pontiac introduced its Strato-Streak V-8 in 1955 as a replacement for its aged inline 6- and 8-cylinder engines to inject excitement and invigorate sales. Displacing 287 ci, it was rated at 180 hp with a 2-barrel carburetor and 200 hp with a 4-barrel. A little more than a decade later, the same basic architecture produced nearly 400 hp and displaced as much as 455 ci.

Over the next few decades Pontiac's straight 6- and 8-cylinder engines gained notoriety for reliability and good general performance, and their popularity remained strong with the mature buyer. As years passed and consumer horsepower expectations within the industry grew, the inline cylinder arrangement proved to have limitations. Under the guidance of General Manager Robert Critchfield, Pontiac introduced a smart V-8 in 1955. Although the engine injected excitement into the 1955 Pontiac lineup, mundane body styling failed to impress young consumers and profits waned.

General Motors appointed Semon "Bunkie" Knudsen as Pontiac's general manager on July 1, 1956, and tasked him with turning the ailing division into a profitable company in short order, or it would be dropped entirely. His plan of making a vehicle that appealed to youthful customers with attractive styling and strong performance was a recipe for success, and he brought to Pontiac the best talent he could find.

Although the mid-1950s Pontiacs were styled attractively, the vehicles didn't portray a youthful image. As a result, Pontiac wasn't popular with younger buyers. The revised appearance for 1956 proved to be a step in the right direction. When Bunkie Knudsen arrived in July 1956, he hired the best talent he could find to aggressively pursue exciting styling and engineering enhancements to rejuvenate the brand. The 1956 model year was the last when bright trim was drawn across the hood.

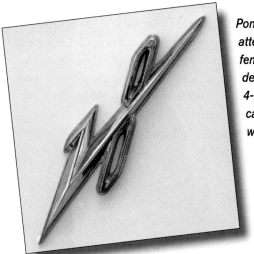

Pontiac heavily marketed its new-for-1955 V-8 engine under its vehicles' hoods. To call attention to it, a die-cast "V-8" logo was affixed to quarter panels in 1955 and the front fender in 1956. Displacement increased to 316.6 ci for 1956. Pontiac's engineering team developed and released an extra horsepower package late in the year that included dual 4-barrel carburetors and corresponding intake manifold, and an aggressive mechanical camshaft. Boosting output to 285 hp, performance and reliability were outstanding. It was the first step that propelled Pontiac toward becoming the division to beat.

Knudsen hired Elliot "Pete" Estes away from Oldsmobile and appointed him as Pontiac's chief engineer. At the same time, he then recruited a young John Z. DeLorean as the director of advanced engineering. The team diligently transformed the Pontiac with conservative styling and notorious reliability into a flashy trendsetter with hot V-8 power. By placing the wheels farther out on its vehicles than that of similar offerings from other makes in 1959, Pontiac's ingenious Wide Track marketing campaign allowed the division to heavily publicize how the feature improved its vehicles' ride and handling qualities. Sales skyrocketed.

Even before the arrival of Knudsen and team, Pontiac toyed with the idea of a two-seat sports car. You may recall such styling exercises as the 1954 Bonneville Special and the 1956 Club de Mer. Although Pontiac couldn't convince the corporate management to allow further development of them, DeLorean, who was promoted to chief engineer when Estes was named the division's general manager in November 1961, forged ahead in developing the two-passenger Monte Carlo built from a 1962 Tempest, complete with an inline 4-cylinder engine boosted by a supercharger.

AMA Policy Against Racing

Although Pontiac continued its corporate battle for a two-seat sports car, it also established itself as a performance leader with the powerful Super Duty 389 and 421 engines available in the midsize Catalina. Ruling

Shedding an unexciting image and making Pontiac profitable was Bunkie Knudsen's mission. He immediately started hiring young, enthusiastic, and innovative engineers to inject a youthful attitude into Pontiac's offerings. The Bonneville was one of Knudsen's innovations and it became the division's performance flagship during the late 1950s. By 1958 the Pontiac was loaded with chrome and had a style its own. Sales began to soar.

oval track and dragstrip racing alike, the success came to an abrupt halt in January 1963 when General Motors elected to enforce a corporate policy it created from the outcome of the Automobile Manufacturer's Association's (AMA) annual meeting held in Detroit on June 6, 1957.

At the 1957 meeting, the AMA directing body, which was comprised of top management from each corporation, reached a gentlemen's agreement recommending that auto manufacturers refrain from the promotion of and/or direct participation in auto racing. Instead,

Pontiac's continued quest for a two-seat sports car resulted in the Monte Carlo show car concept. Created from a modified 1961 Tempest, its frame was shortened, its roof was removed to create roadster styling, and its 195-inch 4-cylinder was supercharged for added performance. The pearlescent white body was trimmed with dual blue racing stripes, possibly the very first Pontiac to feature the styling cue that went on to visually define the first Trans Ams. The Monte Carlo made the early 1960s show circuit before being retired. It's privately owned today. (Photo Courtesy General Motors)

Many hobbyists consider Pontiac's early 1960s styling among the very best the division ever offered. The split-grille theme was solidly in place by 1962, and examples such as this Catalina could be ordered with the Super Duty 421 engine and a host of stamped-aluminum body panels to shed weight for maximum acceleration. Attractive and lightning-quick, Pontiac went from boring styling and straight-8 engines to an industry trendsetter whose V-8 was feared by competitors and revered by enthusiastic consumers.

advertising strategies should be refocused on the safety of more popular passenger cars and station wagons. It signaled the end of factory-owned race teams and factory-backed sponsorship of private race teams, both monetary funding and gratis racing components. Manufacturers

During the late 1950s, Pontiac offered a complete line of heavy-duty driveline components intended for severe off-road applications. They were available through its dealership parts departments. By 1962, the Super Duty engine had grown to 421 inches and was factory assembled and installed into 1962 Catalinas and Grand Prixs. Pontiac rated a competition engine at 405 hp, but the weekly dragstrip and circle tracks wins that racers accumulated suggested that Pontiac's output claim was little more than an arbitrary number. The Super Duty engine carried over to 1963 with a few enhancements, though output remained virtually identical.

sent news of the policy adoption throughout their respective organizations immediately following the meeting.

Although the AMA's 1957 recommendation quelled some activity in the years that immediately followed, General Motors allowed its divisions to interpret the message independently. Pontiac found that because it didn't recommend the use of racing equipment on the street and included a disclaimer at the time of vehicle purchase, it was able to develop its early-1960s Super Duty 389 and 421 engines and install them into certain models without fear of breaching the agreement. Many other manufacturers used similar loopholes to disguise competitive efforts. The horsepower race was on.

By the end of the 1962 calendar year, General Motors owned nearly 52 percent of the new car market, not to mention the market shares of its various other divisions that produced household appliances and diesel locomotives. Many of the corporation's leaders were silently fearful that the U.S. government would force divestment of certain automotive divisions to prevent an auto market monopoly. In lieu of federal intervention, it seems that the corporation decided that foregoing the volume generated by its divisions' association with motorsports entirely would not only promote a safety-conscious image, it could reduce sales enough to prevent outside involvement.

An internal meeting of high-level management took place on January 21, 1963. There, the corporation reaffirmed its stance on racing activity to its divisions, making direct reference to the AMA agreement of

During the early 1960s, the potent Super Duty 421 allowed Pontiac to amass win after win on the circle tracks of the stock car circuit as well as timed quarter-mile runs on the dragstrip. Not only raced by private individuals, many performance-oriented Pontiac dealers campaigned their own race cars every weekend to showcase Pontiac's prowess and publicize their dealership as the location to purchase it. The notoriety was so tremendous that it caused General Motors to review the racing activities of all divisions and reinforce its internal policy to promote safety, not performance.

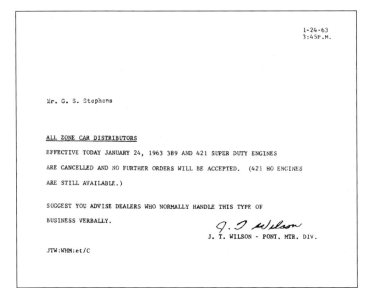

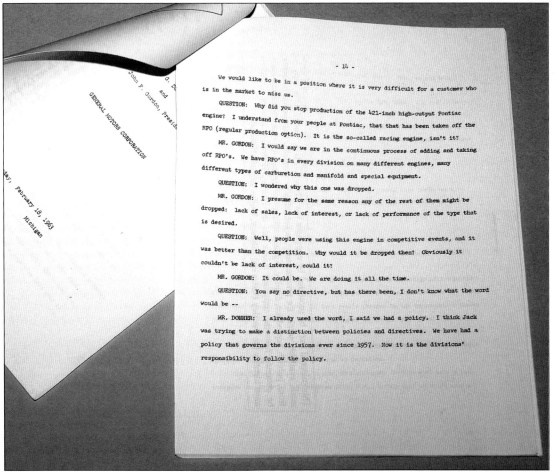

At AMA's 1957 conference, automakers agreed to refrain from advertising speed and performance and showcase a vehicle's safety attributes instead. Many companies, including Pontiac, continued to develop maximum-performance packages, however. That effort eventually resulted in the Super Duty 421 during the early 1960s. This memo, issued by Pontiac's director of car distribution, clearly states that the era ended abruptly on January 24, 1963.

1957. General Motors' then-chairman, Frederic Donner, and its president, John Gordon, made the policy part of their 90-minute general press conference on February 18, 1963. Contrary to modern references, which often describe it as an "edict" or "ban," a transcript of that day reveals that the corporation's top figures adamantly assured media reporters that it wasn't a directive of any sort, but a simple review of corporate policy.

Malcolm "Mac" McKellar, renowned Pontiac engineer responsible for Super Duty 421 development, told me before his passing that it was obvious the corporation was serious this time. Although it was agreed upon in 1957, no one really abided by it. Corporate management made it known in 1963 that any divisional employee who furthered the development of or covertly supplied professional race teams with components would be immediately terminated. Although he knew of no engineer who lost his job bucking the policy, it wasn't a risk that McKellar and many of his coworkers were willing to take.

Pontiac smartly took the performance fight from closed courses to the street for 1964. DeLorean and his team of skilled engineers developed the concept of combining a large-cube engine with an intermediate-size

Have you ever wondered what remarks GM Chairman Frederic Donner and GM President John Gordon made during their annual press conference on February 18, 1963? A copy of the 43-page transcript reveals that just two pages were dedicated to performance-related aspects. Members of the media asked pointed questions and Donner and Gordon reassured attendees that the corporation issued no directive, but instead simply reviewed its policies and reaffirmed its stance on the AMA agreement of 1957.

When Pontiac was no longer able to actively compete in closed-course auto racing, John DeLorean championed the idea of creating the ultimate street car by installing a large-cube engine into an affordable, intermediate-size Tempest. GM's rules limited maximum engine size in the 1964 A-car to 330 ci, however. DeLorean recognized the significance such a car would have with consumers, bucked the corporate rules, and introduced the 1964 GTO in fall of 1963. Its 389-ci engine delivered 348 hp. When combined with the svelte body, it was an instant success with performance enthusiasts. Many hobbyists consider Pontiac's GTO to be the vehicle that initiated the 1960s muscle car craze.

body to create the potent GTO. The division capitalized on a loophole in the corporate rulebook to sidestep the maximum allowable engine displacement for A-body models to make the GTO possible. The entire program progressed in secrecy, not only to preclude corporate meddling, but to prevent other divisions from launching an immediate competitor.

When news of the GTO finally leaked, it was far too late for corporate management to cancel the program. General Motors wasn't pleased with Pontiac's disregard for the policy and might have otherwise taken recourse with Estes and DeLorean, but the profitability associated with the 32,000 GTOs sold during the 1964 model year helped the corporation take a blind eye. No matter how successful the GTO was, however, upper management considered DeLorean a talented rebel and future clashes involving Pontiac concepts frustrated both sides. One such clash ultimately landed Pontiac its hand-me-down F-car for 1967, but not before a series of Experimental Program (XP) concepts were attempted.

XP Programs

As hot as the GTO was for Pontiac during the mid-1960s, the division still pushed for its own small, sporty, two-seater. According to internal documents, General Motors offered Pontiac an opportunity to develop a version of Chevrolet's XP-782 Corvair Monza program in June 1964. The Advanced Studio at GM Styling created a clay model tentatively named Polaris, which it presented to Pontiac in August 1964, but Pontiac wasn't interested in any type of vehicle whose engine was mid- or rear-mounted. Other reports suggest that Pontiac wanted no vehicle correlated to Corvair, whose safety reputation was heavily challenged by internal management and outside critics.

Several new XP programs ensued during the 1960s. Some occurred simultaneously, and have direct lineage to the Pontiac we know today as Firebird. Each has a special place in history and deserves at least a brief review of its influence on the Firebird. As you read the following paragraphs on XP-program vehicles, remember that some of the timelines overlap.

XP-833

Shortly after the GTO's introduction in the fall of 1963, DeLorean and Bill Collins, who was assigned to Pontiac's advanced engineering department at the time, begun pursuing their own sports car program known as XP-833. Unlike XP-782, which was funded by the corporation, initial funding of the XP-833 program fell solely on Pontiac. Covertly devised as a low-buck competitor to the Corvette, the plan called for two- and four-seat variants, but the cost to develop each was too great for Pontiac to incur singlehandedly, so the four-seat concept was dropped.

John DeLorean sponsored a two-door sports car program known as XP-833 in the fall of 1963. At least two running and driving prototypes were assembled as presentation demonstrators to pitch the low-cost two-seat concept to corporate management. The program was ultimately rejected, but both XP-833 prototypes survived and are privately owned today. One was on display at the Pontiac-Oakland Club International's convention in St. Charles, Illinois. A "Banshee" nameplate was added during the 1970s.

The XP-833 was a compact two-seater that was beautifully styled and maintained an aggressive look that was synonymous with Pontiac performance. The flowing body shell was constructed of fiberglass and produced for Pontiac by Dow-Corning, an outside vendor. Notice the body's kinship to the Corvette Stingray that Chevrolet introduced in 1968. As both cars were designed in each division's respective advance studio at GM Styling, it begs the question, which division pioneered the body shape? It's quite likely that Pontiac and Chevrolet influenced each other's product.

According to the work order summary chart, the two-seater took shape in an advance studio in late August 1964. By May 11, 1965, a running and driving prototype had been constructed by Pontiac Engineering and presented to Ed Cole, GM's group executive over cars and trucks. Sleek and sporty, many of its design cues were strikingly similar to the Corvette Stingray that debuted in 1968 and concurrently in development at Chevrolet. Cole enjoyed the XP-833 concept so much that he commissioned a second program, XP-851, as a variant with four-passenger seating so that Pontiac might develop both styles using corporate assets. He requested examples of each for a corporate review in June 1965.

DeLorean was promoted to Pontiac general manager on July 1, 1965. It should have been easy to push the XP-833 program into production. At least two additional running and driving prototypes, one with an OHC-6 and the other a V-8, were developed and proved to be quite popular internally. DeLorean had Collins, whom he promoted to assistant chief engineer, prepare an elaborate proposal, which was presented to GM President James Roche on August 5, 1965. It's quite clear from the original proposal that Pontiac did its homework and made a very strong argument for its need of a low-cost vehicle in the two-passenger marketplace.

DeLorean charged hard for his two-seat XP-833, but Chevrolet argued that even though Pontiac didn't consider it a competitor, the XP-833 would only take away Corvette sales. Additionally, Chevrolet was working on a program that ultimately became the F-car, and General Motors badly needed a high-volume vehicle to combat Ford's Mustang, not snipe at divisional sales volume. After considering Pontiac's proposal, corporate management decided that resources would be better allocated with Pontiac focusing on other projects. On September 13, 1965, the XP-833 and XP-851 programs were consolidated into XP-853, which was already underway. That move effectively ended any chance of either Pontiac concept from moving forward individually.

The XP-833 program didn't go down without one last push, however. In late October 1965 DeLorean approached his former boss, Pete Estes, who was then Chevrolet's general manager, about combining the XP-833 and Corvette into a single program so that each division might have its own two-seat sports car. The proposal apparently fell on deaf ears and the last two operational XP-833 prototypes were placed into storage. Both still exist today and are privately owned. In fact, the V-8 car was originally purchased by Bill Collins years later. He applied a "Banshee" nameplate to it.

XP-853

Mustang's arrival in April 1964 was met with skepticism by corporate management and jeers from divisional staff who'd been asking for a sporty four-seater. "We'd heard through the grapevine that Ford's Mustang was coming, but Ed Cole, the group executive of cars and trucks, felt that it was going to be a flash in the pan," said Pontiac's product planner, Ben Harrison. "He focused on furthering the Corvair Monza instead. As soon as it came out, it sold better than any of us thought, and I went to Cole and told him that the Mustang was here to stay and we better come up with something quick. Ford created a new market with a small, sporty, four-seat sports car with a traditional driveline and an optional V-8 and they had it all to themselves."

On September 1, 1965, Ed Cole proposed an all-new F-body for Chevrolet and Pontiac. The program was named XP-853 and he envisioned it as a sports car capable of carrying two and four passengers. It was aimed toward competing heavily with Mustang as well as the competitors from any other make it spawned. It seems that the concept was a direct result of Pontiac's work on the two-seat XP-833 program as well as the four-seat XP-851 program Cole commissioned months earlier.

Cole requested clay models and interior layouts of the XP-853 from each division's styling staff for a formal review at a product meeting on October 19, 1965. Chevrolet was asked to model a two-passenger convertible while Pontiac was tasked with a four-passenger coupe. Much to the dismay of all involved, the proposed XP-853 program was dropped the day before the meeting. The official reasoning was that corporate determined Chevrolet didn't need an additional car line at that time.

Recognizing the need for a traditional front-engine/rear-drive sports car to combat the Mustang, Chevrolet and Pontiac pushed corporate management to continue program development. By late October 1965, General Motors approved the funding request. Apparently DeLorean wasn't pleased with the program's direction, however. An internal document notes that on November 26, 1965, Pontiac officially requested separation from XP-853 because it felt there was too much interchangeability with Chevrolet and asked to instead pursue its own XP-858 program. Chevrolet forged onward with the XP-853 program, which eventually, in one form or another, evolved into the Camaro that debuted with the 1967 model year.

XP-858

Because of its very short life, details are rather sketchy, but it's obvious that the whirlwind XP-858 program was the result of DeLorean's continued quest for a Pontiac-specific small, sporty vehicle. The XP-858 consisted of two- and four-passenger vehicles that incorporated the

The XP-853 program was initiated by General Motors in September 1965 as an attempt to give Pontiac and Chevrolet a Mustang competitor, but the new F-car was canceled as quickly as it started. With continued fighting, the two divisions received approval for additional development. When DeLorean learned how much component interchangeability the corporation expected between the two division's vehicles, he withdrew Pontiac from the program to seek its own venture. It's easy to see that upon Pontiac's departure from the XP-853 program, the concept was clearly on its way to becoming the 1967 Firebird. (Photo Courtesy General Motors)

design features of the XP-833 and 851 programs as well as Pontiac's contributions to the XP-853 program.

Pontiac Studio started a clay model of the two-passenger XP-858 on November 30, 1965, and in early December the division announced to corporate that it was planned for the 1968 model year introduction. Production was slated to occur in Canada, which hurdled Fisher Body and the costs associated with it. The developmental photos I have of XP-858 are dated January 21, 1966, and reveal roadster styling with very attractive lines that share a strong resemblance to the XP-833 and, again, the Corvette Stingray.

It's not clear what transpired between Pontiac and the corporation during the next few months, but the division wasn't allowed to proceed with the development of its own vehicle. It may once again have been the result of Chevrolet's protest over the possibility of Pontiac producing a Corvette competitor and GM's recognized need for a four-passenger sports car. The work order summary chart reveals that the XP-858 program was officially canceled on April 20, 1966. It states that the decision was due to corporate management's directive that Pontiac use the Chevrolet-developed F-car for 1967.

After withdrawing from the XP-853 program in November 1965, Pontiac Studio immediately started modeling an entirely new two-passenger sports car with plans for a 1968 model year release. Encompassing all prior developmental efforts toward previous XP programs, shades of XP-833 and XP-853 are quite visible in the preliminary styling buck of this program, which was assigned the designation XP-858. I believe this particular program was the first to use the "Banshee" nameplate. It was one of two XP programs that Pontiac actively pursued when General Motors informed Pontiac in March 1966 that it was to immediately rejoin the F-car program that Chevrolet had nearly finished. (Photo Courtesy General Motors)

XP-798

The XP-798 program was initiated by GM Design Chief William L. Mitchell in 1962 as a four-passenger sports coupe intended for Chevrolet and Pontiac. Chevrolet opted out of the program in midyear 1963. By February 1964 Pontiac had taken it on independently and developed a full-scale fiberglass prototype, which it named "Scorpion."

The attractive four-seater contained beautifully styled exterior panels with an aerodynamic fastback shape and an overall body length of nearly 197 inches and a 109-inch wheelbase. The roof featured panels that hinged toward the center of the body to allow for extra headroom while entering or exiting. The doors were also rather unconventional: They were much larger than those of a typical production vehicle, and they hinged outward and then slid forward, lending easier access to the rear seat.

According to the program's work order summary chart, developmental efforts progressed steadily throughout the mid-1960s. Pontiac decided on

Pontiac's XP-798 program dates back to 1962, but the concept is best remembered as the shuttlecock that volleyed between John DeLorean and corporate management at a New York auto show in April 1966. Originally named "Scorpion," and later renamed "Banshee," the four-passenger sports car boasted attractive styling and a number of innovative engineering features. It was actively developed as another potential vehicle and was DeLorean's final push at securing a Pontiac-specific sports car before the division rejoined Chevrolet's F-car program. (Photo Courtesy General Motors)

March 8, 1966, that it would show the XP-798 at the New York International Auto Show that began April 9. The stated intent was to gauge public response for a sporty four-passenger coupe, which DeLorean likely heard as the reason for the cancellation of all preceding two-seat concepts. It was also a Pontiac exclusive. He renamed the prototype the "Banshee" after a U.S. military fighter jet, and a press release was distributed.

On the eve of the show, GM President James Roche made the executive decision to withdraw the Banshee from Pontiac's display, unbeknownst to DeLorean. As DeLorean later made a final pre-show check, he found the Banshee absent and ordered its immediate return. Reportedly, Roche was furious when he found the Banshee again present and banished the rolling prototype to a warehouse where it remained under lock and key for the remainder of the event.

Vintage newspaper reports tell of the volley, treating it almost as if it were a disagreement between parent and child. Roche is quoted as saying that his decision was based solely on the fact that because General Motors had no plans to build such a car, there wasn't a need to display the concept vehicle. To my knowledge, DeLorean never spoke to the media about it and he may have been under a corporate gag order of some sort to prevent continued publicity about the incident.

Despite the fact that the XP-798 would have been expensive to produce, the Banshee was DeLorean's last push at securing Pontiac its own sporty vehicle compliant with four-passenger capacity. General Motors had already made the decision to include Pontiac in the F-car program a month before the New York International Auto Show occurred, so Roche's rationale that Banshee would do nothing but confuse consumers was certainly sound. It may have also been a political play to reaffirm to the notoriously rebellious DeLorean that the corporation always had the upper hand.

Although the Banshee wasn't displayed at the 1966 event, the XP-798 program remained in GM's system for the next few years until it was officially canceled in 1970. I'm told by those from within General Motors that the concept vehicle was stored for several years, but was eventually crushed. Definite traces of its design are, however, visible in the Pontiac's production Firebirds, both first and second generations.

General Motors Styling

The unique relationship between GM Styling (renamed GM Design Staff on May 1, 1972) and Pontiac during the 1960s deserves explanation. Pontiac didn't actually employ designers. General Motors had its own styling organization separate from its automotive divisions, and William L. Mitchell was its vice president. During the mid-1960s, Styling employed more than 1,500 people and its groups included industrial equipment designers, draftsmen and skilled craftsmen, model builders, and, of course, automotive designers.

Styling staffed and maintained advance and production studios in its own facility as a service for GM's automotive divisions. Each studio was led by a head designer who reported directly to Mitchell. Bunkie Knudsen considered vehicle styling an essential part of his vehicle's salability and while general manager of the Pontiac Division, he routinely visited Pontiac's production studio at GM Styling to provide feedback on vehicle development. Pete Estes and John DeLorean followed suit in subsequent years. Mitchell ultimately had final approval for production, however.

"It was a situation where Bill Mitchell was our boss and the Pontiac Motor Division was like our customer," explained Bill Porter, who was studio chief at Pontiac's exterior studio during the late 1960s. "Mitchell was in the studio daily to inspect our work and inject his influence. I remember he always liked flats and creases and can remember him using lines like, 'Your trousers have a crease. Now put one on there.' Mitchell would approve our work and we would then present it to Pontiac. It was a fine line because it had to satisfy both Mitchell and DeLorean, and the two didn't always agree on a particular style."

Pontiac Camaro

Vintage General Motors work order summary charts reveal that Bill Mitchell initiated the XP-836 program on July 15, 1964, in an advanced studio. The project was a small sport coupe for Chevrolet with the goal of creating a low-cost vehicle aimed at competing with the Mustang. On November 10, 1964, Ed Cole gave approval for the vehicle that was expected to reach production in 1967. This project was combined with XP-853 along the way. With more than two years of developmental work, it eventually resulted in Chevrolet's 1967 F-car, the Camaro, introduced in September 1966.

Beyond Pontiac's initial efforts toward the XP-853, the production 1967 F-car was developed entirely by Chevrolet. It was nearly ready for release when General Motors decided in early March 1966 that Pontiac would join Chevrolet's 1967 F-car program. As foolish as it might seem to Pontiac loyalists, the corporation had its reasoning, however, and it was based on financial soundness. How it was implemented is an amazing story best told by some of those directly involved at the time.

"We had been working on another project, the XP-798, and everyone including me thought it was a really good-looking car," recollected Tom Schreitmueller, who held the title of staff project engineer at the time. "DeLorean named it the Banshee and as opposed to using GM's Fisher Body Division, we looked to outsource its fiberglass body production to Dow-Corning in northern Michigan. As a Pontiac liaison with that company, I had spent a couple of days with them working on program setup. Within a short time they provided us with a quote for building the fiberglass-reinforced body, which was used to develop a complete project financial picture. The project was submitted to corporate management for approval but it was not approved, primarily because from a corporate standpoint, Fisher Body would be seriously impacted."

Fisher Body argued that outsourcing XP-798 body production would negatively impact General Motors profitability in two ways. First, taking body production away from the corporation would impact Fisher Body's bottom line. And second, it was Fisher Body's opinion that the XP-798 would cut into Camaro sales and take even more body production jobs away from Fisher. "The corporation agreed that Pontiac had successfully made its case for needing a small, very sporty entry but felt that its body should be made in-house if at all possible. Fisher Body was directed to prepare a cost estimate to replace that provided by Dow-Corning," added Schreitmueller.

Dow-Corning sent Schreitmueller two copies of its cost proposal for XP-798 body builds and corporate management insisted that one be provided to Fisher for use in preparing its cost and tooling estimate for the body. "In a move that only John DeLorean could have dreamed up, he instructed me to deduct 10 percent from the Dow-Corning body quote, then write that number on the proposal in pencil and lightly erase it," explained Schreitmueller. "He was trying to force Fisher Body into meeting Dow-Corning's low-dollar bid or go crazy trying to figure out how Dow-Corning could do it for that amount!"

After considering Fisher Body's arguments as well as other factors, however, corporate management denied Pontiac's request to produce the four-seat XP-798. "When that was turned down, we were handed the Camaro in which to create our sporty four-passenger vehicle," Schreitmueller added. Neither division was happy with the corporation's decision to include Pontiac in the 1967 F-car program. Each felt that it eroded vehicle exclusivity; Chevrolet protested that it expended nearly all of the resources necessary for developing the 1967 F-car. Pontiac was simply given a completed project to customize to create a Chevrolet competitor.

The XP-798 Banshee's body shape was quite attractive. Door length was extended to allow easy passenger access to the rear seating area, but it proved to be a concern as the car neared production. An internal memo discussed Engineering's search for a cost-effective solution. DeLorean planned to have the fiberglass body produced by Dow-Corning, an outside vendor, and GM's Fisher Body Division took exception. Its argument was among the reasons GM management prevented Pontiac from moving forward with the Banshee. (Photo Courtesy General Motors)

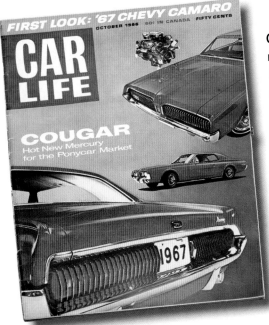

Car Life *magazine is credited with coining the term "pony car" to describe the small, sporty car segment that emerged as other manufacturers introduced competitors to Ford's Mustang. I believe its first use was the October 1966 issue when the Mercury Cougar and Chevrolet Camaro were introduced. An editorial details the intent behind the term "pony car" and the word is used several times throughout the magazine, including its cover.*

Pontiac argued that any of its unsuccessful attempts at unique, sporty two- and four-seaters it so passionately created was a better fit for the performance-oriented division than using Chevrolet's F-car. "DeLorean was really frustrated. From the outset we were figuring ways to Pontiac-ize our version of the Camaro. The styling limitations the corporation imposed upon us made the F-car project seem very unappealing, but we all knew we had to make the Camaro work. I spent a good deal of time developing financial reports as to their impact on profitability," added Schreitmueller.

Developmental work on Pontiac's F-car had begun in advance of the New York International Auto Show that April, yet DeLorean pushed ahead with plans to display the already-canceled XP-798 concept at that show. Knowing that Pontiac would be producing its own F-car and the XP-798 had been officially shelved, only now might Roche's decision to pull the Banshee from the event seem fortuitous. It gives merit to his comment that the corporation had no plans to build it.

General Motors thought long and hard about Pontiac's entry into the F-car market before arriving at its decision. Market studies indicated that a sporty four-passenger vehicle that directly competed with the Mustang would sell in good quantity. Developing the Camaro was an immense expense. The corporation also understood that Chevrolet's volume alone wasn't enough to pay for the F-car tooling. It also knew that Pontiacs sold notoriously well and expected a sporty Pontiac F-car to move well. Its volume would help make the entire F-car program financially successful sooner. To further assist in that financial success, the corporation required that F-car

structuring be used in the redesigned X-car for 1968.

General Motors was also aware that Mercury was actively developing the Cougar as a plusher, larger, and higher-priced cousin to the Mustang. With Pontiac one rung higher on the corporate ladder than Chevrolet, consumers would pay Pontiac's higher base cost but expected entry-level content and up-level component quality to accompany it. With the low-priced Camaro aimed as the Mustang competitor, increasing the standard content of Pontiac's F-car would allow it to command a higher price point. General Motors planned to position the Pontiac as the Cougar competitor.

It's certainly possible that management also used the F-car as a pawn to defiantly fulfill DeLorean's continued requests for a small, sporty Pontiac. One retired GM employee with first-hand knowledge of the program said, while claiming anonymity, "DeLorean had his clashes with the corporation and when his last project was shot down, he made some pointed comments about the group. Management was so frustrated with him that handing him Chevrolet's F-car was the machine's way of saying, 'Well, you wanted one. Now do something with it.' And in true DeLorean fashion, boy, did he ever!"

Without time for unique body panel tooling or funding for major structural changes and engineering enhancements, General Motors permitted Pontiac only limited platform changes in which to create its F-car and to reach the public as quickly as possible. Management required the use of Camaro's body shell and chassis architecture, but permitted Pontiac to install its own drivetrains and create new bolt-on pieces that would allow the division to maintain its unique exterior and interior identity.

The Transformation

Once past the disappointment and frustration of the failed two- and four-seat programs that so many within the division so strongly believed in, and then being told it could simply tart up a Camaro, Pontiac recognized that this was its only opportunity to build the sports car it desired. DeLorean vowed to make his F-car even more exciting than Chevrolet's and pushed his team to widely separate it from Chevrolet's with improved engineering

After General Motors rejected several attempts by Pontiac to secure its own two-seat sports car, the company decided that the F-car would not only fulfill Pontiac's request for a sporty car but also increase overall program volume. Management handed Pontiac the nearly completed Chevrolet Camaro in March 1966. To ensure it reached consumers quickly, the corporation limited Pontiac's exterior and interior changes to simple cosmetics. This vintage Pontiac press photo depicts a few iterations of the front-end styling as it evolved from the Chevrolet's Camaro into the Pontiac Firebird we know today. (Photo Courtesy General Motors)

The basic details of Pontiac's four-seat F-car had been developed by May 1966. Chevrolet's Camaro was nearly ready for pilot production, but Pontiac's late entry and the quest to distinctly separate its F-car from its sister brand delayed Pontiac's vehicle release by several months. Pontiac designers were quite successful in taking a Camaro and giving it a unique appearance that identified it as a Pontiac from any angle. (Photo Courtesy General Motors)

When Pontiac rejoined the 1967 F-car program in March 1966, Chevrolet's Camaro was completely engineered and practically ready for production. General Motors handed DeLorean a Camaro with which he was to create Pontiac's F-car with limited changes. For at least a while, the corporation considered a two-seat variant of the F-car complete with a wheelbase shortened by 8 inches. Pontiac modeled the concept in its studio at GM Styling to assess the effect, but it ended there.

Pontiac charged ahead to visually separate its F-car from Chevrolet's by adding features that gave it a strong Pontiac identity. There was little chance consumers could mistake Chevrolet's F-car for Pontiac's. Borrowed from the 1967 GTO, louvered taillights were a feature that Pontiac incorporated into its 1967 F-car, in an attempt to integrate it into Pontiac's potent performance car lineup. The chrome-plated rear bumper was styled differently also.

practicality and performance-minded features and styling that youthful customers found appealing. He also understood that injecting the cues that contributed to GTO's success would allow customers to think of it as being closer to the GTO than to the Camaro.

"John DeLorean was determined to make the Firebird successful and he put its development on the fast track," Pontiac's product planner, Ben Harrison said. "Just as the project began he called a group of us to the [Milford] Proving Grounds one Saturday to view a pre-production Camaro. Our job was to determine what could be modified to make it look like a Pontiac. We agreed that it needed our bumper and hood, and the taillight treatment was taken directly from the GTO. We got the corporation to approve all that."

DeLorean worked closely with exterior design chief Jack Humbert, who headed Pontiac Studio at the time, to ensure the look of Pontiac's F-car was on target. GM designer Ron Hill was Humbert's assistant and he said, "Pontiac's 1967 F-car was basically a Camaro facelift and I remember the project being very hurried. There was no real funding and very little developmental time. We simply took the approach, 'We have to do this,' so we sat down and did it."

Humbert and his team hurriedly pushed the F-car ahead of 1968 Pontiac projects already in progress. The division's signature split-grille theme was crafted into a full-width front bumper whose central point created an

A full-width chrome-plated bumper, distinct split-grille theme, and quad headlight treatment were among the features that Pontiac borrowed from 1968 A-car development and incorporated into its 1967 F-car. Pontiac's highest performance F-car was equipped with a 400-inch V-8 and a dual-scooped hood adorned with bright "400" callouts that lent an aggressive appearance and maintained separation from other Firebirds in the lineup. The scoops' shape was borrowed from the 1968 GTO.

overall body length greater than Camaro's by more than 4 inches. The taillights took on the shape of those from the 1967 GTO. Side louvers had become a trademark of 1960s Pontiac performance, and Wayne Vieira added the feature to each rear quarter to create visual separation from a side perspective. Hill said, "We were reasonably happy with our F-car under the circumstances. It looked totally unique despite being equipped with the same body panels as the Camaro."

As the performance division within General Motors, Pontiac wanted its F-car more powerful than Chevrolet's as well. Its base 6-cylinder engine was rated at 165 hp, whereas Camaro's 6 was rated at 140. The GTO's 400-inch V-8 was specifically chosen because it was larger than Camaro's 396. It was, however, detuned to remain compliant with the corporation's new policy on maximum weight-to-horsepower ratio, which kept performance reasonable and promoted the safety-conscious image.

The hot-performance 400 model was equipped with a pair of dual scoops molded into the hood for immediate visual identification. Although the scoop's shape was pilfered from the 1968 GTO designed alongside Pontiac's 1967 F-car, its true origin points to earlier Pontiac show cars. Merlyn Boyden, a supervisor in Pontiac's Engineering garage, recalls being tasked with installing the first Pontiac 400 into a 1967 F-car in 1966. "We modified a pre-production Camaro by adding prototype body panels and the 400 engine, for which we had to fabricate frame mounts. We then installed a hand-crafted fiberglass 400

Although Pontiac used extra brightwork to trim its F-car, simulated air louvers with chrome-plated accents were added to distinguish the Firebird from the Camaro in a side perspective. Pontiac had used this feature previously on its show cars but never on a production vehicle until midyear 1967. Fender louvers, both functional and ornamental, became a Pontiac performance car staple.

hood to ensure we had sufficient clearance. I remember the prototype hood buckling badly from the underhood heat during subsequent tests, but it really looked good."

Within weeks, Styling's exterior designers had transformed the Camaro into an aggressive-looking sports car easily recognizable as a Pontiac. "Everyone started following DeLorean's lead and bought into the F-car program," said Ben Harrison. "His determination to make it better than the competition in every aspect made it a very exciting project to work on. As the package started coming together, I think we all recognized that Pontiac's F-car was going to be something really special."

Pontiac wanted an instrument panel exclusive to its F-car. Fedele Bianco, interior design chief at Pontiac Studio, modeled a mockup in clay, but time and lack of funding prevented it from moving forward. Just as with the exterior styling, Bianco and his team were left with injecting superficial Pontiac flavor into the Chevrolet-designed Camaro interior.

Bob Luyckx was Bianco's assistant at the time, and he recollected, "We knew the 1967 F-car was basically a facelift situation and were unable to modify the Camaro interior much. We added a few small details to give it individuality, but it remained very much Chevrolet's design. We improved upon it over the next couple of years, but the second-generation Firebird worked out much better for Pontiac in my opinion. A designer always wants to start with a clean sheet and we were unable to do that for 1967."

Ben Harrison added, "We just didn't have the funding for anything major inside the car, but we needed it to have the Pontiac look. We used the steering wheel from our full-size Pontiac and created thick vinyl seat covers with our own pattern. We added woodgrain vinyl appliques on the dash and die-cast badges on the door panels to maintain elevated consumer perception. The entire situation wasn't ideal, but we made do despite the limitations. It was a clever transformation that produced an attractive car inside and out, and in record time."

To make its F-car a better handler than the Camaro, Pontiac's John Seaton and his suspension team took a larger-diameter front sway bar and tuned it for a firmer ride. Seaton found the Camaro's mono-leaf rear springs a great detriment because they allowed axle hop during heavy acceleration and/or braking. A phenomenon common to leaf-sprung vehicles raced on the dragstrip, racers combatted it with "traction bars," which limited axle travel. Seaton conjured up a "radius rod" that solidly linked the rear axle with the frame, effectively eliminating the condition.

Pontiac's F-car was marketed with a wheelbase of 108.1 inches, which was minutely larger than Camaro's at 108. The front wheel track of each F-car measured 59 inches, but the rear wheel track of Pontiac's edged Chevrolet's by more than 1 inch, giving it the widest track among all competitors in the market. It also allowed Pontiac to include its F-car in its aggressive Wide Track marketing campaign.

Birth of the Firebird

You've probably noticed by now that the "Firebird" name has been omitted when discussing the development of Pontiac's F-car. Why? you might ask. Well, there's a simple reason for it. Pontiac didn't officially name its F-car the "Firebird" until pilot production was just about to begin.

As Chevrolet and Pontiac's respective F-car programs neared production status, each division was tasked with creating names for its variant. Chevrolet had strongly considered "Panther," but "Camaro" was specifically chosen for its French derivation, which loosely translated into "friend."

The May 20, 1966, printing of the *El Paso Herald Post* was among the very first publications to report that Pontiac would have its own sports car in February 1967 with an anticipated nameplate of "Banshee." DeLorean liked the Banshee name and had used it when renaming the XP-798 for the New York International Auto Show that spring. In fact, he even spent $6,000 that summer to purchase its rights from FiberFab, a West Coast–based kit-car manufacturer that trademarked "Banshee" for one of its models. From that point forward, Pontiac referred to its F-car as the Banshee.

Chevrolet's Camaro was introduced to the buying public in September 1966 as a four-passenger sports car aggressively developed to be better than the Mustang in every respect. Camaro's exterior was aerodynamically styled for an exciting visual appeal. Its cockpit-type interior had traces of Corvair and Corvette overtones and was slightly larger to provide greater passenger comfort. Where Ford essentially carried over its Falcon suspension, which contributed to Mustang's stiffer ride, Camaro's underpinnings were a fresh design using the latest computer-aided technology to soften the ride while providing superior handling characteristics.

The Camaro hit the ground running. According to GM production records, Chevrolet produced more than 15,000 its first month. Because of its late entry into the F-car program, Pontiac wasn't able to finish and release its variant until months later. Camaro sales went unabated during that time. In the fall of 1966, word spread that Pontiac was working on its own F-car, but many media outlets treated its anticipated February 1967 arrival with skepticism, simply assuming Pontiac's version would be little more than a rebadged Camaro, unaware of what the performance division had in store for them.

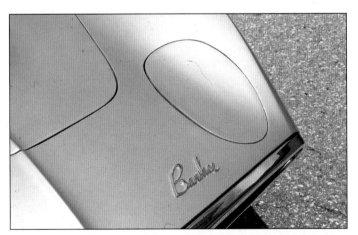

Pontiac had initially planned to use the "Banshee" name for its F-car and actively worked on preparing emblems for production. Not long before the vehicle was scheduled for its public release, the Banshee name was dropped because of its association with death. The prototype Banshee emblems left over from the F-car program were used to decorate the otherwise nameless XP-833 prototype vehicles before they entered private hands in the 1970s. (Photo Courtesy Don Keefe)

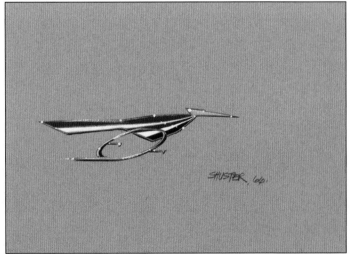

Many new names were proposed for consideration after the Banshee name was dropped. "Roadrunner" was among them and Stuart Schuster, a stylist in GM Styling's Automotive Identification department, created this sketch as a possible logo. It predated Plymouth's involvement with the name by nearly two model years. (Photo Courtesy Stu Shuster)

Development of "Banshee" badging began as Pontiac's production F-car neared, but that came to an abrupt halt. "Shortly after the Camaro was released, some writers pointed out that 'camaro' also meant 'shrimp' in Spanish," Harrison said. "Chevrolet did all it could to draw attention away from that in its marketing, but it still generated some negative publicity. I decided I should check on 'Banshee' and found an acceptable definition was a female spirit whose wail foretold of pending death. I read that definition to DeLorean and without hesitation, he dropped the Banshee name and never considered it again. He wanted to avoid any negativity with our new F-car."

With production just weeks away, Pontiac frantically conjured up exciting new names for its now nameless F-car. Some possibilities included GM-X, Phantom,

Scorpion, T/T (which stood for "Tourist Trophy," the oldest car race in the world), and Road Runner. Pontiac even went so far as to have a concept sketch of a possible "Road Runner" emblem created. Stuart Shuster of GM Styling's Automotive Identification department told me, "I created the original sketch. The Plymouth Road Runner was several months off and a designer in Pontiac studio took the name 'Roadrunner' to Chrysler when he went to work there."

The gas turbine–powered XP-21 program of the early 1950s was a joint experimental project between Harley Earl, vice president of GM's Styling, and the GM Research Laboratories, to further the development of aerodynamic shapes and turbine propulsion as an alternative power source. It was displayed at GM's 1954 Motorama. The single-seat fiberglass body, which took on the appearance of a high-speed jet airplane and a top-speed claim of 200 mph, was America's first gas turbine vehicle. High exhaust temperatures (reportedly in the range of 1,250 degrees F) plagued later development.

When Pontiac abandoned "Banshee" for its F-car, John DeLorean considered a number of proposals but ultimately chose to borrow the "Firebird" name from the series of experimental jet-powered vehicles in GM's system. A press release followed shortly thereafter announcing the F-car's official name, explaining how the folkloric Firebird exuded youth and power, and describing the F-car's correlation to a series of experimental cars. This photo accompanied it. (Photo Courtesy General Motors)

Expanding on the technology of Firebird I, the titanium-bodied Firebird II created a media frenzy at GM's Motorama in 1956 with its four seats and greater appeal as a family vehicle. Excessive exhaust heat from the gas turbine engine (though reduced by a third) was still a concern. Equipped with technology that allowed it to follow an electric wire imbedded in the roadway and display road and weather conditions to passengers, Firebird II was capable of being operated conventionally or automatically (without any hands on the steering wheel or controls).

The futuristic shape of the two-seat Firebird III with its twin bubble canopies and drive-by-wire technology arrived in 1958. Exhaust heat was reduced to an acceptable range and a small, 2-cylinder, internal combustion engine was used to drive the accessories. All three original Firebird concepts are on display at the General Motors Heritage Center in Warren, Michigan.

Another name Pontiac considered was "Firebird." General Motors had already trademarked and used it for its series of experimental jet-age vehicles that featured gas-turbine propulsion, so there were no copyright or licensing issues to delay obtaining new emblems and badging. At least one vintage newspaper reported that Pontiac announced on November 1, 1966, that its F-car had been officially named "Firebird." The original logo drawings reveal an initiation date of late-October 1966.

It's unknown who suggested the Firebird name, but DeLorean ultimately approved the mid-October name choice. In a Pontiac press release distributed weeks later, he was quoted as saying the Firebird was "a legendary Indian symbol which promised action, power, beauty, and youth." It simply couldn't have fit the way Pontiac hoped to market its F-car any better.

With the Firebird name secured, designers went to work creating an emblem and Shuster was commissioned to pen the design for Pontiac. Remaining true to DeLorean's definition, the result was a bird with outstretched wings rotated downward and a squinted eye whose overall appearance and shape were strongly influenced by western Native American tribes.

Pontiac buyers expected greater basic content when compared to a similar Chevrolet model so to substantiate that value, Firebird featured full-length rocker panel trim and a series of bright accents to the vertical louvers on each quarter panel. Where some manufacturers may have used cloth seating surfaces and a rubber floor mat to reduce the cost of entry-level models, Pontiac marketed its Firebird equipped with the same materials found in its luxurious-yet-sporty Grand Prix, whose base cost was several hundred dollars higher. Firebird's suspension was also revised to make it sit slightly lower than the Camaro and E70 x 14 tires were made standard equipment.

Despite pushback from GM's legal team about infringement concerns for a British company using the name for its outboard motor, the corporation selected "Firebird" as the name of its gas-turbine XP-21 program. Each vehicle was adorned with a Firebird. Depending on the year, its shape and appearance differed. All had clear delineation to the bird associated with western Native American tribes. This final iteration was created for Firebird III and today is found on all three vehicles.

After reviewing a number of possibilities, Pontiac decided to use the Firebird nameplate for its 1967 F-car in October 1966. An emblem was created, and holding true to the name borrowed from the series of experimental vehicles, a Native American bird with downward-facing wings was created. This particular version remains synonymous with the first-generation Firebird.

General Motors priced the Camaro to compete with Ford's Mustang while Pontiac's up-level Firebird was priced to compete directly with Mercury's Cougar. Pontiac didn't agree with that, however. The division expected the Firebird to cut into GTO sales, but Pontiac saw its two performance vehicles aimed at separate consumer segments. Pony car sales were hot for 1967 and the Camaro was on track to sell more than 120,000 by the time the Firebird was released. Pontiac sought to capitalize on the customer base that went on to purchase more than 220,000 Camaros, nearly 475,000 Mustangs, and 150,000 Cougars during the 1967 model year.

Pontiac planned to flood the market with exciting marketing to sway undecided first-time buyers into purchasing the youthful and powerful Firebird. Its ultimate goal, however, was to attract current Mustang owners seeking to take a step up for their next purchase. With convertible styling as hot as it was at the time, it only made sense that Pontiac offered a Firebird convertible to secure as many takeaway sales as possible.

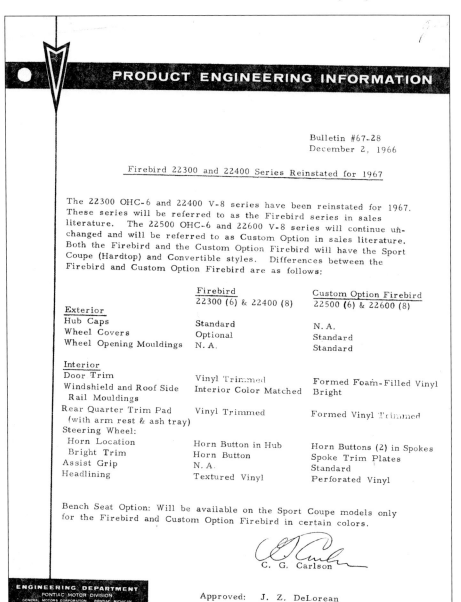

Internal Engineering Bulletin 67-28 dated December 2, 1966, is among the earliest documents that discusses Pontiac's new 1967 Firebird by name. The direct reference to its reinstatement suggests that the F-car was planned and canceled at some point. It likely coincides with the division's decision to opt out of the initial F-car program to focus on various other XP projects. It's obvious that Pontiac had the trim levels and equipment well defined at the time this bulletin was printed. The Firebird was truly as classy as any other 1967 Pontiac in the lineup.

The First Firebirds

With production just around the corner, Pontiac anxiously awaited consumer response to its new F-car. The scheduled release was February 23, 1967, in Pontiac's display at the Chicago Auto Show. A number of prototype Firebirds were made available to Pontiac staffers, but in order for Pontiac dealers to have vehicles on hand for showroom displays to coincide with Firebird's February release, regular production was scheduled to begin in January 1967.

Prior to regular production, Pontiac was busy building un-saleable pilot vehicles as well as a small fleet of specially built Firebirds intended for promotional use and show duties to introduce the line to consumers. According to vintage newspaper reports, Pontiac announced that pilot production of the new 1967 Firebird began on or about December 13, 1966, at the General Motors Assembly Division (GMAD) plant in Lordstown, Ohio. Having located the first units produced, that fact can be confirmed.

The first two V-8 Firebirds were assigned production Vehicle Identification Numbers (VINs) 223677U100001 and 223377U100002. "SHOW" was stamped into their cowl-mounted data tags, apparently indicating the intended purpose. The tag of 100001 is stamped "SHOW1" and that of 100002 is stamped "SHOW4." Other Firebirds with subsequent VINs were built along with these two and they, too, likely had an intended usage, also containing data tags that were stamped accordingly.

The billing history card for Firebird 100001 reveals that it was Regimental Red with a black convertible top and equipped with a 326 2-barrel engine and a 2-speed automatic transmission. Firebird 100002 was a hardtop that featured a Silverglaze exterior with a black Cordova top and Rally II wheels. It was equipped with a 326 H.O. 4-barrel engine and backed by a 4-speed manual transmission.

After their tenure in Pontiac's marketing department, the first two V-8 Firebirds made their way into public hands, sort of. Originally purchased by Pontiac employees at the end of the 1967 model year, subsequent owners remained fellow employees or close friends. To the best of my knowledge, Firebird 100001 remained in the Detroit area for decades. According to a former owner of Firebird 100002, it was sold during the mid-1970s to a friend living in Arizona.

The first two V-8 Firebirds were reunited in the early 1990s when the owner of 100001 purchased 100002. A restoration was planned and the two were partially disassembled, but the project stalled and the two remained in that state until 2012, when they were put up for auction on eBay. Hobbyists were abuzz when news of the two surfaced. The duo was ultimately purchased by a private individual at the auction's close.

Firebirds 100001 and 100002 were nationally renowned in 2014 when they became the subject of a reality-based auto enthusiast television show. The partially sensationalized plot portrayed them as abandoned 1967 Firebird prototypes that were newly discovered and not the production-line-built promotional vehicles that

were previously on eBay, as knowledgeable hobbyists knew them to be. The show shop purchased the Firebirds and performed complete restorations in record time. The Firebirds reportedly now reside in an auto museum in the Midwest.

When show promoters shared the "discovery" of these two Firebirds with media outlets, the instant headlines that resulted generated significant interest and attention not only for the Firebird model line, but for the entire Pontiac hobby market in general. It's quite amazing to think that these two Firebirds, originally used to promote the new-for-1967 Firebird model line, are still doing today exactly what they were intended to do when produced in December 1966.

Although there's no question (based solely on VIN sequence) that 100001 was the first V-8 Firebird produced, it's not clear whether it was actually the *first* 1967 Firebird to roll off the assembly line at Lordstown. Because Firebirds equipped with 6-cylinder (OHC-6) engines had a VIN sequence beginning with a "6," there's a chance that the 1967 Firebird with VIN 600001 could have been assembled ahead of it, making it the first Firebird truly produced. No documentation to support either argument has surfaced, however.

The whereabouts of the first OHC-6 Firebirds or any previous or current owners is uncertain, but the billing history cards for VINs 600001 and 600002 are available from PHS Automotive Services. It appears that they were assembled at the same time as their V-8 brethren and assigned to Pontiac's internal fleet for promotional usage. It then seems that they, too, were sold at the end of the 1967 model year. As of this writing in 2016, no additional details beyond what's gleaned from the billing histories of either car have yet to surface.

Both 6-cylinder Firebirds were hardtop models. Firebird 600001 was a basic Montreux Blue complete with the standard 1-barrel engine, column-shift manual

PHS Automotive Services has the billing history of virtually every first-generation Firebird on file. That includes the first 1967 unit to (theoretically) roll off the assembly line at the Lordstown, Ohio, assembly plant. VIN 223677U100001 and several others that followed were destined for show use at major events across the country and have "SHOW" stamped into the cowl-mounted data tag.

transmission, and basic wheel ornamentation. In Cameo Ivory, 600002 received sportier equipment such as the Sprint-6 engine backed by an automatic transmission and Rally II wheels. Until additional information comes forth, I can only speculate on their lineage, but it's reasonable that the first two 6-cylinder Firebirds were built in series with the first two V-8 examples.

It's amazing to consider that the Firebird went from ideas on paper to assembly plant production in nine months. And although you may not agree with the corporation's decision to disallow Pontiac its own two-seater, force the Chevrolet F-car on it, and limit it to mostly cosmetic changes, it not only saved General Motors millions of developmental dollars, it allowed Pontiac to bring the Firebird to market in short order.

The first two V-8 Firebirds were purchased by Pontiac employees at the close of the 1967 model year. The pair were eventually reunited years later, and were first available for sale in an eBay auction in 2012. They became the subject of a reality television show episode that documented their restoration. Once completed, they were shown together a few times before becoming part of a museum collection in the Midwest. (Photo Courtesy Frank Johengen)

The billing history from the first 1967 Firebird equipped with a 6-cylinder engine indicates that 223377U600001 was very basic. It was unexcitingly equipped with a single-barrel carburetor and a 3-speed manual transmission with column-mounted shifter. With little to draw hobbyist interest beyond a pilot VIN, its current whereabouts is unknown.

CHAPTER TWO

1967 FIREBIRD

With the 1967 F-car completed and production ramping up for dealer inventory, Pontiac planned to formally introduce its new and exciting four-seat Firebird to the buying public at the Chicago Auto Show on February 25, 1967. The division was notorious for its elaborate displays at the high-traffic Midwestern venue, and with the spring driving season just around the corner, the late-February show seemed perfectly timed for a midyear model unveiling. At that same time, the Firebird went on sale nationwide as the newest addition to Pontiac's 1967 model year lineup.

During the weeks prior to the Firebird's debut, Pontiac began circulating information to its dealership sales staff and media outlets about its new four-passenger sports car. The first correspondence of any type occurred on January 3, 1967, when Pontiac's sales promotion manager sent zone management a memo urging dealers to pre-sell as many Firebirds as possible so that each dealership might have sufficient on-hand inventory for the upcoming release. Details of the new model were, however, rather limited.

Revered as a performance leader among its peers, Pontiac was at the top of its game during the mid-1960s. GTO sales peaked in 1966 and developmental work was underway to create a second Pontiac super car to complement it. The 1967 GTO hit the ground running and when the 1967 Firebird was introduced mid–model year, it simply reinforced Pontiac's image as GM's performance division. Many Pontiac purists consider the 1967 Firebird a venerable classic. It's easy to understand why with beautiful examples like this. (Photo Courtesy Tom DeMauro)

Official announcement of Pontiac's entry into the sports car market came with the issuance of a Firebird-specific press release on January 27, 1967. It stated that vehicles would be available for purchase in late February 1967 and that its styling would have strong Pontiac identity including the split grille theme. Emblems designating engine displacement affixed to the raised portion of the hood gave attention to performance.

Over the course of the decade preceding the Firebird's debut, Pontiac earned an image as a hip manufacturer of youthfully inspired performance cars. When the 1967 Firebird debuted on February 25, the sporty car market included many competitive options. One vintage report claims that when Pontiac dealers learned that its F-car would share such a close kinship with Chevrolet's, they were as unhappy as the Pontiac design team had been just months earlier when handed a Camaro to transform. Pontiac's efforts to distinguish the Firebird's appearance and performance were handsomely welcomed by consumers and media alike. With the copious amounts of showroom traffic it generated, dealers quickly shrugged off its perceived shortcomings.

Magazine writers praised Pontiac for its efforts in giving the Firebird distinction over the Camaro, not only visually, but for its superior ride and handling qualities as well. Some even noted that the Firebird seemingly emanated performance. One stated it was a quality that Camaro inherently lacked. Writers were enamored with the multitude of optional Firebird equipment, which allowed buyers to create a uniquely equipped example to specifically suit their needs.

The Firebird Lineup

To give the Firebird maximum consumer appeal and position it as a solid contender against every competitor in class, Pontiac created a number of option packages that distinctly adjusted the Firebird's sporty attitude to complement the driving personality and budget of its targeted buyer. Advertised as The Magnificent Five, the ingenious marketing concept purportedly suggested by Pontiac's ad agency, McManus, John & Adams, lent the perception of five distinct Firebird models and played on the idea that the division cared so much for its customers that it thoughtfully created a Firebird for every buyer. The process was, in fact, nothing more than checking boxes on the order form. Certain components were automatically included.

FORM 662

PONTIAC MOTOR DIVISION
GENERAL MOTORS CORPORATION
AIR MAIL LETTER

TO	Mr. G. S. Stephens	ADDRESS	
FROM	C. L. Copeland	ADDRESS	Pontiac, Michigan
SUBJECT	1957 FIREBIRD Advance Information Guide	DATE	January 3, 1967

CONFIDENTIAL

ATTENTION: Zone Managers

Under separate cover we are shipping each Zone a prorate of the attached subject Advance Information Guide. The quantities will allow Zones to provide one copy of the Guide to all field personnel and to each dealer plus a small extra supply to be used at the Zone Manager's discretion.

This Advance Information Guide is being provided as a helpful aid to dealers and it should be used as reference when writing initial orders for FIREBIRD models. Quantities of the Advance Information Guide and the Wholesale Car Orders (mailed by Car Distribution) are scheduled to arrive in each Zone during the week of January 2. Since this material is preliminary in nature, changes may occur without notice prior to Dealer Announcement.

We recognize that this material will reveal some of the basic FIREBIRD features to dealers before they attend the Announcement Meetings to be conducted by Management. However, this advance information should in no way take the "edge" off of the Announcement Meetings, but it will rather add to dealer interest to personally see the car. Also, it is very important that we develop a large initial bank of bonafide retail orders for FIREBIRD models. To do so, dealers must do some preselling, so as many retail orders as possible can be put into the system very early. This will allow us to preference a large number of sold orders for arrival on or shortly after FIREBIRD Announcement Day.

In view of the above, the Wholesale Car Orders and Advance Information Guide must be distributed to each dealer as soon as possible. Dealers could then contact preferred customers, write initial retail FIREBIRD orders and submit them to the Zone for early preferencing.

This letter, dated January 3, 1967, and sent via air mail is among the earliest correspondence between Pontiac and its dealers that mentions the 1967 Firebird. It explains that an Advanced Information Guide would follow and urged dealers to place Firebird orders so they could have inventory in stock upon its formal debut. Dealers were also urged to pre-sell Firebirds to preferred customers for immediate delivery on that day.

What happened if you were identified as a preferred customer by your local Pontiac dealer in 1967? You received an invitation to attend a special viewing of the new Firebird a few days ahead of the general public release. The package was tastefully decorated in glossy red cardstock with an embossed Firebird emblem in gold on the cover. It included a glossy press photo of the new model.

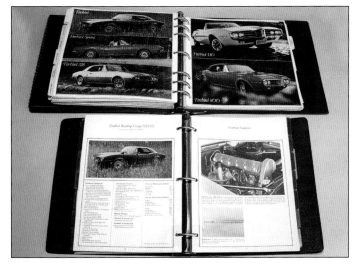

Dealership staff used a pair of minutely detailed binders that contained photos, optional equipment, and exterior and interior choices for educational purposes and to aid customers. It was rare for a dealership to have or need more than a single copy of each and examples in excellent condition can be quite valuable today.

In the decades I have spent collecting Pontiac literature, I have come across only a handful of them for the 1967 model year. None were equipped with the supplemental Firebird material. In fact, many literature collectors were unsure if such a supplement even existed. I happened across this pair at auction. Pontiac distributed a Firebird packet to dealers just after the model release with instructions to insert the material into their Sales Manual (bottom) and Colors and Interior binder (top). This directive was rarely followed. I am proud to have both as part of my collection.

A short deck was common among sports cars and Pontiac's F-car was no exception. To ensure consumers didn't mistake a Firebird for a Camaro, Pontiac stylists included a beefy, wrap-around rear bumper, added individual block letters to the deck lid, and placed a bright Firebird logo on the fuel filler door. The Firebird 400 was further differentiated from its divisional siblings with a die-cast "400" badge at the rear.

Firebird

The base model was aimed at entry-level buyers who were conscious of price and economy. Pontiac played on the Firebird's performance image, promoting that its 165-hp overhead cam 6-cylinder (OHC-6) engine offered 20 to 45 more horsepower than its competitors in the pony car category. Additional standard equipment included a column-shifted 3-speed manual transmission and

Although Firebird details leaked out and a general press release was distributed in January 1967, the first opportunity most consumers had to view Pontiac's newest model was in the division's display at the Chicago Auto Show that began February 25, 1967. If you look closely at this photo from that event, you find the first four production Firebirds with VINs 100001, 100002, 600001, and 600002 (further discussed in Chapter 1): two V-8 Firebirds (front center and right) and the first two 6-cylinder Firebirds (left and right rear). On the center turntable is Pontiac's customized Firebird convertible show car, "Skydiver," which featured pearlescent orange paint and a similar interior treatment. It was intended to attract youth interested in the sport of skydiving. (Photo Courtesy Chicago Auto Show)

1967 FIREBIRD SERIES AND MODEL IDENTIFICATION

The two Firebird body styles (Hardtop Coupe-22337 and Convertible-22367) will each be available in five (5) different versions to appeal to a broad range of sports car prospects. These major versions will be merchandised as "The Magnificent Five Firebirds" (Firebird - Firebird Sprint - Firebird 326 - Firebird H.O. - Firebird 400) and each will use the same series prefix # (223--).

The following standard equipment is distinctive to each version and indicates the major differences between each of the "Magnificent Five" Firebirds.

Firebird

- 230 cu.in., 1 bbl., reg. fuel, Overhead Cam 6-Cyl. Engine 165 horsepower
- 3-speed manual trans., fully synchronized - column mounted
- 7.35 x 14 blackwall tires

Firebird 326

- 326 cu.in., 2 bbl., reg. fuel V-8 Engine, 250 horsepower
- 3-speed manual trans., fully synchronized - column mounted
- E:70 x 14 Wide Oval blackwall tires

Firebird Sprint

- 230 cu.in., 4 bbl., Quadra-jet Overhead Cam 6-Cyl. Engine 215 horsepower
- Heavy rated front and rear springs
- H.D. clutch
- 3-speed manual trans., fully synchronized - floor mounted
- E:70 x 14 Wide Oval blackwall tires

Firebird H.O.

- 326 cu.in., high output, 4 bbl., prem. fuel, V-8 Eng., 285 hp
- Dual exhaust system
- Heavy rated front and rear springs
- Special sports side striping with H.O. block letters
- 3-speed manual trans., fully synchronized - column mounted
- E:70 x 14 Wide Oval blackwall tires

Firebird 400

- 400 cu.in., 4 bbl., Quadra-jet prem. fuel, V-8 Eng., 325 hp
- Dual exhaust system
- Chrome air cleaner, rocker arm covers and oil filler cap
- Special hood with dual air scoops
- H.D. battery and starting motor
- H.D. radiator
- Declutching engine fan
- Heavy rated front and rear springs
- 3-speed H.D. manual trans., fully synchronized - floor mounted
- E:70 x 14 Wide Oval <u>Red Line</u> tires

Effective 12-30-66

-2-

As of December 30, 1966, the details of model level content were clearly defined and the Firebird lineup was marketed as The Magnificent Five. This particular document was part of a complete package sent to dealers communicating many details of the 1967 Firebird. Correspondence such as this lends insight into Pontiac's true intent to target each Firebird model toward various customer audiences.

7.35 x 14 black-sidewall tires. Coupe pricing started at $2,666; the convertible at $2,903.

Firebird Sprint

Improved 6-cylinder performance was available by selecting the W53 Sprint Option. For $105.60 more, buyers transformed their Firebird into a Sprint that included a 4-barrel version of the OHC-6 engine designed for premium-fuel operation, a floor-shifted 3-speed manual transmission with heavy-duty clutch assembly, E70 x 14 black-sidewall Wide Oval tires, and heavy-duty suspension. Specific Sprint ornamentation was added to the rocker panel for visual identification.

Firebird 326

Most buyers in the market for a new Firebird were interested in the model for its sporty attitude and they expected V-8 power to accompany it. L30 326 Option delivered a combination of comfort and performance at the reasonable cost of $95.04 above the base-model Firebird. It included a 326-inch V-8 with 2-barrel carburetor, a column-shifted 3-speed manual transmission, and E70 x 14 black-sidewall Wide Oval tires. Pontiac played on the fact that its smallest V-8 was the largest in class, boasting 40 to 70 more horsepower than its competitors while at a comparable cost.

Firebird H.O.

L76 H.O. Option transformed the Firebird 326 into the Firebird H.O., which boasted increased performance with a sporty flair. For $169.70 over the base-model price, buyers received a high-output variant of the 326-ci with 4-barrel carburetor, dual exhaust, heavy-duty springs and shocks, heavy-duty battery, and an attractive, body-length side stripe containing specific H.O. ornamentation. The column-shifted 3-speed manual and E70 x 14 black-sidewall tires remained standard equipment.

Firebird 400

W66 400 Sport Option was the ultimate offering for performance-minded consumers. The option transformed the base model into the Firebird 400. At its heart was a hot 400-ci 4-barrel V-8 adorned with chrome accents. It also contained a host of other items (detailed elsewhere in the chapter). With the standard 3-speed manual, the Firebird 400 added $358.09 to the base Fire-

The Firebird 400 hood was adorned with dual scoops that protruded upward, which tends to de-emphasize the "ironing board" feature of the basic Firebird hood. The standard hood makes the slender spine that continues rearward from the center point of the front bumper more noticeable.

bird cost. If a 4-speed manual or automatic was preferred, the package cost dropped to $273.83, with the transmission purchased separately.

Exterior and Interior

Vintage Firebird literature shows the new model available in 15 exterior colors that spanned the entire color spectrum. According to a memo dated February 15, 1967, Starlight Black, Plum Mist, and Montego Cream were planned as standard colors, but canceled just before production began. They were treated as SPS (Special

VIN Decoding

Pontiac typically affixed its vehicles' stamped-metal VIN tag on the portion of the cowl visible when opening the driver's door, and the 1967 Firebird is no exception. For identification purposes, Pontiac numbered its Firebird Coupe and Convertible body styles differently, and VINs should begin with 22337 and 22367, respectively. The next two characters identify model year and assembly plant detail. The last six digits are a particular Firebird's build number and always begins with a "1" for a V-8 while 6-cylinder Firebirds begin with a "6." Here's an example of a typical 1967 Firebird VIN:

2 2337 7 U 100001

2	Pontiac Motor Division identifier
2337	Model styling
7	Last digit of model year
U	Assembly Plant
100001	Sequential build number

As with most Pontiacs, the VIN tag of any 1967 Firebird was riveted to the cowl in the driver's doorjamb. Beginning in 1968, federal rules required that the VIN be visible from the exterior. Although it remained on the cowl, it was subsequently relocated to the driver's side of the instrument panel behind the windshield.

The 1967 Firebird used Chevrolet's Camaro body shell. Although the silhouettes were quite similar, Pontiac used specific front and rear treatments as well as unique exterior styling cues to create a four-seat sports car that exuded Pontiac identity and looked very much unlike a Camaro from this angle. A pillared hardtop was not an option, but retractable quarter windows lent the appearance. The fixed-roof F-car was marketed as a "hardtop coupe" or "sport coupe" in sales literature. Verdoro Green was limited to the Firebird in 1967, but its availability expanded to other Pontiacs in subsequent years.

With Firebird production already underway at the Lordstown plant to fill the distribution pipeline and just before its public release, Pontiac had its zone offices notify all dealers within their respective areas with instructions on handling special-order colors Starlight Black, Plum Mist, and Montego Cream. The February 15, 1967, memo included pricing and combination availability.

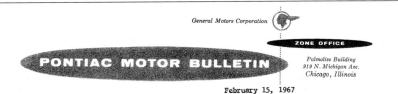

General Motors Corporation

ZONE OFFICE

PONTIAC MOTOR BULLETIN

Palmolive Building
919 N. Michigan Ave.
Chicago, Illinois

February 15, 1967

TO ALL DEALERS IN THE CHICAGO ZONE

SUBJECT: FIREBIRD SPECIAL PAINT ORDERS

We are now accepting special paint orders for the Firebird models.

Special Paints will fall into two groups:

1. STARLIGHT BLACK   CODE A
   PLUM MIST   CODE M
   MONTEGO CREAM   CODE T

   As you know, these colors have been cancelled as standard colors for the Firebird models and are in the category of a "Special - Special" since they can be ordered, punched and transceived in the regular manner.

   The price structure for these three "Special - Special" paints (Code A, T, & M) is as follows:

Dealer Net	$ 7.60
F.D.H.	.53
List	10.00
Label	10.53

   There is no special paint charge when these three paints are ordred as part of a two-tone in combination with a standard paint - the regular two-tone charge is all that applies.

2. All paints, other than the 15 standard colors and the 3 "Special - Special" paints mentioned above, are special paints and the orderes must be submitted to the Chicago Zone Office.

   The special paint charges are:

	SOLID OR WITH CORDOVA TOP	TWO-TONE
Dealer Net	$60.00	$ 82.40
F.D.H.	4.20	5.77
List	79.00	108.50
Label	83.20	114.27

   H. E. Duling,
   Office Manager & Car Distributor

HED/ddh

Solid Paint) colors on the Firebird, costing $10.53 extra. In some instances a buyer was charged for purchasing Starlight Black, but it's unclear whether Pontiac actually charged for Plum Mist and/or Montego Cream. Coronado Gold, Mayfair Maize, and Verdoro Green were additional exterior colors Pontiac made available in the spring of 1967 at no extra charge.

As a way for buyers to create a personalized Firebird, Pontiac also offered SPS colors for $83.20 that expanded the color palette to almost any GM color available that model year. Any such order had to be submitted to the zone office for approval before being released for production, however. Pontiac also offered its own custom colors, which were available on Firebird, including Blue Charcoal, Copper Blaze, Sierra Red, and Silver Turquoise.

A convertible top in five colors was available at every level and it was surprisingly popular considering the Firebird's sporty-car target market. Convertibles accounted for nearly one-fifth of all 1967 units and it was most often ordered in the Custom Option Firebird V-8 that model year. Interestingly the preservation or restoration of first-generation Firebird convertibles is overwhelmingly more popular than of hardtop models.

The Firebird's instrument panel was practically identical to the Camaro's. A color-keyed three-spoke steering wheel was standard equipment. The N30 Deluxe Steering Wheel, complete with brushed-chrome spokes, was borrowed from Pontiac's full-size models. The A-car wheel (shown) with slightly different dimensions from the full-size wheel was a midyear change for Firebird. A column-shifted manual transmission was standard; a column-shifted automatic was available at extra cost.

A Cordova top was available on coupe styling for $84.26 extra. Those who opted for a Firebird convertible had five color choices for the cloth top. A two-tone paint treatment in any standard color combination (RTT for $31.07) or with special colors (STT for $114.27) was also available.

The Firebird interior was very Camaro-like and many components were directly interchangeable. The Firebird dash panel consisted of a formed metal structure with a padded upper overlay and woodgrain trim at the center. Two large nacelles protruded outward and housed instrumentation that included a 120-mph speedometer on the left and a fuel gauge and a series of warning lamps on the right as standard equipment. For $10.53, buyers could opt for U15 Safeguard Speedometer, which warned drivers of accelerating past a pre-set speed. The W63 Rally Gauge Cluster replaced warning lamps with analog gauges for $31.60.

Another innovation was Pontiac's popular hood-mounted tachometer. The concept was developed by GM designer Ron Hill as a solution to an overly crowded mid-1960s Grand Prix and 2+2 instrument panel with the H.O. engine. "Pontiac was placing its tachometer wherever it could, like the center console, steering column, and

A-pillar," he explained to me. "While I was in the Pontiac studio, I came up with the idea of placing it outside the vehicle on the hood and designed its shape. Critics said, 'That will never work. How are you supposed to see it in the snow?' To which I replied, 'You don't use a tach in the snow!' The GM patent was issued in my name."

The electric Hood-Mounted Tachometer was a dealer-installed option at the 1967 model year startup. The complete kit included the tachometer, all electrical connections, a paper template for cutting the hood, and complete instructions. Pontiac added it to the factory-installed-option UPC list as U16 in November 1966; it appears to have reached the assembly plants

In the left pod of the instrument cluster was a 120-mph speedometer taken directly from the Camaro. It was a somewhat realistic top speed for the Firebird, particularly with the 400-ci, but the dial's color and font was atypical for Pontiac. The division created a unique hood-mounted tachometer with matching font specifically for Firebirds equipped with the option to maintain visual continuity.

Although the right pod of the instrument cluster was typically occupied by a fuel gauge and a host of warning lamps, the optional W63 Rally Gauge Cluster provided buyers with analog gauges that displayed engine oil pressure, coolant temperature, and charging system state. An in-dash tachometer wasn't available for 1967.

Among Pontiac's popular innovations during the 1960s, the Hood-Mounted Tachometer placed the engine RPM gauge outside the vehicle on its hood, directly in the driver's line of sight for easy reference. The housing of the 1967 unit stood nearly 3 inches tall and 8.5 inches long. Its redline began at either 5,100 (V-8) or 6,500 (OHC-6) rpm. Initially available as a dealer-installed item at model year startup, Pontiac made it a factory-installed option in midyear 1967. It was available on Firebird as a standalone option for $63.19 (U16), or in concert with the W63 Rally Gauge Cluster.

To increase the Firebird's trunk capacity and boast in sales materials that its F-car offered the greatest storage volume among its competitors, Pontiac made the newly developed collapsible spare tire a standard feature. The "Space Saver" tire, as Goodyear marketed it, gave the Firebird a total trunk compartment volume of nearly 10 cubic feet.

sometime after January 1967. (Research continues for a bulletin or press release that confirms it.) The tach was available on the Firebird, with or without the W63 Rally Gauge Cluster for $63.19.

A rather ordinary color-coordinated three-spoke steering wheel borrowed from entry-level Pontiacs was standard on the Firebird. The N10 Deluxe Steering Wheel with brushed-aluminum spokes was a popular option that gave the Firebird's interior an air of class for $12.11. It was included as standard equipment on the Custom Option Firebird and was a mandatory option with the 400

Sport Option. N34 Custom Sport Steering Wheel option with simulated woodgrain rim and brushed spokes was available on all Firebirds for $42.13.

Pontiac modified the Firebird's standard and deluxe steering wheels in midyear 1967. Based on information gathered from vintage Pontiac parts manuals, I have determined that the Firebird's standard and deluxe steering wheels were pirated directly from the full-size Pontiac and contained a diameter of 16.5 inches, a dish of 6.188 inches, and possibly a transparent upper rim. Most likely related to increasing driver comfort, Pontiac began

STANDARD VERSUS DELUXE

When the Firebird was introduced to consumers, Pontiac created two distinct series based solely on the selection of a single option, W54 Custom Trim. The option was advertised as "providing the ultimate in luxury and appearance" with the ability to transform a base-model Firebird into a "highly sophisticated personal sports car." When equipped with W54, Pontiac intended to refer to the model as "Custom Option Firebird," whereas no additional nomenclature was added to a Firebird with standard interior.

The transformation to a Custom Option Firebird cost $108.48. W54 Custom Trim delivered items that were otherwise extra-cost (PO1 Deluxe Wheel Discs, N30 Deluxe Steering Wheel, and UO5 Dual Horns) and added exterior

bright moldings to the front and rear wheelwells, side roof rails, and windshield pillars.

The interior was noticeably plusher with several up-level appointments. Front door panels and rear-seat side trim were padded for extra comfort and featured full-length armrests. The seating surfaces retained the same seat cover and pattern, but an assist bar was added to the passenger side of the dash panel. A perforated vinyl headliner replaced the cloth unit on hardtop styles. A total of 48,180 Firebirds were equipped with the option that year.

A 1967 Pontiac document clarifies that Pontiac's sales and accounting departments used 2337 and 2367 series identifiers to differentiate fixed-roof Firebirds from convertibles without regard to interior styling or engine type.

Although the Custom Option Firebird shared the same Morrokide seating and loop-pile carpeting with a Firebird in basic trim, door panels and rear quarter trim were plusher, and a passenger-assist grip was added to the instrument panel. Headliner material was unique to each trim level as well. The Custom Option added a level of class that most buyers opted for.

using A-car steering wheels in the Firebird, which looked identical but had a diameter of 16 inches with a depth of 5 inches.

Basic Firebird comfort features included plush loop-pile carpeting and seats covered in expanded Morrokide, a durable material constructed of a cloth backing coated with pliable vinyl that simulates the appearance of leather while remaining waterproof and stain resistant. Two-point lap belts front and rear were among the list of standard safety equipment on the Firebird. Increasing front-seat passenger safety was possible with the AS1

Shoulder Belt option, which incorporated a second belt to create a three-point restraint system. The A39 Custom Seat Belts option available for $6.32 gave buyers the opportunity to equip their particular Firebird with restraint belts that were color-keyed with the interior and included brushed-chrome buckles.

AL4 Front Bench Seat with fold-down center armrest was available to replace the front buckets on hardtop Firebirds, increasing passenger capacity to five. It was available in standard and custom styling for $31.60. Color choices were, however, limited to Blue, Gold, and Black,

Pontiac's engineering, materials, and production departments as well as Fisher Body assigned numbers 2400, 2500, and 2600 to differentiate body styling, interior type, and engine detail to precisely identify models internally, using the terms "Standard" or "Deluxe" to differentiate basic Firebirds from Custom Option Firebirds, respectively.

A list of those series identification codes is shown below. These numbers are *not* associated with the VIN in any way. My reason for detailing Pontiac's internal extended identifiers is to provide clarification should you see them elsewhere in the book or in other reference materials as you attempt to document a particular 1967 to 1969 Firebird.

Code	Body Style	Engine
2337	Standard Coupe	6-cylinder
2367	Standard Convertible	6-cylinder
2537	Deluxe Coupe	6-cylinder
2567	Deluxe Convertible	6-cylinder
2437	Standard Coupe	V-8
2467	Standard Convertible	V-8
2637	Deluxe Coupe	V-8
2667	Deluxe Convertible	V-8

Throughout this book, the Deluxe Firebird is referred to as the "Custom Option Firebird" just as Pontiac intended, but remember that Deluxe Firebirds and Custom Option Firebirds are synonymous.

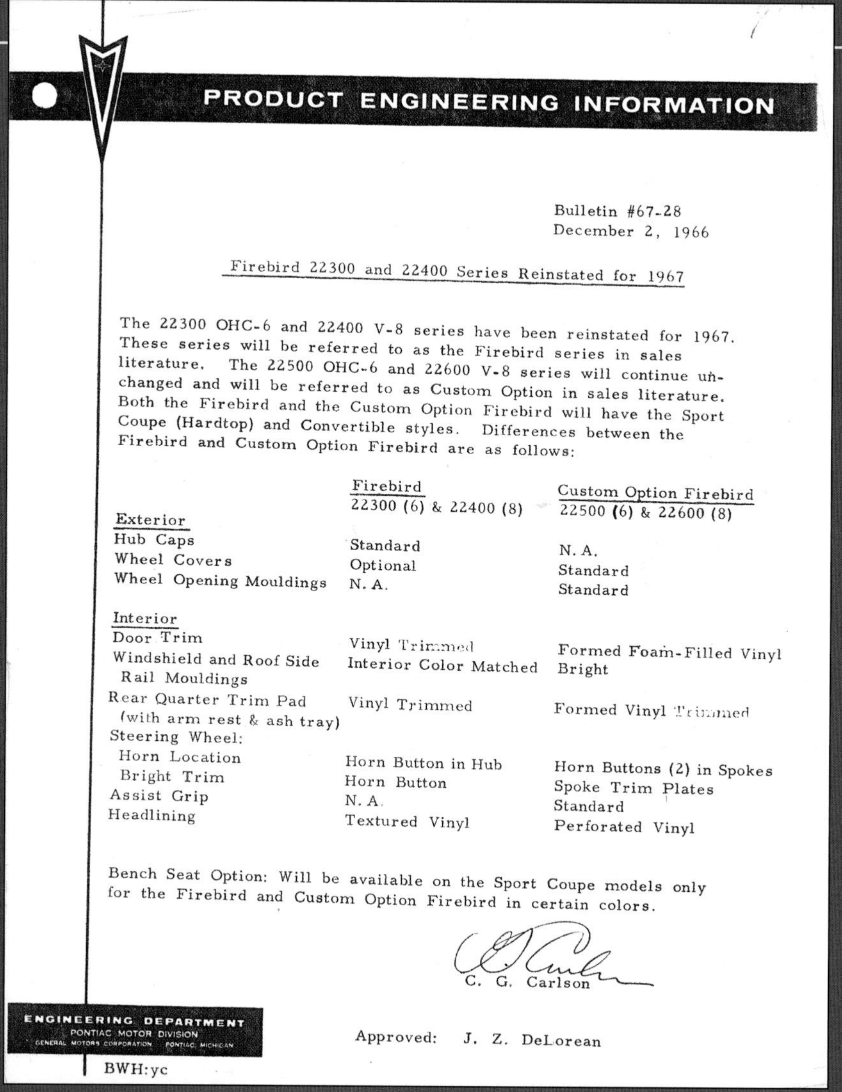

PRODUCT ENGINEERING INFORMATION

Bulletin #67-28
December 2, 1966

Firebird 22300 and 22400 Series Reinstated for 1967

The 22300 OHC-6 and 22400 V-8 series have been reinstated for 1967. These series will be referred to as the Firebird series in sales literature. The 22500 OHC-6 and 22600 V-8 series will continue unchanged and will be referred to as Custom Option in sales literature. Both the Firebird and the Custom Option Firebird will have the Sport Coupe (Hardtop) and Convertible styles. Differences between the Firebird and Custom Option Firebird are as follows:

	Firebird 22300 (6) & 22400 (8)	Custom Option Firebird 22500 (6) & 22600 (8)
Exterior		
Hub Caps	Standard	N.A.
Wheel Covers	Optional	Standard
Wheel Opening Mouldings	N.A.	Standard
Interior		
Door Trim	Vinyl Trimmed	Formed Foam-Filled Vinyl
Windshield and Roof Side Rail Mouldings	Interior Color Matched	Bright
Rear Quarter Trim Pad (with arm rest & ash tray)	Vinyl Trimmed	Formed Vinyl Trimmed
Steering Wheel:		
Horn Location	Horn Button in Hub	Horn Buttons (2) in Spokes
Bright Trim	Horn Button	Spoke Trim Plates
Assist Grip	N.A.	Standard
Headlining	Textured Vinyl	Perforated Vinyl

Bench Seat Option: Will be available on the Sport Coupe models only for the Firebird and Custom Option Firebird in certain colors.

C. G. Carlson

ENGINEERING DEPARTMENT
PONTIAC MOTOR DIVISION
GENERAL MOTORS CORPORATION • PONTIAC, MICHIGAN

BWH:yc

Approved: J. Z. DeLorean

It's unclear what Pontiac intended by stating in this internal bulletin dated December 2, 1966, that the Firebird had been reinstated for 1967, but it likely relates to DeLorean's plan to withdraw from the joint F-car project early on and pursue a Pontiac-only venture. No matter the case, the Firebird's standard equipment was sorted out well in advance of its February 1967 release.

Despite being forced to deal with Camaro's design limitations, Pontiac smartly modified the Firebird's interior to achieve the same sense of individuality it sought with the exterior. Plush and inviting, and available in an array of colors, buyers were treated to the level of comfort they expected when purchasing a Pontiac. Many options were available.

Because of Pontiac's late entry into the F-car program, interior development was limited. Many of the Firebird's appointments were taken directly from Camaro. Front bucket seats covered in Morrokide and loop-pile floor carpeting were borrowed directly from the prestigious Grand Prix. A padded trim panel adorned with the "Firebird" nameplate covered most of the door and further ensured Pontiac's F-car's distinction from Chevrolet's.

and a column-shifted transmission was required. For buyers who needed a bit of extra interior storage space, the A67 Folding Rear Seat option was available for $36.86.

When compared to larger models, the sporty Firebird's trunk was at a spatial disadvantage. Pontiac took notice and included an inflatable spare as standard equipment, which allowed the division to boast Firebird's 9.9 cubic feet of trunk capacity as the highest among its direct competitors. The N64 Conventional Spare Tire was available at no extra charge for buyers who were skeptical of the inflatable spare's capability and/or for those who customarily used the spare tire during regular rotations to extend the overall service life of their tire set.

Engine Lineup

In the years preceding the Firebird's debut, Pontiac had developed an inline 6-cylinder engine featuring a single overhead cam (OHC-6) under the direction of Chief Engineer John DeLorean. The intent was to give A-car buyers a small-displacement 6 that offered good fuel economy and moderate acceleration in a unique package to compete with Buick's 231-ci V-6 and 215-ci V-8. Like Chevrolet's 6 with an inline cylinder arrangement, Pontiac's 6 displaced 230 ci and it seemed as if many of the bolt-on components were interchangeable. Pontiac's was, however, its own design and to maintain individuality, the division went to great lengths to incorporate technology measureable by output.

Overhead cam engines were common to sporty European vehicles but were considered rather exotic in America in the late 1960s. DeLorean felt an overhead camshaft would give Pontiac an engineering edge on its domestic competitors, one that marketing could exploit. The design carried the stigma of being very complex with

Pontiac's overhead cam inline 6-cylinder (OHC-6) was the division's attempt to create an exotic, small-displacement engine like that found in European vehicles. It was capable of delivering a suitable combination of good economy and satisfactory performance. As the standard engine in the entry-level Firebird when fitted with a 1-barrel carburetor, the 230-ci 6-cylinder was rated at 165 hp.

No matter the model level, Pontiac affixed displacement badges onto the raised portion of its hood to denote engine sizing and draw attention toward the Firebird's performance image. It was a feature Camaro lacked. Remaining true to its European influence, the OHC-6 emblem displayed its volume in liters.

To increase the performance of the OHC-6 in Sprint applications, Pontiac added a 4-barrel Rochester Quadrajet carburetor and a camshaft with greater duration and valve lift. The effort boosted horsepower by 50 to a total of 215 and rewarded buyers with a Firebird that performed spiritedly while still delivering good economy.

high maintenance costs, however, and DeLorean and his engineering team, which included the capable Malcolm R. McKellar, worked hard to develop a highly reliable OHC-6 that required little maintenance.

Introduced on the Tempest line in 1966, Pontiac's OHC-6 was highly publicized and generated a significant amount of media attention. Its most innovative feature

The Sprint-6 engine also included a unique exhaust manifold that was actually two streamlined units that gathered and collected exhaust gas separately, and merged it into a single Y-pipe. The intent was to reduce the number of exhaust pulsations in the manifold at a given time. That improved scavenging at high engine speed. Independent dyno testing indicated that the Sprint-6 manifold added about 6 to 10 hp over the standard manifold in an otherwise stock combination. This particular engine is on display at Speedway Motor's Museum of American Speed in Lincoln, Nebraska.

was a rubber belt reinforced with fiberglass to drive the camshaft instead of a costly mechanical chain. In retrospect, the OHC-6 was only moderately successful with consumers, who were mostly skeptical because of the perceived shortcomings associated with overhead cam engines in general. In reality, it was very well built.

It was only fitting that Pontiac included its OHC-6 engine in the Firebird when it was introduced. As the Firebird's base mill, the OHC-6 included a 1-barrel carburetor and a cylinder head combustion chamber volume of 78 to 80 cc that produced a compression ratio of 9:1. The number-9782012 camshaft featured 228 degrees of duration and .400-inch valve lift. The 230-ci was rated at 165 hp at 4,700 rpm and 216 ft-lbs at 2,600 rpm.

The Sprint-6 was a high-performance version of the OHC-6 and boasted a 4-barrel Quadrajet carburetor, a number-9782212 camshaft with 244 degrees of duration and .438-inch valve lift, oversize intake and

The hood plateau on V-8 Firebirds proudly displayed the engine's displacement in cubic inches using chrome-plated badges accented with red paint. Firebird 400s received a similar emblem on the deck lid. Small touches like these separated Firebird from Camaro, and gave it an edge in its perceived performance value.

exhaust valves, and a split-exhaust manifold that exited into the same single-exhaust muffler used on the Firebird 326. With combustion chamber volume reduced to 66 to 67 cc, the advertised compression ratio jumped to 10.5:1, and output increased to 215 hp at 5,200 and 240 ft-lbs at 3,800 rpm. It was a formidable performer.

Pontiac's smallest displacement V-8 in 1967 was the 326-ci. It provided the typical V-8 power that buyers expected from the sporty Firebird without significantly hampering fuel economy when compared to the OHC-6

engines. The basic 326-ci (L30) was equipped with a 2-barrel carburetor, a 269/277-degree number-254 camshaft, number-140 cylinder heads with 1.92/1.66-inch valves, and a combustion chamber volume of 67 cc, which produced an advertised compression ratio of 9.2:1 for operation on regular-grade fuel. It was rated at 250 hp at 4,600 rpm and 333 ft-lbs at 2,800 rpm.

The L76 326 H.O. featured a number-9782896 4-barrel intake manifold and a Carter AFB carburetor. An advertised compression ratio of 10.5:1 was accomplished with number-141 cylinder heads, which retained the 1.92/1.66-inch valve sizing, but contained a reduced combustion chamber volume of 58 cc. Like the 2-barrel

Although dual 4-barrel carburetors were found on Pontiac's competition engines from 1956 to 1963, Pontiac used a trio of 2-barrel carburetors for its maximum performance street engines beginning in 1957. Marketed as Tri-Power, it used the center carburetor for normal operating conditions and a progressive linkage added the outer carburetors as engine demand required it. To portray a safety-conscious image, General Motors banned the use of multiple carburetors for all of its 1967 vehicles with the exception of Chevrolet's Corvette.

The Firebird 400 was the hottest Firebird in the lineup. It was equipped with high compression, large valve cylinder heads, a Quadrajet carburetor, and dual exhaust. Its 400-ci V-8, which was rated at 325 hp at 4,800 rpm was borrowed directly from the 1967 GTO. It even wore the same chromed-plated louvered air cleaner and valvecovers as the midsize offering.

The number-97 eventually morphed into the number-997, where the identification number was actually cast into the head. Its features are identical to the number-97. It's unclear exactly which version was originally installed on the 400 Ram Air in the 1967 Ram Air Firebird, but based on cylinder head production dates, 97 or 997 is correct. (Photo Courtesy Chris Haggerty)

To improve block rigidity, Pontiac equipped its 400 with four-bolt main caps beginning in midyear 1967. The casting number was relocated to a pad near the number-8 cylinder, and the very first blocks produced in April 1967 had a part number that was difficult to interpret. It seems that "9792510" is generally accepted as the number, but it may have simply been a foundry error as the block was apparently re-numbered 9792506 during subsequent runs. With so few 1967 Ram Air Firebirds documented thus far, it's unclear if the Firebird's late-year 400 Ram Air V-8 used the existing two-bolt block and/or the new four-bolt casting. (Photo Courtesy Chris Haggerty)

contains a higher chromium content to improve high-temperature strength. A single valvespring package boasted higher seat and open pressures than with typical 670s despite being installed at 1.58 inches. The added spring pressure was required to control the increased valve action associated with the 301/313 duration and lobe dwell area of the 744 cam.

Many have asked how Pontiac differentiated between typical 670s and those assembled to 400 Ram Air specs in the engine assembly plant. According to Pontiac engine expert Nunzi Romano of Nunzi's Automotive in Brooklyn, New York, Pontiac stamped a small "X" on the circular pad cast into the center exhaust port of the Ram Air units. "I don't know if they were all that way," he said, "but the 400 Ram Air 670s I worked with definitely had it." I consider his suggested identification method quite plausible because Pontiac used "XX" and "XO" stampings to denote GTO-spec cylinder heads in preceding years.

Valvetrain reliability issues, reportedly from broken valvesprings caused by coil bind and/or the single valvespring oscillating, induced valve float. That forced Pontiac to revise the 400 Ram Air cylinder head in midyear 1967. It's well documented in Pontiac parts literature that beginning with Engine Unit Number (EUN) 646616, which likely reached a production vehicle in late May or early June 1967, a second type of Ram Air engine was released and it received several new components.

Pontiac then modified the 400 Ram Air's cylinder head by removing about .125 inch more from the valvespring pocket during machining, which increased the install height to 1.72 inches. A dual-valvespring package boosted spring pressure over the single spring piece for even greater control. Additionally, while overall valve length remained at about 5.1 inches, Pontiac used a swirl-polished version of the 8440-alloy valve to further improve reliability by eliminating the sharp edges where stress cracks can develop.

According to vintage Pontiac parts manuals, 9783097 was the number of the modified 400 Ram Air cylinder head introduced with EUN 646616, and two variants seemingly exist. The first used a modified number-670 casting; the "6" and "0" of the casting identification numbers found on the center exhaust port were ground away and a "9" was stamped into place. The second features a larger "997" embossed into the casting to the right of the center exhaust port.

Some experienced hobbyists argue that Pontiac never produced a number-97 casting where the "9" was stamped. Instead, it's thought the derivation of this casting was from savvy racers who were looking to fool tech inspectors, hoping to run taller valvesprings in their 1967 400-ci when competing in a racing series such as NHRA where class rules limited component choices. However, there are just too many "97" castings out there for this to be the case in every instance.

It's certain that some hobbyists (or even unscrupulous sellers) have converted a 670 into a bogus 97 casting, but a handful of claimed originals exist and in each instance the casting was produced during April or May 1967. That seemingly coincides with the point at which the second-type 400 Ram Air with EUN 646616 was introduced. Romano's opinion is that the number-97 cylinder head with the "9" stamped into the casting is absolutely authentic and he has no reason to doubt that Pontiac made them.

P&A EXTRA 67-24   - 2 -   October 30, 1967

New Engine Block Released

A new service Engine Block Assembly, fitted with pistons, pins and rings, has been released for the 1967-68 GTO and Firebird Ram Air Engines.

The new block, part number 9794075 (F-3), incorporates the 4-bolt bearing cap construction. The present released blocks are of 2-bolt bearing cap construction and should not be used as a replacement for a GTO or Firebird Ram Air Engine.

Part 9794075 will appear in the December 1st catalog replacement pages. In addition, part numbers 9787916 and 9792280 will be revised to include the 2-bolt bearing cap information.

Pontiac notified its dealership parts departments through its newsletter, Parts & Accessories Extra 67-24 *issued on October 30, 1967, that a new-fitted 400-ci block with four-bolt main caps was the correct service replacement piece from that point forward for any Firebird or GTO with the 400 Ram Air. It seems that 9794075 was the part number for the fitted 400 Ram Air block, which included the number-9792506 block casting and cast pistons with rings and wrist pins.*

Pontiac also introduced a new block casting for the 400 Ram Air. Until the changeover, the 400 Ram Air used a typical number-9786133 400-inch block with two-bolt main journal caps. After the changeover, that gave way to a new block that was functionally identical to its predecessor but featured four-bolt caps on journal numbers two, three, and four for added bulkhead rigidity and overall block strength.

Part number 9792506 was assigned to the new block, and Pontiac relocated its casting identification number from the horizontal pad at the rear of the previous block to a ledge just behind the number-8 cylinder on the new block. The new block was mistakenly misidentified on its very first run, however. Only a handful of four-bolt blocks cast on D247 (or April 24, 1967) have been located and all appear to have "9792510" as the casting number. The last digit is very difficult to decipher and "0" is the best guess from those familiar with the block.

Interestingly, Pontiac shows no 9792510 block in its part numbering system and the main caps were sequentially numbered 9792513 to 9792517 from front to rear. All remaining part numbers in the 979251X series are accounted for and unrelated to the block. As opposed to explaining the 9792506 misidentification, it's much simpler for hobbyists to simply refer to the oddly numbered four-bolt casting as the 9792510.

The 9792510 block is so rare that it was assumed to be limited to 400 Ram Air applications and was introduced with other second-type features on EUN 646616. The number-9792510 block with that particular EUN exists today and is coded "XS" for GTO use. With that information, it's absolutely certain that four-bolt caps were in production in certain applications by the time the second-type 400 Ram Air was introduced.

1967 Ram Air Firebird

The 400 Ram Air had been installed into several hundred GTOs by the time the Firebird was released in February 1967. It seems that Pontiac planned to offer the GTO's top engine option in the Firebird from the onset of model production, and at least one vintage 1967 Pontiac price schedule dated February 23, 1967, reveals that the L67 option contained a retail price of $236.30 in the Firebird. Transmission cost was above that.

Corporate policy restricted the 400 Ram Air to 360 hp when installed into the 3,600-pound GTO, and Pontiac not-so-coincidentally rated its 1967 400 Ram Air engine at that same number. As any racer or enthusiast familiar with the performance capability of that engine can attest, the factory rating was rather conservative. Based on its actual on-track performance, the mill really generated closer to 400 hp. Use of that same engine in

To remain compliant with General Motors' standard of no more than 1 horsepower per 10 pounds of vehicle weight, Pontiac devised an ingenious method of limiting the output of the GTO's 400 for use in the lighter Firebird. The throttle linkage actuating the secondary barrels was uniquely shaped to delay secondary circuit activation and prevent the secondary throttle plates from reaching 90 degrees F. Savvy owners simply bent the tab so that full travel was restored. In a matter of seconds, output of the Firebird's 325 hp 400-ci equaled that of the GTO's.

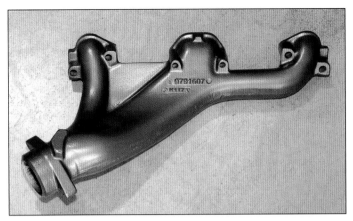

To increase the potency of the 400 Ram Air for 1967, Pontiac included high-flow units developed for the 421 H.O. in mid-1960s full-size models but also fit the Firebird chassis. Based on a design similar to the cast headers from the Super Duty 421, the tuned "long branch" manifolds bested the 1967 A-car 400 Ram Air's streamlined units by a few horsepower and rivaled the performance of aftermarket tubular headers on the street. High-quality reproductions are readily available today.

the 3,250-pound Firebird meant its horsepower rating could not exceed 325.

Pontiac effectively limited the output of the 400-ci V-8 in all of its Firebird 400s by developing a unique carburetor linkage that prevented the secondary barrels of the Rochester Quadrajet from fully opening. As with the basic L78 400 4-barrel, Pontiac rated the Firebird's 400 Ram Air at 325 hp and 410 ft-lbs, but raised the RPM points at which power peaked to 5,200 and 3,600, respectively. By simply adjusting the carburetor to reach full-throttle travel, the Firebird's 400 Ram Air was capable of equaling the output of the GTO's 360-hp engine.

Many vintage magazines discussed the 400 Ram Air in articles about the 1967 Firebird, but only one reported its delayed availability until a few months after production startup, though no explanation was offered. A hobbyist who ordered a Ram Air Firebird in April 1967 explained that he pestered Pontiac Engineering to investigate the cause of his vehicle's production delay. He claimed that at least two high-level engineers claimed that the holdup was in securing certification for California emissions. Although there hasn't been any factory documentation to support it, it could be true.

Ordering a Ram Air Firebird was a multilayer process and a rather costly proposition. It required selecting the W66 400 Sport Option ($273.83) on the standard Firebird order form and the L67 400 Ram Air engine ($263.30) under the Firebird section of the Special Equipment order form. Depending on transmission choice, the M20 Muncie 4-speed or M40 Turbo-400 added $184.31 or $226.40, respectively. Total package cost was at least $721.44 and possibly as much as $763.57. When corrected for inflation, that's equivalent to about $5,500 today.

Like the GTO, the Firebird's Ram Air assembly was shipped in the trunk and a typical air cleaner was installed at the time of production. The selling dealer was tasked with modifying the underhood bracing to accommodate the stamped sheet-metal baffle and cutting open and finishing a second set of hood scoops before customer delivery. Because there were no provisions to keep the offending elements out with the Ram Air assembly installed, the intent was for the owner to install the Ram Air components as needed, and reinstall the originals in inclement weather conditions.

The Ram Air Firebird for 1967 was Pontiac's most potent F-car. It was a relatively unknown combination intended for maximum performance on the dragstrip. Just 65 were produced that model year and only a handful of survivors have been documented so far. It seems most succumbed to the harsh operating conditions associated with the racetrack.

Production records reveal that 65 Firebirds were equipped with the 400 Ram Air during the 1967 model year. All were produced between the last week of June and the end of July 1967. Of that total, 45 were backed by the M20 4-speed manual; the remaining 20 were backed by the M40 Turbo-400. Eight were convertibles, just two of which were equipped with the M40 automatic transmission. According to production info, the only axle ratio available was 3.90:1 despite the fact that gearing as deep as 4.33 was available on the basic 400-ci engine.

Jim Mattison of PHS Automotive Services confirmed that the first 1967 Ram Air Firebird was produced on June 28. According to the billing history card for that particular example, the EUN of the 400 Ram Air is 649713. Although EUNs do jump around a bit, Mattison said he had yet to find any 400 Ram Air in a Firebird with an EUN prior to the 646616 date in which the second-type Ram Air engine was introduced. He also confirmed that the last Ram Air Firebird was produced on July 27, 1967, and that all examples, regardless of transmission, were equipped with a 3.90:1 rear axle ratio.

Less than a dozen Ram Air Firebirds have been documented and some of those are no longer equipped with their original drivetrain. That makes documenting any Ram Air Firebird without its original engine or transmission a difficult task because nothing immediately visual separates a Ram Air Firebird from a typical Firebird 400. The only real way to document an authentic Ram Air Firebird is to obtain a copy of the original billing history card, which PHS Automotive Services can provide for you at a nominal cost with quick turnaround.

Few of the documented Ram Air Firebirds exist that today are equipped with their original 400 Ram Air engine, which makes it difficult to determine if any other than number-997 cylinder heads were used. Because the EUNs of the 400s used in the Ram Air Firebirds succeed the aforementioned EUN 646616 introduction date, the number-997 should be correct for the application despite the build date of any 1967 Ram Air Firebird.

The four-bolt number-9792510 block is more common to GTOs than Firebirds. As to Firebird applications, 20 code-XN engines were used with the automatic transmission, 42 code-WI engines were teamed with the M20 Muncie 4-speed, and 3 code-WQ engines were used for 400 Ram Air engines equipped with a manual transmission and K19 California emissions equipment. It's unknown just how many of them used the 9792510 casting. Although there were definitely some, based on the Firebird-coded 400 Ram Air blocks that have surfaced, the standard two-bolt 9786133 400-ci block is more common, particularly in code-XN applications.

Transmission Lineup

Six-cylinder Firebirds equipped with manual transmissions received Saginaw-built units exclusively. A column-shifted M12 3-speed with 2.85:1 first-gear ratio (code-FK) was standard equipment with the 1-barrel; a floor-mounted shifter was available for $42.13 extra. That same M12 with a floor-mounted shifter was standard with the Sprint-6 and a floor-shifted M20 4-speed with 3.11:1 first-gear ratio (code-FH) was available for $184.31.

A Saginaw-built M12 3-speed manual with 2.54:1 first-gear ratio (code-RJ) was used with the 326-ci V-8. As with the OHC-6, a column shift was standard and a floor-mounted shifter was optional for $42.13. The standard transmission with the Firebird 400 was a Warner-built M13 heavy-duty 3-speed manual with a 2.42:1 first gear (code-ST) and floor-mounted shifter. A Muncie-built M20 4-speed manual with a 2.52:1 first gear (code-FF) was optional with either V-8 at $184.13 extra. A Muncie-built M20 with a 2.20:1 first gear (code-FX) was the only 4-speed manual available with the 400 Ram Air.

Although all of General Motors' automatic transmissions during the 1960s were filled with a special hydraulic fluid that was pressurized by a crank-driven pump for proper operation, in most instances, an auxiliary cooler was an integral part of the radiator. The coolant in the radiator drew heat away from the transmission fluid, which served to limit the transmission's maximum operating

A column-shifted 3-speed manual was the standard transmission in 1967. Both a floor-mounted shifter and a 4-speed were extra-cost options. The floor shifter was supplied by Inland Tool and Manufacturing (ITM) and pirated directly from the Camaro. Featuring a chrome-plated flat-stock handle without any markings whatsoever, it was a relatively low-budget shifter known for notchy gear changes. (Photo Courtesy Bill Krause)

The Firebird cockpit offered a racy look, especially with the handsome three-spoke steering wheel and floor-mounted manual-transmission shifter. Due to the rush to production, Pontiac used the Chevrolet-spec ITM floor-shifter, but many owners quickly replaced the low-cost unit with an aftermarket Hurst assembly, which greatly improved shifting precision.

temperature and increase its service life. It wasn't uncommon to find entry-level automatic transmissions in low-performance applications during that era without provisions for an external fluid cooler, however. In those instances, air wash beneath the car while traveling at speed sufficiently cooled the transmission fluid and additional cooling from a radiator-mounted cooler wasn't required.

An air-cooled M30 Super Turbine 300 2-speed automatic was available with either 6-cylinder for $194.84. A radiator-cooled variant, the M31 Super Turbine 300 2-speed, was available with the 326-ci V-8 for the same amount. The M40 Turbo-400 3-speed was the only automatic available with the Firebird 400 at $226.44 extra.

As far as transmission production is concerned, 3,413 Firebirds with OHC-6 and 326 2-barrel engines were equipped with the standard column-shifted M12 3-speed manual, but any additional breakdown is unknown. An option often associated with floor-shifted manual transmissions is the M09 Custom Gear Shift Knob. This attractive, simulated-woodgrain shifter knob replaced the standard round ball for $3.69 and 1,784 Firebird buyers opted for it during the 1967 model year. Of that, 531 were combined with the M12 3-speed and the remaining 1,253 units with the M20 4-speed.

Rear Axle

The Firebird used a Pontiac-built rear axle assembly similar to that of the A-body line. Ring-gear diameter measured 8.2 inches and it was held to the differential case by ten 3/8-inch bolts. Gear ratios ranged from 2.56 to 4.33:1 depending on the application. Although a single track (or open) differential was standard equipment with all ratios up to 3.55:1, opting for a limited-slip differential was as easy as selecting the G80 Safe-T-Track Differential for $42.13 extra.

A two-digit code was assigned to each axle assembly to denote gear ratio and differential type. Pontiac placed a paper sticker on the driver-side brake drum for easy identification during vehicle production, but very few remain today. That same two-digit code was stamped more permanently into the rear of the passenger-side axle tube near the brake-line clip.

Despite a rather negative reputation brought on by component failures in preceding years, the Pontiac axle had been revised enough that by the 1967 model year it was quite reliable. The G83 Safe-T-Track Differential Heavy-Duty was the very best of the bunch, and it was automatically included at $63.19 when a limited-slip differential was combined with 3.36 and 3.55:1 ratios, and in all 3.90 and 4.33:1 applications where limited slip was mandatory.

The G83 option included a host of up-level components to beef up durability. The differential case assembly was redesigned to use four pinion gears rather than two as found in the standard limited-slip unit. By increasing the number of pinion gears, side-gear loading was more evenly distributed, improving strength. Contrary to what some report, however, the original blueprint for the heavy-duty four-pinion case reveal that it is actually constructed of the same pearlitic malleable iron as the standard-duty two-pinion case.

Buyers also received forged steel axle shafts (number-9787654) that were heat treated for maximum durability as well as a 10-bolt differential housing (or center section) constructed of cast nodular iron as opposed to gray iron in typical applications. The latter is identifiable by a large "N" cast on the top near the pinion flange and/ or its part number, 9788647, which is cast into it. Some report that the nodular housing may have made its way into non–heavy-duty Firebird applications, but it's believed any such instance is an exception and not the norm.

Largely unpublicized, the 4.33:1 axle ratio was a special-order option for certain Firebird applications. I have at least one 1967 Firebird Rear Axle Identification Chart that confirms it was combined with the heavy-duty limited-slip differential only, and availability was limited to the Firebird 400 equipped with a base engine and manual transmission. Reportedly just 13 Firebird 400s were equipped with the code-ZR axle assembly. None have surfaced yet.

PONTIAC MOTOR DIVISION   Number   67-I-74   Section   3   Date   7/14/67

'67

Dealer
Service
Information
Bulletin

Attention: Service Manager

Subject: FIRM RIDE SENSATION ON 1967 FIREBIRD MODELS

Our Firebird has been well received in all parts of the country. Sales, as you undoubtedly know, are continuing to soar. Our decision to enter into the sports car field has proven a wise one.

The introduction of the Firebird model, however, has brought a new dimension of performance into our Pontiac family. Many former Pontiac and Tempest owners, when first experiencing a demonstration ride in the Firebird, are quick to comment on the firm ride they experience. This firm ride is typically a sports car feature and to obtain a true sports car image this feature is carried over into the Firebird. It is true that some Firebird owners, when first experiencing this ride, will undoubtedly comment on the difference between it and the Pontiac ride they had become accustomed to.

The purpose of this bulletin is twofold. Should complaints of firm ride come to your attention:

1. Check to make sure that there is no unbalance condition of wheels and tires which would result in an abnormal vibration. Pay particular attention to tire pressures. Tire pressures set higher than those recommended always result in an abnormally firm ride.

2. If no unbalance of wheels and tires or other vibration condition is apparent, assure your customer that the firm ride he is experiencing is a design characteristic of the vehicle. This feature provides for the easy handling and sports car ride for which the Firebird has become so popular. No attempt to change springs, shocks, etc. should be made since the only available customizing of this ride is with the use of the optional Koni shock absorbers which increase the firmness of the ride referred to in our bulletin 67-I-57.

SERVICE DEPARTMENT
PONTIAC MOTOR DIVISION
GENERAL MOTORS CORPORATION

Read, Initial & Pass On • Service Supervision   Parts   Accounting

It's obvious from the issuance of Technical Service Bulletin 67-I-74 on July 14, 1967, that Pontiac customers were finding the Firebird's ride a bit too taut for their liking. The division reaffirmed the Firebird's position as a sports car and that its ride and handling qualities were not atypical of a vehicle in that class. Adjustable Koni shock absorbers were quietly made an available option during the 1967 model year, and it allowed owners to customize their Firebird's ride and handling. Pontiac reported that 154 buyers added them to their order that model year.

When Chevrolet engineers developed the Camaro suspension, it included a solid rear axle suspended on mono-leaf springs. The single-leaf package provided good ride quality at a reasonable cost. When Pontiac engineers began developmental work on the Firebird, they found that the spring was prone to uncontrollable flexing while accelerating and braking. Most well-used 1967 Firebirds have been converted to multi-leaf rear spring assemblies today, but a few examples like this still exist.

The 1967 Firebird used the underpinnings that Chevrolet designed for its Camaro. Although the original rear leaf springs of this particular example have been replaced, the 1967 Firebird was equipped with mono-leaf units, which Pontiac engineers found to deflect under heavy acceleration and braking. Pontiac developed a unique "radius rod" that solidly linked the axle to the frame, effectively limiting deflection.

Suspension

Chevrolet developed the F-car's basic suspension package and Pontiac had little time to meaningfully modify its attitude. Unitized body construction consisted of integral rear frame rails that played a major role in the body structure. The front suspension was housed within a separate stub-frame that connected to the body at four locations. A front sway bar measuring .6875 inch in diameter was standard equipment and no larger options were available. A rear sway bar was never used.

Depending on the engine and transmission combination and the manner in which its torque was applied, Pontiac specified none, one, or two radius rods for the F-car to attain maximum ride quality and controllability. This 1967 Service Bulletin dated February, 13, 1967, clarified application inclusion for dealership service staff. F-car suspension revisions for 1968 saw the elimination of the radius rod at the close of the 1967 model year.

The base-model Firebird offered the softest ride with front and rear spring rates of 275 and 100 pounds per inch, respectively. Firebird Sprints, 326s, and H.O.s received slightly higher rates of 320 and 115 pounds, respectively. The Firebird 400 offered the tautest ride with 345- and 135-pound springs and firm-control shock absorbers. An up-level option, the Y96 Ride and Handling package, available for $9.32 on all option levels but Firebird 400, netted the buyer with the same high-rate springs and firm-control shock absorbers found on the 400.

The rear axle was suspended from the body using a single-leaf spring on each side and the rear shock absorbers were positioned ahead of each axle tube. Pontiac engineers determined that during heavy acceleration or braking with certain engine and transmission packages, the single-leaf spring assembly lacked sufficient rigidity and often wound up, causing axle shudder. The solution was a radius rod (or traction bar) that acted like a control arm and connected the axle housing solidly to the frame.

Every 1967 Firebird rear axle has provisions to accommodate a radius rod beneath each axle tube, but the actual number of rods used varied with application. A single rod located at the passenger-side rear was used on Firebirds equipped with the basic OHC-6 engine with automatic transmission and an axle ratio of 3.23:1 or greater, the basic OHC-6 with manual transmission, the Sprint-6 with automatic transmission, and a V-8 with automatic transmission. A second radius rod on the driver-side rear was added whenever the Sprint-6 or V-8 engine was mated to a manual transmission. No radius rod was used with the OHC-6 engine or any axle ratio less than 3.23:1.

Front and rear drum brakes with manual assist were standard issue. Front drums were finned for additional cooling. Buyers who wanted the latest technology in vehicle braking could opt for J52 Front Disc Brakes for $63.19. Optional J50 Wonder Touch Power Brakes were available with either setup for $41.60 extra.

Wheels and Tires

Because numerous choices were available for 1967, Firebird wheel and tire combinations can be quite confusing. A 14 x 6–inch stamped-steel wheel fitted with a small hubcap was standard equipment. Although the wheel was painted black with most of Firebird's available exterior colors, there were a few exceptions. It was color-matched with Montreux Blue and Mariner Turquoise exteriors, and color-coordinated with Gulf Turquoise, Signet Gold, and Champagne.

Three full-wheel cover options were available as premium upgrades on the Firebird. They included P01 Deluxe Wheel Discs for $16.85, P02 Custom Wheel Discs for $36.33, and N95 Wire Wheel Discs for $69.41. Wherever an optional full-wheel cover was selected, the wheel was always black. Because the W54 Custom Trim option included P01 Deluxe Wheel Discs as part of the package, any up-level cover or wheel on a Custom Option Firebird was $16.85 less than the amount noted above.

Pontiac's popular Rally wheel (code-P05), a styled, stamped-steel unit introduced on the A-car for 1965, was also available on the Firebird for 1967. Including a bright center cap and trim ring, the .60-inch offset of the 14 x 6–inch wheel made it incompatible with Firebird's finned

A 14 x 6–inch steel wheel with a small hubcap was entry-level equipment on the standard Firebird. Although the attractive, no-nonsense look it lends is popular today, it was the lowest-cost wheel ornamentation Pontiac offered. It was most often found on Firebirds where the buyer simply sought a no-frills racer, or planned to replace them with an aftermarket mag-type wheel after delivery. Coker Tire offers quality reproductions of the original steel wheel in various sizes and Ames Performance reproduces the hubcap.

The P01 Deluxe Wheel Cover was a $16.85 option on the standard Firebird, but was included in the Custom Option package. The Deluxe Wheel Cover was practically identical to that found on the Tempest lineup, but the center medallion was red instead of black. The cover gave the Firebird a touch of sophistication associated with more expensive Pontiacs.

The Custom Wheel Cover gave the Firebird a sporty look with its large vent holes and knockoff-type center cap. Coded UPC P02, it was an up-level option across all Firebird models. Pricing ranged from $19.48 to $36.33, depending on other equipment. This same cover was also available on the Tempest model line.

Wire-spoked wheels were expensive to produce and popular with high-end vehicles. To incorporate that appearance into its 1967 model lineup, Pontiac created the N95 Wire Wheel Disc option as a full wheel cover that simulated the look of an authentic wire-spoked wheel. The option added as much as $69 to the final price of a Firebird that model year.

Pontiac's styled-steel Rally wheel was a popular A-car option during the mid-1960s that gave consumers an attractive unit directly from the factory. The stamped 14 x 6 unit was also available on the 1967 Firebird as UPC PO5 for $56.87. Any Firebird owner seeking to replicate the unique appearance can find correct reproductions of the E70-14 Firestone Wide Oval tire and Rally from Coker Tire (shown). The Rally I is also available in a number of sizes that are popular with consumers today.

Pontiac's Rally II wheel was introduced in 1967 as a premium wheel option intended to give buyers a mag-type unit as a factory-installed option. Adorned with a bright trim ring and a center cap with a black plastic center, the stamped-steel unit was heavily marketed and proved to be immensely popular with consumers. It remained in the Pontiac system for more than 20 model years. (Photo Courtesy General Motors)

During the mid-1960s, Pontiac created its exciting "Tiger" marketing campaign for the GTO and the attractive code-O Tiger Gold exterior finish was a key component of that. Renamed Coronado Gold for 1967, the color was among three choices Pontiac added to the 1967 Firebird palette for its spring sales promotion. It's quite apparent how far Pontiac went to relate its new Firebird to its popular GTO by using distinctive features and equipment that made its high-performance A-car iconic. As with the GTO, Coronado Gold beautifully accented the new F-car's sporty silhouette and gave it a very classy appearance. (Photo Courtesy Larry Delay)

front brake drums. Pontiac required that J52 Front Disc Brakes be added wherever the $56.87 Rally wheel option was ordered. Despite the uniquely attractive appearance, the restriction apparently limited popularity of the P05 option with consumers and ultimately led to the wheel's demise for 1968.

Although referred to as "Sprint" wheels a few times in Pontiac publications, the beautifully styled Rally II (code-N98) wheel was all new for 1967. Developed by Pontiac and produced by Motor Wheel Corporation, the stamped-steel wheel featured five individual spokes, each with an embossed area that created a subtle break for contrasting paint accents. According to Trevor Brown, a former Pontiac engineer who oversaw wheel development at the time, the division's Rally (or Rally I, as it came to be known) and Rally II wheels were considered up-level wheels that were relatively affordable to produce but could be priced as premium options. As such, they were good money makers. The Rally II was available in 14 x 6 inch only and included a bright center cap and trim ring for $72.67.

Although a 7.35 x 14–inch tire was initially slated as entry-level equipment, by the time production began, a bias-ply Wide Oval tire by Firestone in E70 x 14 sizing had replaced it and a black sidewall was standard on every 1967 Firebird but the Firebird 400. That same tire accented with a thin white-line sidewall (PX2) or a red-line sidewall (PX3) was available for $31.60 extra. The white-line tire was standard equipment on the Firebird 400 and buyers could opt for the red-line at no extra charge. Optional on all Firebirds was a radial-ply white-line sidewall tire in 185R x 14 sizing. Because a premium tire was already included with the W66 400 Sport Option, the radial tire option (code P33) was just $10.53 extra on the Firebird 400, but was otherwise a $42.13 option over the basic black-sidewall tire standard on all other Firebirds.

Production and Options

Pontiac viewed its Firebird as an opportunity to capture buyers moving to smaller, sporty cars. Hot on the heels of GTO's success, one report claimed that the division's sales goal for Firebird was 50,000 to 60,000 units and it expected very little of that as takeaway volume from the GTO. In reality, during its first few weeks of production, the Firebird claimed the shortest on-hand supply of all its competitors. The midyear addition was so successful that final production exceeded intended capacity by nearly 50 percent!

A total of 82,560 Firebirds were produced during the months that remained of the 1967 model year, and according to a Pontiac production report, all but 48 of the 2537-series vehicles were assembled at the General Motors Assembly Division plant in Lordstown, Ohio. As you might expect, the Firebird 326 was Pontiac's hottest seller. One Pontiac report that recapped 1967 model year sales stated that nearly 80 percent of all Firebird buyers opted for a V-8, and 48,180 buyers opted for the Custom Option trim level. It adds that the Firebird 400 sold even better than the division expected and that both 6-cylinder variants underperformed with consumers.

Appendix A reveals total production by Firebird series as well as a detailed breakdown of engine and transmission combinations. Also, the recent discovery of a group of random production figures for the 1967 model year at General Motors Heritage Center is being shared with hobbyists for the very first time.

Of the 5,316 Sprint-6 engines equipped with a manual transmission, 405 were fitted with K19 Air Injector

Exhaust Control. K19 was also installed on 349 of the 326 H.O. engines equipped with manual transmissions. C60 Air Conditioning was installed onto 851 Firebirds with the OHC-6 engine, and of that total, 198 were manual transmission examples.

Six 1967 Firebirds were built with the C48 Heater Delete option. Just 26 Firebird Sprint

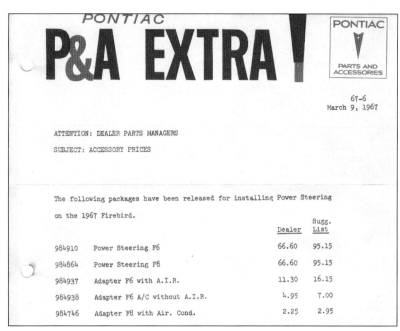

PONTIAC
P&A EXTRA!

PONTIAC
PARTS AND ACCESSORIES

67-6
March 9, 1967

ATTENTION: DEALER PARTS MANAGERS

SUBJECT: ACCESSORY PRICES

The following packages have been released for installing Power Steering on the 1967 Firebird.

		Dealer	Sugg. List
984910	Power Steering F6	66.60	95.15
984864	Power Steering F8	66.60	95.15
984937	Adapter F6 with A.I.R.	11.30	16.15
984938	Adapter F6 A/C without A.I.R.	4.95	7.00
984746	Adapter F8 with Air. Cond.	2.25	2.95

An electric clock was available on the Firebird by selecting UPC U35, which added $15.80 to the final price. Mounted onto the transmission tunnel or console (if so equipped), the clock could not be ordered in conjunction with a U57 Stereo Tape Player, which was otherwise located in the same possible positions.

Have you ever found a 1967 Firebird seemingly equipped with the N40 Power Steering option, but its original paperwork suggests it wasn't factory installed? P&A Extra 67-6 dated March 9, 1967, announced the release of a dealer-installed power steering kit for Firebirds that weren't equipped with the factory-installed option but whose buyers wanted it. The components in the dealer-installed option were identical to those used at the Lordstown assembly plant, which made it appear factory correct.

The Firebird H.O. was a hot package that combined small-cube V-8 performance with exciting styling. It included a 326-ci V-8 with 4-barrel carburetor rated at 285 hp, dual exhaust, and distinctive side striping. This particular example is equipped with N95 Wire Wheel Discs, which was an extra-cost option at all levels.

convertibles were equipped with C60 Air Conditioning. N25 Exhaust Extensions were installed on 803 Firebirds. Of that, 72 were Firebird Sprints and just 5 were Ram Air Firebirds. K30 Cruise Control availability was limited to the V-8 with an automatic transmission.

The 48 6-cylinder 2537-series Firebirds previously noted as built outside the Lordstown, Ohio, facility were part of the CKD program, which stood for "Completely Knocked Down." Such models were partially assembled in the United States and shipped overseas in containers to one of GM's various assembly plants for final assembly. It was a method that allowed vehicle sales in countries where domestic assembly was required or to hurdle high import taxes and/or tariffs.

Although a manually retractable top was most popular with Firebird buyers, a select number of them opted for a C06 Power Convertible Top, which used an electrically operated hydraulic pump to automatically open or close the cloth top with the touch of a button. The control switch was located on the instrument panel to the left of the steering column in 1967 and 1968.

At year's end, Pontiac produced 15,528 1967 Firebird convertibles. Body rigidity was compromised by the lack of roof support and vibrations over moderate-to-harsh bumps were common. F-car engineers combatted the phenomena with a Body Vibration Dampener, or a canister containing a sprung weight suspended in oil at each corner of the vehicle to effectively dampen harmonics. It was first used by General Motors on the early-1960s Corvair. Hobbyists most often refer to the dampener as a "cocktail shaker" because of its appearance and function.

The Firebird Sprint was differentiated from the basic Firebird on the exterior only by specific rocker-mounted badging. Its 4-barrel engine, floor-mounted manual transmission shifter, and taut suspension defined its attitude from the driver's seat. When equipped with the entry-level hubcap, the steel wheel matched the exterior color in certain applications. (Photo Courtesy Bob Wilson)

W66 400 SPORT OPTION

W66 400 Sport Option transformed the basic Firebird into the Firebird 400. In addition to the L78 400-ci 4-barrel engine rated at 325 hp, it included a host of ancillary equipment to visually and physically differentiate it from its brethren.

The exterior of the Firebird 400 featured a unique dual scooped hood with strategically placed "400" badges, the Pontiac crest on the front bumper, and specific grille finishing. Heavy-duty springs and shock absorbers stiffened the ride and improved handling. Chromed engine accents, N10 Dual Exhaust, T60 Heavy-Duty Battery, and PX3 E70 x 14 Wide-Oval tires with sporty red-line trim completed the package.

The W66 option cost $358.09 and included a floor-shifted M13 3-speed manual transmission as standard equipment. Package cost dropped to $273.83 when teamed with a 4-speed manual or M40 Turbo-400 automatic, but the transmissions were purchased separately at extra cost. N30 Deluxe Steering Wheel was a mandatory option that added $12.11 to the cost.

The Firebird 400 was the most exciting Pontiac available during the 1967 model year. A total of 18,698 were produced. Appendix A details exact production numbers. Those below reveal production numbers for specific option combinations that made certain examples even more unique.

- D55 Front Console was installed on 15,380 Firebird 400s. Of that, 9,379 were equipped with the M40 Turbo-400 automatic transmission, 5,543 with the M20 4-speed manual, and 908 with the M13 3-speed manual.
- J52 Front Disc Brake option was installed on 3,745 Firebird 400s.

The Firebird 400 was Pontiac's hottest F-car option for the 1967 model year. Sporty styling was paramount to the model line's success and injected even more performance personality. Externally differentiating the Firebird 400 were a pair of ornamental hood scoops styled much like those of the 1968 GTO. They were accented by die-cast "400" badges.

- N33 Tilt Steering Wheel was installed in 290 Firebird 400s, of which 276 were equipped with the M20 4-speed manual.
- N64 Conventional Spare was installed on 6,828 Firebird 400s.
- PX2 E70 x 14 Wide Oval tires with white-line trim were installed on 8,399 Firebird 400s at no extra charge.
- P33 185R x 14 Radial tires with white sidewall trim were installed on 373 Firebird 400s for $10.53 extra.
- K19 Air Injection Reactor system was installed on 1,199 Firebird 400s equipped with a manual transmission.

Firebird's chrome-plated bumper featured Pontiac's classic split-grille treatment. Its pointed peak on the Firebird 400 was adorned by a flexible arrowhead logo that not only further identified it as a premium Pontiac product, but served as an energy absorber to prevent bumper damage during minor impacts.

Interestingly, all 48 CKD Firebirds were Sprints fully equipped with the Sprint-6 engine and a manual transmission. Exactly half were equipped with M12 3-speed and M20 4-speed, and each was equipped with the D28 Delete Outside Rearview Mirror option. It's not clear which plant and/or country these Firebirds were sent to and the specific reasoning behind the unique build pattern is a mystery. Research continues, but the answer may be lost to history.

Pontiac offered a wide array of exterior colors for its 1967 Firebird that spanned the spectrum. Buyers seeking a vehicle with a customized look could choose virtually any General Motors paint as a special order color available at extra cost. Silverglaze was among the list of Pontiac's standard offerings and the beautiful hue seemed a rather rare choice with Firebird buyers. The white accent stripe of the Firebird H.O. creates a beautiful contrast. (Photo Courtesy Larry Delay)

CHAPTER THREE

1968 FIREBIRD

Pontiac's 1968 Firebird went on sale September 21, 1967. Model year production began in late August or early September. With the late introduction of the 1967 model and its overwhelming consumer response, exterior changes were neither possible from a styling standpoint nor required by lack of sales. Some additions were, however, mandated by the National Traffic and Motor Vehicle Safety Act of 1966, which required compliance by January 1, 1968. Exterior modifications were limited to cosmetic revisions while interior plushness increased to a level that Pontiac buyers had come to expect while remaining compliant with federal safety regulations.

To thwart theft of vehicles and components, the Act required that manufacturers make the VIN visible from outside without moving any part of the body. Pontiac placed its "public" VIN tag on the driver's side of the dash panel for easy viewing through the windshield, eliminating the need for a doorjamb tag. A "federal" VIN, which generally consisted of a portion of a particular vehicle's complete VIN was required on major components. Pontiac began stamping partial VINs on the body, engine, and transmission.

The Firebird Lineup

The 1968 Firebird series was again marketed as The Magnificent Five and the cars were practically identical to those of 1967 except for a slight displacement increase of

On the heels of a very successful midyear introduction for 1967, Pontiac's Firebird was an essential carryover for the 1968 model year. Retaining the aggressive styling that separated it from the Camaro in 1967, changes for 1968 were mostly limited to subtle exterior appointments and a handful of engineering revisions. To comply with new federal requirements, wraparound lighting lenses served as front parking and side marking turn signals.

Required for all new 1968 vehicles, Pontiac relocated its cowl-mounted VIN tag from the driver-side doorjamb to the driver's side of the instrument panel where it was easily viewable through the windshield. The tag remained in that position until Firebird production ceased in 2002. The last six digits of this particular VIN have been digitally removed for owner security. Also beginning in 1968, engines and transmissions were marked with a portion of the VIN as well.

Newly enacted federal requirements for 1968 included stamping a vehicle's VIN into its major driveline components to thwart theft. Pontiac stamped a partial VIN into the engine block and transmission case. On the V-8, the intended location was the on front of the block, just left of the timing cover, and the 9-digit sequence contained critical information. In this instance, "2" signified Pontiac, "8" signified the last digit of the model year, "U" signified the Lordstown, Ohio, assembly plant, and the remaining six digits match those of the VIN. The last two in this particular example were digitally removed from this photo for owner security.

Not long after Pontiac distributed its 1967 Firebird sales material, it began working on that for 1968. The 1968 Sales Manual (or Dealer Album) contained several pages of handsome photos and intricate details dedicated to the various Firebird levels. Originally intended as a dealership sales aid when selling new vehicles, the vintage sales manuals are an invaluable resource to researchers today.

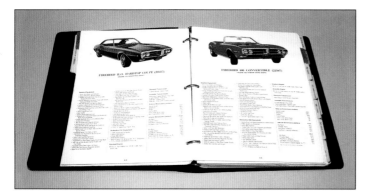

The Magnificent Five marketing campaign went unchanged for 1968 and the Firebird 400 remained very popular with performance enthusiasts. W66 400 Sport Option contained virtually the same equipment from 1967. Although this photograph may look flopped, sharp eyes will notice that the steering wheel and hood-mounted tachometer were actually relocated during its conversion to right-hand drive. It is one of reportedly four 400 Ram Air Firebirds exported to Australia that year.

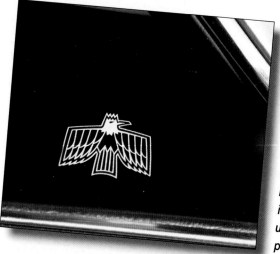

Although a side-vent window was characteristic of the 1967 F-car, revisions to the Firebird's for draft-free circulation allowed its elimination for 1968. Side glass covering the entire door opening replaced 1967's sectional, two-piece design. A Firebird logo (white ceramic paint stenciled onto the glass and cured during the tempering process) added an elegant touch and it was planned to be a standard feature on all 1968 Firebirds. However, in accordance with Federal Motor Vehicle Safety Standard (FMVSS) number-205, it was discontinued to prevent a potential obstruction when using the outside rearview mirror(s). Pontiac added the feature shortly after 1968 Firebird production began and removed it by December 1967. Its use was sporadic. Although its presence is most common in Firebirds built during November and December, the assembly plants continued using aged inventory as it became available until the cessation of model year production in July 1968.

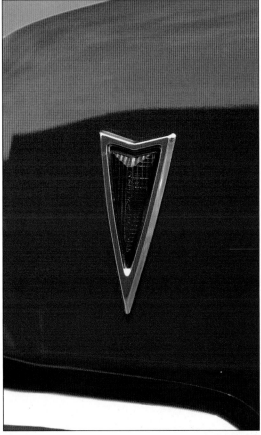

Federal Motor Vehicle Safety Standard (FMVSS) number-108 required that 1968 vehicles be equipped with side markers that were reflective for vehicle detection in all conditions and illuminative so fellow motorists were certain of signaled intentions. Pontiac stylists found wraparound parking lights an easy solution for frontal compliance. Rear side markers took on the shape of the division's arrowhead logo. It was an ingenious way of incorporating the new requirement.

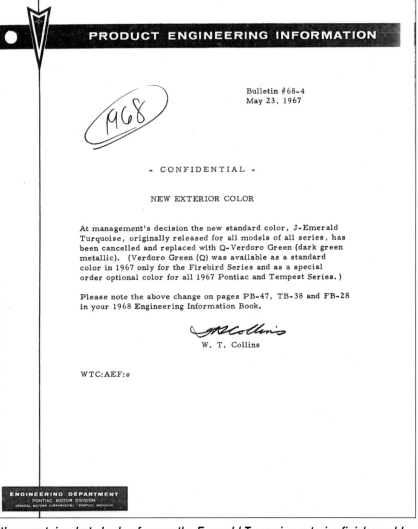

It's uncertain what shade of green the Emerald Turquoise exterior finish would have been, but it seems from this internal engineering bulletin issued by Bill Collins on May 23, 1967, that Pontiac hadn't initially planned to carry over Verdoro Green into the 1968 model year. This bulletin may indicate that Pontiac recognized the Verdoro Green popularity with consumers during 1967, creating the need to extend its availability.

the 6-cylinder and small V-8 engines. Most buyers found the five levels quite convenient. Ordering a Firebird equipped to suit a particular need was as easy as ordering a base-model Firebird and checking the appropriate Sport Option for the level desired on the order form.

The base price of an entry-level Firebird with the larger OHC-6 1-barrel for 1968 was $2,908. The W53 Firebird Sprint with larger Sprint-6 engine and 4-barrel carburetor added $116.16 to the sticker price. The Firebird V-8 with a 2-barrel carburetor, billed as the L30 Firebird 350, was priced at $105.60. The L76 Firebird H.O. with a 4-barrel carburetor, dual exhaust, and body accent stripes included the new 350 H.O. at a cost of $180.58. The W66 Firebird 400 was offered with virtually identical options as the 1967 and was priced at $273.83.

Exterior and Interior

The exterior of the 1968 Firebird was almost identical to that of the 1967 model. Changes were limited to new front and side marker lights and a revised ventilation system on Firebirds not equipped with air conditioning. In those instances, cable-controlled dash vents and doorjamb outlets allowed draft-free circulation. The enhanced ventilation led to the elimination of the side vent (or wing) windows, which meant a quieter ride with a sufficient volume of air circulation.

Pontiac marketed the Firebird's new, one-piece side glass as giving the interior a more spacious, picture-window effect. For additional character, a small Firebird logo was placed on the leading edge of the side glass, but for reasons most likely related to visibility concerns, not all 1968 Firebirds were equipped with the treatment.

The Firebird was available in any of Pontiac's 15 standard color choices for 1968. Only one, Starlight Black (code-A), required special preparation and Pontiac charged customers $10.53 for the SPS Solid Special Paint choice. Non-production special-order colors were available as SPS Special Solid Color for $83.20, and two-tone treatment options carried over from 1967. Identical color choices were available for SVT Cordova Tops at $84.26 on hardtop Firebirds and the cloth top on Firebird convertibles.

On December 15, 1967, Pontiac issued Sales Manual Release number-6 announcing that Autumn Bronze (code-I) replaced Starlight Black (code-A) on the Firebird line. Starlight Black required special-order treatment and a slight upcharge, but Autumn Bronze was considered a standard exterior color without any surcharge. According to Pontiac production records 1,003 Firebirds received the attractive hue during the remainder of the 1968 model year.

In late March 1968, Pontiac announced that Carnival Red, Marigold Yellow, Pink Mist, and Windward Blue were new SPS Firebird exterior colors for its spring promotion. They were treated like other SPS colors from a cost standpoint and the finishes are quite rare. Of these colors, Pink Mist may be most recognizable for its bold

Although the front and rear seats of Firebirds equipped with the standard interior carried over for 1968, door panels received additional padding and a section of carpet on the lower edge for a luxurious touch. Rear quarter trim panels were plusher, and soft armrests and padded front windshield pillars added to passenger safety. On Firebirds so equipped, the center console received a simulated woodgrain overlay.

During the 1967 and 1968 model years, Pontiac's standard steering wheel was a good-looking three-spoke unit with a hard rim that was molded in color to match the interior and accented by a bright horn button at the center. Despite the fact that thousands were installed in Firebirds during the two model years, the standard wheel is quite the rare sight today. (Photo Courtesy Tom DeMauro)

The 1967 instrument panel returned, but the dash was padded more heavily to comply with new federal safety standards. Round vent outlets were included on all models. When a car was not equipped with air conditioning, the vents were cable controlled to provide fresh air circulation. The N30 Deluxe Steering Wheel was redesigned for 1968 and included a soft vinyl horn button adorned with the Firebird emblem. It remained optional on the basic Firebird for $14.74, was included with the Custom Option Firebird, and continued as a mandatory option on the Firebird 400.

Consumers often gauged a particular vehicle's performance potential by the maximum speed indicated on its speedometer. Keenly aware of this, Pontiac increased its F-car's speedometer to 160 mph for 1968 to further bolster Firebird's performance image. Backlighting changed from green in 1967 to light blue for 1968 to achieve a more aesthetically pleasing effect and maintain uniformity with other Pontiacs. The conical shape of the cluster lens was muted to eliminate distortion and the font was changed to make instruments easier to read.

Pontiac significantly increased the luxuriousness of the interior package of Custom Option Firebirds for 1968. When equipped with W54 Custom Interior, seats were covered in a combination of expanded and knit Morrokide, and door panels and quarter trim were of a much more handsome design. Approximately one-third of 1968 Firebird buyers selected the custom interior option that model year. There has been at least one report of an early 1968 Firebird that wasn't equipped with the updated seat covering and was instead fitted with standard seats.

The UB5 Hood-Mounted Tachometer was a popular option with performance enthusiasts and its availability continued for 1968, but not without a few modifications. Most likely to comply with FMVSS number-205, housing height and length was reduced by .75 inch, which made it less obtrusive from the driver's seat. That, in turn, required revising the dial face, which retained a redline of 5,100 rpm with V-8 engines and 5,500 rpm with the 6-cylinder. The angle of the glass covering within the housing was also revised to reduce glare and improve legibility.

appearance on a Firebird. Several were produced and at least one was affiliated with Nancy Sinatra. A handful of 1967 Firebirds were painted pink, but it's not known if the 1967 hue is identical to 1968's Pink Mist.

With the short lead time that Pontiac stylists had to distinguish the 1967 Firebird from the Camaro, they were forced to use much of Chevrolet's interior equipment. For 1968, however, Pontiac was able to inject a rather significant amount of divisional character into the Firebird, making its interior quality comparable to the midsize LeMans.

To improve appearance and increase passenger protection, Pontiac developed full-length door panels constructed of a padded vinyl upper and carpeted lower, and padded vinyl rear quarter trim. Armrests from 1967 were now soft rubber instead of the hard plastic used previously. Padding was added to the dash panel and windshield pillar trim, and stamped-steel door handles replaced Camaro's die-cast units for safety reasons.

With seemingly greater emphasis on improved occupant safety, Pontiac noted in Firebird sales literature that its padded interior appointments not only looked attractive, but more important, they were functional. Shoulder belts were slated to be standard equipment on all coupes, and they were even marketed that way, but an internal document dated August 23, 1967, rescinded that order, reverting them to optional content with availability identical to 1967. A buzzer reminded drivers whenever the key was in the ignition switch with it in the "off" position and the driver's door open.

The Custom Option Firebird was created by selecting W54 Custom Trim for $114.80. The package contained up-level appointments similar to 1967, but with a number of material improvements. Whereas W54 used standard Firebird seating in 1967, a handsomely designed Morrokide seat cover with knit-vinyl inserts was new for 1968. W54 again included N30 Deluxe Steering Wheel, but it featured a new, color-coordinated plastic rim with brushed-chrome spokes and was complemented by a molded vinyl horn button complete with the Firebird emblem. The N34 Custom Sport Steering Wheel with simulated woodgrain rim was carried over from 1967 except that the depth of its "dish" was revised.

On January 26, 1968, Pontiac issued Sales Blueprint 68-30 announcing a new leather seating option that gave buyers the ability to create a Custom Option Firebird with even greater luxury for $263.30. Specifying trim code 281 netted the same appointments as W54, but bucket seats trimmed with genuine leather and Morrokide replaced the Morrokide and knit-vinyl units. Production availability was scheduled for February 1, 1968, and color choice was limited to Saddle. No known production numbers of Firebirds equipped with the leather interior option exist but, surprisingly, quite a few have been documented.

Pontiac Sales Blueprint 68-30 announced that a new interior choice for Custom Option Firebirds was scheduled to reach production on February 1, 1968. With color choice limited to Saddle, genuine leather replaced Morrokide seating surfaces on front and rear covers, adding a greater air of luxury. Although there are no known figures that indicate the total number of 1968 Firebirds produced with the leather interior option, and several have been documented, the option is rather rare.

Front bucket seats could be replaced by a full-length bench when buyers selected the AL4 Contoured Bench Seat option. It provided front occupants with a center armrest when lowered, and increased passenger capacity by one when raised. The AL4 option also required a column-mounted transmission shifter. With 3,721 produced in 1968, it wasn't uncommon to find a first-generation Firebird with a bench seat back then, but it's rather uncommon today. (Photo Courtesy Tom DeMauro)

Stack and Company in Sydney, Australia, had been importing American vehicles for decades by the late-1960s. Part of the importation process included the conversion to right-hand drive prior to delivery. The interior of this particular 1968 Firebird was so faithfully converted by Stack that it looks as if it left the Lordstown, Ohio, assembly plant in this manner. It was loaded with options.

To maintain its performance image over Camaro, Pontiac carried over the prominently displayed engine size on the Firebird's hood. The bright, die-cast badges were revised to accommodate the 1968 displacement increase to 4.1 liters for the 6-cylinder and 350 for the small V-8.

Buyers could add capacity for one more passenger on hardtop Firebirds by selecting the AL4 Bench Seat for $31.60. The bench was available in any standard-interior color choice, but was limited to Black and Parchment with W54 Custom Trim. A bulletin issued on April 26, 1968, immediately canceled the bench seat option with Parchment Custom, but there were no other restrictions throughout the model year. A total of 3,721 Firebirds were so equipped.

A46 Power Bucket Seat option equipped the driver's front bucket with an electric motor that allowed four-way adjustments for $69.51. It was relatively unpopular, however, as only 278 were installed.

Pontiac issued a bulletin on April 19, 1968, announcing immediate availability of A90 Deck Lid Release for $13.69, which consisted of a button located within the glove compartment that remotely unlocked the deck lid for easy access to the luggage compartment. A total of 698 were installed that model year.

Engine Lineup

For 1968, Pontiac increased the displacement of its smallest engine offerings. All now featured a closed-crankcase ventilation system as well as the thermostatically controlled carburetor pre-heater system to improve cold-weather drivability.

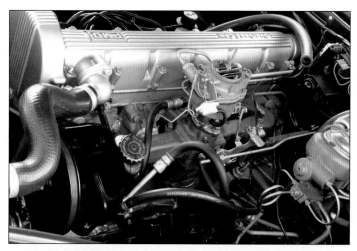

To boost performance and drivability, Pontiac fitted its OHC-6 with a new crankshaft with greater stroke length, which increased displacement from 230 to 250 ci. With a 1-barrel carburetor, it remained the standard engine in base-model Firebirds and was rated at 175 hp at 4,800 rpm and 240 ft-lbs at 2,600 rpm.

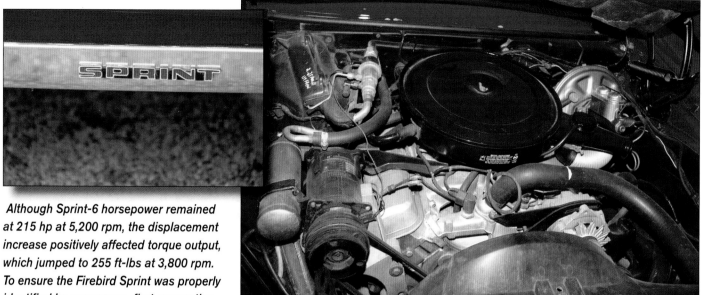

Although Sprint-6 horsepower remained at 215 hp at 5,200 rpm, the displacement increase positively affected torque output, which jumped to 255 ft-lbs at 3,800 rpm. To ensure the Firebird Sprint was properly identified by consumers, first-generation Firebirds were equipped with die-cast "Sprint" badges positioned on the lower end of the front fender, directly behind the wheelwell. This particular emblem was used in 1968 and 1969.

A bore diameter increase to 3.88 inches jumped Pontiac's small V-8 from 326 to 350 ci for 1968. A 2-barrel carburetor not only boosted performance to 265 hp at 4,600 rpm and 355 ft-lbs at 2,800 rpm, it also increased its commonality with the 400-ci for assembly line ease. As the Firebird 350's standard engine when equipped with a 2-barrel carburetor, a 4-barrel variation boasting a hotter camshaft and increased compression ratio rated at 320 hp at 5,100 rpm and 380 ft-lbs at 3,200 rpm was included with the Firebird H.O.

The OHC-6 remained the Firebird's standard engine, but Pontiac had reengineered many components to improve performance and reliability. Increasing crankshaft stroke length from 3.25 to 3.625 inches added 20 ci, taking total displacement to 250. Additional counterweighting was added for smoother operation at all operating speeds. The cylinder head combustion chamber was slightly modified to further reduce emissions and enlarged to maintain its target compression ratio at 9:1.

Along with greater displacement, Pontiac also increased camshaft duration of the standard OHC-6 with a 1-barrel carburetor to 240 degrees; output jumped to 175 hp at 4,800 rpm and 240 ft-lbs at 2,600. A total of 13,832 were installed into entry-level Firebirds during the 1968 model year.

The L72 Sprint-6 again included the Quadrajet carburetor, a 244-degree camshaft, and an advertised compression ratio of 10.5:1. It retained its horsepower rating of 215 at 5,200 rpm, but torque increased to 255 ft-lbs at 3,800 rpm as a result of displacement boost.

With an emphasis on performance perception, Pontiac's smallest-displacement V-8 (the 326) grew to 354 ci for 1968 by way of a bore diameter increase from 3.710 to 3.875 inches. Despite its actual displacement being slightly larger, the small-cube V-8 was marketed as a 350-ci. When compared to the outgoing 326, the new 350 idled smoother, offered improved performance throughout the entire operating range, and, by incorporating design features associated with the 400-ci, reduced exhaust emissions simultaneously.

The increased bore diameter of the 350-ci block allowed the use of a larger 1.96-inch-diameter intake valve to improve airflow and performance, and the number-17 cylinder head featured a new open-design combustion chamber to increase efficiency. Retaining a 2-barrel carburetor, the 269/277-degree number-254 camshaft, and a 9.2:1 compression ratio for compatibility with regular-grade fuel, the additional 28 cubes pushed total horsepower upward 15 units to 265 at 4,600 rpm and added more than 20 ft-lbs of torque, boosting that total to 355 at 2,800 rpm.

The 326 H.O. package matured into the 350 H.O. for 1968 and its number-18 cylinder heads were very much akin to the 2-barrel's number-17 casting. However, its combustion chambers displaced 66 cc for a compression ratio compatible with premium-grade fuel that was advertised at 10.5:1. The L76 350 H.O. (newly fitted with a Quadrajet carburetor in place of the Carter AFB) was rated at 320 hp at 5,100 rpm and 380 ft-lbs at 3,200 rpm. Those backed by an automatic transmission (code-YM) received the number-254 camshaft with 269/277 degrees of duration, whereas the number-066 with 273/282

Pontiac's attractive and high-quality die-cast badging with bright plating and painted accents continued for 1968. The hood-mounted emblem was used to call out engine displacement and was revised to reflect the increase from 326 to 350 ci that model year. Such ornamentation was a staple of the features that enhanced the division's performance image.

The W66 400 Sport Option remained the top 1968 Firebird for performance enthusiasts. With an advertised compression ratio of 10.75:1, large-diameter intake and exhaust valves, and a 4-barrel carburetor, it delivered 330 hp at 4,800 rpm and 430 ft-lbs at 3,300 rpm. For buyers who wanted a bit more performance without sacrificing drivability, the 400 H.O. boasted the high-flow exhaust manifolds from the Ram Air and an output increase of 5 hp. The Firebird 400's air cleaner lid and valvecovers were chrome plated for extra flash.

degrees of duration was specific to a manual (code-WK). It was an excellent combination that performed very well and delivered good fuel economy.

The L78 400-ci 4-barrel remained the base engine with W66 400 Sport Option. It featured a new 400-inch block (number-9790071) which, according to its original drawing, differed from its predecessor only in the placement of its cylinder-wall scallops, which serve to provide valve clearance. Its number-16 cylinder head was also new and retained large 2.11/1.77-inch valves, but featured a new open-style combustion chamber that displaced 72 to 74 cc. Although the 400's advertised compression ratio was 10.75:1, its actual ratio measured closer to 10:1. The compression ratio disparity was quite common in Pontiac sales literature during the 1960s, and it was a direct attempt to provide buyers with an engine that performed at that stated level, but with a slightly lower actual ratio to quell the possibility of detonation or run-on with low-quality fuel.

Code-YT was specified for automatic transmission applications; Code-WZ was used with manual transmissions. Either application used the same number-067 camshaft with 273/289 degrees of duration and about .407-inch valve lift. When compared to 1967, horsepower increased 5 units to 330 at 4,800 rpm and torque jumped to 430 ft-lbs at 3,300 rpm. The Quadrajet's

unique throttle linkage that restricted secondary function remained for 1968 and kept the Firebird compliant with GM's corporate vehicle-weight-to-horsepower ratio policy. The horsepower increase suggested a slightly greater curb weight.

The L74 400 H.O. was borrowed from the GTO engine lineup as a way to give Firebird 400 buyers a performance engine option in which air conditioning was available. The 400 H.O. option added $76.88 to the price of the Firebird 400 and consisted of the same two-bolt 400 block and number-16 cylinder heads used on the basic Firebird 400-ci, but the 067 camshaft was limited to automatic transmission applications (code-YW). The 288/302-degree 068 was used with the manual (code-WQ). Equipped with the same high-flow exhaust manifolds as the 400 Ram Air, the 400 H.O. was rated at 335 hp at 5,000 rpm and 430 ft-lbs at 3,400 rpm.

1968 400 Ram Air

The 400 Ram Air carried over into the 1968 model year with very few changes. The number-670 and -997 cylinder heads of 1967 were replaced with the number-31 casting (often called "37" from the appearance of the numbers cast on the center exhaust port) for 1968. Specific to 400 Ram Air, the 31 was essentially the same as the number-16 found on standard 1968 400s except that its valvespring pads were machined deeper for Ram Air–spec valvesprings, and it was fitted with swirl-polished valves for improved durability. Combustion chamber volume measured about 72 cc and actual compression ratio measured about 10:1 despite the 400 Ram Air's advertised rating of 10.75:1.

Any 9792510 blocks left over at the close of the 1967 model year were used for early-1968 400 Ram Air engines before number-9792506 replaced it. There has been no proof to determine that these two blocks actually differ, but both appear identical in virtually every respect and share the same four-bolt main caps with part numbers. It begs the question, if the last digit in the 9792510 sequence is difficult to decipher, could it be possible that "9792510" was actually a foundry error that was corrected to "9792506" during the second casting run that occurred in the fall of 1967? The answer will likely remain a mystery unless factory documentation surfaces to support it.

Some within Pontiac were concerned about the drivability characteristics of the 1967 400 Ram Air with the 301/313-degree number-744 cam and an automatic

9790140 AND 9794234 MANIFOLDS

When Pontiac redesigned its cast-iron 4-barrel intake manifold to accommodate the new Rochester Quadrajet for 1967, its number-9786286 was amazingly similar to the single 4-barrel on the Super Duty 421 that terrorized high-speed oval competitors. The manifold was revised slightly for 1968. Most notable was the elimination of the exhaust passage found on the carburetor mounting flange. The intent was to superheat the carburetor, ensuring optimal fuel atomization in all weather conditions, but Pontiac deemed it unnecessary after a single model year.

Production of the 1968 4-barrel manifold (number-9790140) began in August 1967. Without fanfare, it was replaced by a second manifold (number-9794234) during the 1968 model year. Some hobbyists feel that the 9794234 manifold and Ram Air II engine were released concurrently in mid-May 1968, and some sources state that 9794234 was limited to Ram Air II; 9790140 remained on all other engines. Both theories have gone unsubstantiated with any sort of factory documentation, however.

The earliest cast date for the 9794234 manifold has been March 25, 1968 (C258), and it appeared original to the entry-level 400 it was removed from. The engine serial number (ESN) of that particular 400 also predates the release of the RAM AIR II by a few weeks. It's believed that 9794234 simply replaced 9790140 as the standard 4-barrel manifold in V-8 production during April 1968, but didn't have any differences to support a part number change.

With the recent discovery of the original drawing for each 1968 manifold, you can understand the actual differences between them. According to those documents, development of the 9794234 began in February 1968 and it differs from 9790140 in two respects. First, the unused material left over from the elimination of the under-carburetor exhaust passage on the 9790140 was removed on 9794234. Second, the plenum area where 9794234 transitions into the number-8 runner was enlarged slightly, perhaps to balance overall airflow through the casting.

Although it's very difficult to say if Pontiac's modifications actually translated into any additional engine performance, after considering this newly found information, it's safe to say that any 4-barrel Pontiac V-8 produced from April 1968 onward should be equipped with the 9794234 manifold. This includes the last few Ram Air I engines and all Ram Air II units.

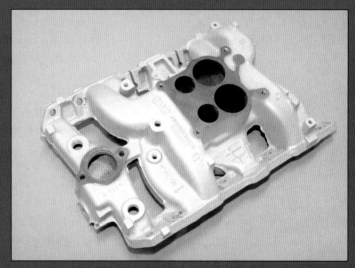

At 1968 model year startup, all 4-barrel Pontiac V-8s were equipped with the number-9790140 cast-iron intake manifold. The casting was revised slightly in March 1968 and number-9794234 superseded 9790140 as the 4-barrel intake manifold on all V-8 applications from that point forward. No reason for the change was ever published, but a comparison of original drawings of the two reveals minor internal changes.

The 400 Ram Air was advertised as Pontiac's top performance option for 1968. The basic package was carried over from 1967 and again included functional Ram Air and high-flow exhaust manifolds. Instead of the 301/313-degree number-744 camshaft for both manual and automatic transmissions as in 1967, the 288/302-degree number-068 was specified whenever the 400 Ram Air was backed by an automatic for 1968. To remain compliant with GM's horsepower-to-weight standard, the Quadrajet's secondary action was limited by a specific carburetor linkage that restricted the GTO's 360 hp engine output to 335 hp at 5,300 rpm and 430 ft-lbs at 3,600 rpm in the Firebird.

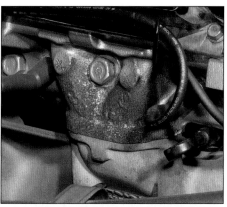

The 1968 400 Ram Air was equipped with specific D-port cylinder heads fitted with 2.11/1.77-inch valves constructed of a specific alloy and swirl polished for maximum durability and unique valvesprings designed to handle the valve action and high-RPM capability. Although the 1968 400 Ram Air cylinder head is technically identified by "31" cast into the center exhaust ports, the shape of the "1" can sometimes be mistaken for a "7," which leads some hobbyists to also refer to it as a "37" casting. And then there are odd castings like this, where "37" is actually found on the center exhaust port. Even Pontiac's foundry workers found it confusing. Notice the stamped "X," which denotes the special valvetrain.

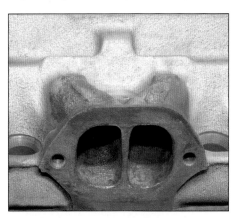

When Pontiac engineers developed the new-for-1955 V-8, the intake and exhaust port routing was configured for compact packaging. As a result, the center exhaust ports shared a common wall, which caused the otherwise oval-shaped port outlet to take on a pronounced "D" shape. As years passed, the identifying characteristic led to the nickname "D-port" when referring to cylinder heads of that type.

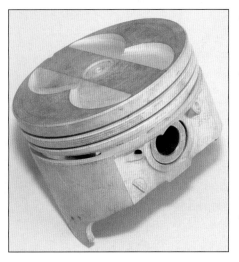

Along with every other Pontiac V-8 from 1967 and 1968, the Ram Air I was equipped with the division's cast aluminum pistons. The high-quality unit was ideal for typical passenger car engines because it was produced affordably, was relatively lightweight yet durable, and operated quietly and reliably throughout its lifetime. The cast piston wasn't suited for high-RPM engines pushed to the limit, however. If it made contact with a valve during an unexpected valvetrain failure, the cast piston was prone to breakage, potentially taking the rest of the block with it.

transmission. For 1968, Pontiac specified the 288/302-degree number-068 camshaft for 400 Ram Air automatic transmission applications (code-XN); the 744 remained with the manual (code-WI). Despite the difference in camshaft duration, Pontiac rated the 1968 400 Ram Air at 335 hp at 5,300 rpm and 430 ft-lbs at 3,600 rpm regardless of transmission choice, an increase of 10 hp and 20 ft-lbs over 1967.

At 1968 model year production startup, Pontiac set the retail price of the L67 400 Ram Air engine at $342.29. Order Code-347 didn't appear on the typical Firebird order form and instead required checking the appropriate box on the Special Equipment order form. The window

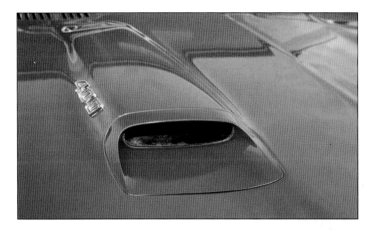

Although the molded plastic scoop inserts of the Firebird 400 hood were sealed off during manufacturing, pre-delivery preparation of any 1967–1968 Ram Air Firebird included carefully cutting away the louvered section, which, when combined with the corresponding air cleaner pan, then allowed the carburetor to directly ingest cooler outside air.

Pontiac Sales Promotion BLUEPRINT

May 16, 1968   P.S.B. 68-57

GTO AND FIREBIRD RAM AIR II ENGINES

More and more young performance enthusiasts around the country are being bitten by the GTO and Firebird 400 bugs! In addition, requests for Ram Air engines for both series are increasing daily.

To meet this demand for maximum performance, Pontiac Engineering has developed an <u>all-new Ram Air Engine Option</u>. It is designated Ram Air II and replaces the original Ram Air Option.

The Ram Air II Option is designed to provide the ultimate in action-packed performance. Cool outside air is inducted through the twin air scoops located on the hood of the Firebird 400 and GTO. The air enters the intake system directly through a plenum chamber to the carburetor and this unrestricted flow significantly increases engine efficiency and assists in developing full engine power. The "open" air scoops are meant to be only <u>temporarily</u> installed and the original scoops and air cleaner should be reinstalled for driving in inclement weather.

The 400 Ram Air II Option utilizes a 10.75:1 compression ratio with a four barrel quadra-jet carburetor. Cylinder heads and combustion chambers have been redesigned to effect maximum engine breathing. Exhaust manifolds have been revised to accommodate the larger round exhaust ports. Other new features include: higher lift cam shaft, lighter weight valves, new valve springs and larger push rods, forged aluminum pistons, new crank shaft, new distributor with revised advance curve and a new tuned harmonic balancer.

The Ram Air II Option is available on Firebird 400 and GTO models with either 4-speed manual transmission or Hydra-Matic transmission. It can be ordered by specifying Code 347 on the Special Equipment Wholesale Car Order Form No. 516. Horsepower and torque specifications for this new engine are as follows:

FIREBIRD	GTO
340 horsepower at 5300 rpm	366 horsepower at 5400 rpm
430 lb. ft. at 3600 rpm	445 lb. ft. at 3800 rpm

PONTIAC MOTOR DIVISION ▼ GENERAL MOTORS CORPORATION

Although Pontiac engineers were developing a new high-performance 400-ci for 1969, racers complained that the 1968 400 Ram Air was becoming uncompetitive against the latest engine offerings from other manufacturers. In response, Pontiac introduced some of its newest technology ahead of the 1969 engine with the midyear release of the Ram Air II. The new 400-ci V-8 available to Firebird and GTO buyers was announced with this bulletin issued on May 16, 1968.

sticker of such Firebirds listed the cost at $616.12. Although that is a large price disparity, the amount shown on the sticker included $273.83 for the W66 400 Sport option, which was required when ordering L67.

On January 1, 1968, Pontiac increased the cost of the 400 Ram Air by $15 to a total of $357.12, and window sticker pricing subsequently reflected a revised package cost of $631.16. The reason for the increase is not known, and it seems that all other optional equipment on the Firebird was unaffected.

You've probably noticed the purposeful effort to refrain from referring to the 1967–1968 400 Ram Air as the Ram Air I and may be wondering why. There's a simple answer for that. Pontiac never originally referred to its 400 Ram Air as Ram Air I until about April 1968, when it began marketing a modified 400 Ram Air offering billed as Ram Air II. It's only logical that the preceding Ram Air engine package assume "I" nomenclature. From this point forward (in this book), I refer to the 400 Ram Air as the Ram Air I (or R/A I), but it should be noted that it's quite acceptable to use 400 Ram Air and Ram Air I interchangeably.

According to Pontiac production documents, when Ram Air I production ended in mid-May 1968, a total of 413 Ram Air Firebirds had been assembled. Of that total, 321 were backed by M20 4-speed manual transmissions and the remaining 92 received the M40 Turbo-400 automatic. A 3.90:1 axle ratio was used in all applications regardless of transmission choice. These Firebirds were excellent performers and remain highly coveted by performance enthusiasts and collectors.

1968½ Ram Air II

The Ram Air I was Pontiac's hottest engine for 1967 and at 1968 startup. As other manufacturers raised the performance bar, Pontiac developed ways to make its 400 even more competitive. Throughout the 1967 calendar

The Ram Air II superseded the 400 Ram Air as Pontiac's top performance engine in May 1968. Although its advertised rating increased by 5 hp on paper to 340 hp at 5,300 rpm, new cylinder heads with round exhaust outlets and a long-duration camshaft with high valve lift made the mill considerably more potent than its predecessor. Shortly after being phased out, the original 400 Ram Air was renamed Ram Air I by Pontiac (and most hobbyists ever since).

year, Pontiac's engineering team was hard at work creating a new high-performance 400-ci with planned availability for the 1969 model year. Although the foundation consisted of a typical 400-inch block with four-bolt main caps and a cast crankshaft and connecting rods, Pontiac developed forged aluminum pistons for added durability.

The greatest performance gains from the new 400-ci came from valvetrain and cylinder head enhancements.

In May 1967, Pontiac began developing an entirely new hydraulic camshaft with extended duration intended for a high-revving 400-ci for the 1969 model year. In December 1967, development began on a new cylinder head with increased airflow capacity.

In contrast to the typical oval exhaust ports, where the pronounced "D" shape of the siamesed center ports lends the descriptive term "D-port," the new Ram Air cylinder head featured round exhaust outlets that, according to renowned Pontiac engineer Malcolm McKellar, were intended to make installing tubular headers easier for racers. The cylinder head also featured oversize intake ports, which not only increased airflow, but also increased port volume to support operation up to 6,000 rpm.

Although Pontiac was in the midst of developing its new-for-1969 400, the division recognized that its then-current Ram Air 400 needed a technology injection. "Racers complained that our 400 was falling behind," said McKellar, "so we took some of what we developed for the 1969 engine and applied it to the 1968 Ram Air I to create the Ram Air II, which we introduced late in the year. It was a rush design that we needed to get into production quickly, so we used only what we had finished developing up to that point."

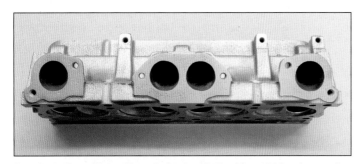

Pontiac's "round-port" era began with the May 1968 release of the Ram Air II. The division updated the Ram Air I cylinder head to include the redesigned exhaust ports it was developing for a 1969 extra-horsepower 400. The port was modified internally to greatly improve airflow capacity when compared to the standard casting, and it featured a round outlet shape measuring 1.75 inches in diameter. The round shape had no real effect on airflow, however. It was simply intended as an installation convenience for racers who typically replaced factory-issued exhaust manifolds with tubular headers.

The Ram Air II was equipped with forged aluminum pistons for increased durability and it was heavier than the cast pistons used in other 400-ci engines. That required specific crankshaft balancing, so Pontiac created the number-9794054 cast ArmaSteel piston with journals machined for an additional .001 inch of oil clearance. The "9794054" of original Ram Air II cranks was cast in place, but later service replacements were constructed from a typical cast nodular iron 400-ci unit and machined to Ram Air II specifications. The cast part number of the replacement crankshaft was ground away and "9794054" was messily stamped into place.

In conjunction with TRW, Pontiac developed a forged aluminum version (number-9794056) of its standard 400-ci piston that was introduced with the Ram Air II. Constructed of SAE-328 alloy, the new piston increased the durability of the Ram Air II, particularly at high engine speeds where a cast piston is most vulnerable. TRW continued to offer Pontiac's forged piston in its aftermarket piston lineup; Federal-Mogul offers them today.

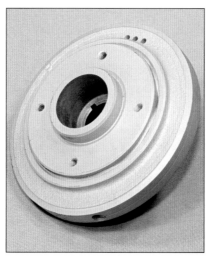

Pontiac developed a new V-8 harmonic balancer for the 1968 model year. Unlike the previously used multi-piece units that bolted together, the revised component featured unitized construction and its outer ring (or inertia weight) is separated from the crankshaft hub by a rubber absorber. The design was claimed to offer greater balancing qualities for improved operational smoothness. A revised balancer (number-9794058) was developed to complement the high-RPM capability of the Ram Air II and it differs from the standard V-8 balancer in the durometer of its rubber absorber. It carried over into 1969 for use on the Ram Air IV.

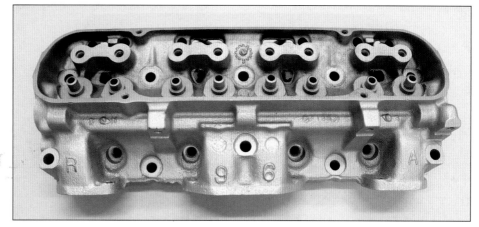

The new round-port Ram Air II cylinder head is identified by a large "R" and "A" on the end exhaust ports. Production began as early as April 19, 1968 (A198). Beginning on April 23, 1968 (A238), a large "96" was added to the center exhaust ports to further identify the specialty casting. Pontiac apparently last produced the Ram Air II cylinder head in January 1969 and it remained in the parts system through the 1970s.

The new Ram Air II (or R/A II) was comprised of the same foundation as the original 1968 Ram Air 400, using a 400-inch block with four-bolt main caps (number-9792506) and typical cast connecting rods. Its cast Arma Steel crankshaft (number-9794054) was specifically balanced for use with new, highly durable forged aluminum pistons (number-9794056). Number-9792506 blocks were apparently cast in larger runs and stockpiled for Ram Air engine use. The last examples were cast on March 11, 1968 (C118). Once the supply of number-9792506 blocks was exhausted, typical number-9790071 400-inch castings modified to accept four-bolt caps were phased into Ram Air II production.

The Ram Air II cylinder head was a hybrid variant that combined intake port sizing of the 1968 Ram Air 400 number-31 casting with the round exhaust port arrangement of the new-for-1969 Ram Air cylinder head. The Ram Air II casting (number-9793596) is identified by the letters "R" and "A" on the end exhaust ports. As production continued, Pontiac added a large "96" to the center exhaust ports for easier identification. Although "96" was reused in 1971 to identify a 400-inch D-port cylinder head, the two are not related in any way.

The Ram Air II number-96 casting had an intake port volume that measured approximately 155 cc and contained a maximum airflow capacity of about 205 cfm at 28 inches of pressure. Although most believe that the exhaust port outlet's round shape lent additional airflow, Pontiac modified the internal port shape to improve peak airflow; subsequently, it flowed some 15 to 20 percent better than a typical D-port exhaust port, or around 195 cfm at peak. It created one of the highest exhaust-to-intake flow percentages of any Pontiac cylinder head casting, and that contributed to the Ram Air II's potency.

Although Pontiac transitioned into an open-wedge chamber design to improve the combustion efficiency of its V-8s for 1968, the Ram Air II used a modified version of that chamber. Marketed as a "spherized wedge," the chamber shape became synonymous with the series of round-port castings that were produced through the 1974 model year. Additional relieving around the intake valve worked in concert with the valveseat to further improve low- and mid-lift airflow. Its spark plug was repositioned slightly to enhance flame propagation. Despite the Ram Air II's advertised compression ratio of 10.75:1, combustion chamber volume of the number-96 casting measured 72 to 73 cc in stock form, which produced an actual compression ratio of about 10:1 on a standard-bore 400-ci.

The Ram Air II valvetrain consisted of many unique components. At the heart was the new number-9794041 (or 041) hydraulic camshaft, which featured an advertised duration of 308/320 degrees. To accommodate the

CAM CHOICE WITH R/A II AND AUTOMATIC TRANSMISSION

It's well understood that the number-041 camshaft was newly introduced with the Ram Air II engine in midyear 1968. A technical data sheet for the Firebird-spec Ram Air II engine dated June 5, 1968, lists the 308/320-degree grind as the only camshaft available with that engine. Some contend, however, that the 041 was used with the manual transmission Ram Air II only, and that those with an automatic were actually equipped with the 288/302-degree number-068 camshaft (as with the Ram Air I) that the new engine superseded.

Upon further investigation of the highly detailed data sheet, it appears that Pontiac may have printed it with NHRA-type technical inspections in mind. As such, it's quite possible that the division's intent in stating that the number-041 was the only cam used was to give class racers competing with automatic-equipped Ram Air II Firebirds performance that equaled those racing manual transmission cars.

Proving the theory that the number-068 was the factory-installed cam in Ram Air II automatic transmission applications has been a challenge. Aside from finding an original,

1968 FIREBIRD & TEMPEST 8-CYL. ENGINE IDENTIFICATION CHART

IDENTIFICATION LETTER CODE STAMPED IMMEDIATELY BELOW PRODUCTION ENGINE NUMBER ON FRONT OF RIGHT HAND SIDE OF BLOCK. DO NOT ORDER ENGINES OR PARTS FROM THIS CHART.

S – STANDARD EQUIPMENT   O – OPTIONAL OR SPECIAL EQUIPMENT

Letter Code	Trans. Type	350 Cubic Inch	400 Cubic Inch	Engine No. (Last Two Digits)	2 Bbl. Carb.	4 Bbl. Carb. (Quadrajet)	8.6 Comp. Ratio	9.2 Comp. Ratio	10.5 Comp. Ratio	10.75 Comp. Ratio	2337-67	3327-69	3527-37-39-67-69	3535, 3935	3127-37-39-67	4237-67	Camshaft (9777254)	Camshaft (9779066)	Camshaft (9779067)	Camshaft (9779068)	Camshaft (9785744)	Camshaft (9794041)	Distributor (1112281)	Distributor (1112282)	Distributor (1111447)	Distributor (1111270)	Distributor (1111272)	Distributor (1111449)	Distributor (1111940)	Distributor (1111165)	Distributor (1111941)	Valve Springs (Std.)	Valve Springs (H.D.)	Valve Springs (Ram Air)	Horsepower
YZ	HMT		X	71		X				X						O		X									▲					X		X	350
WY	MAN		X	73		X				X						O				X				X								X		X	360
XW	HMT		X	74		X				X						O			X													X		X	360
WS	MAN		X	76		X				X						O			X						▲								X	X	360
XS	MAN		X	77		X				X						O				X					▲								X	X	360
WT	MAN		X	78		X				X						S			X					▲								X	X	360
YS	HMT		X	79		X				X						O			X					▲							X		X	350
XP	HMT		X	81		X				X						O			X					▲							X		X	360
XM	HMT		X	83	X		X									O	X									X	X				X		X	265
WP	MAN	X		92	X			X			O	O	O	O			X								X						X			265
WR	MAN	X		94		X		X			O	O	O	O			X			X							X				X			320
YN	AT	X		96	X			X			O	O	O	O			X								X■						X			265
YP	AT	X		97		X		X			O	O	O					X								X					X			320
WC	MAN	X		21	X			S									X							X							X			265
YJ	AT	X		24	X			O									X								X■			X●			X			265
WK	MAN	X		27		X		O										X					X								X			320
YM	AT	X		29		X		O									X							X						X			320
WU	MAN		X	41		X	O										X								▲					X			360
XT	HMT	X		42	X		X	O										X													X			360
XN	HMT	X		43		X	O							X																X		X	335
WQ	MAN	X		44		X	O							X																X		X	335
WI	MAN	X		45		X	O								X											▲				X		X	335
WZ	MAN	X		46		X	O						X													▲				X		X	335
YW	HMT	X		47		X	O						X										▲							X		X	330
YT	HMT	X		48		X	O						X										▲							X		X	330

▲NOTE: With 60 P.S.I. Oil Pump Spring   ■Early Production   ●Late Production

02-1-5 & 04-1-5

© 1968 PONTIAC MOTOR DIVISION, GENERAL MOTORS CORPORATION

C-206   Revised 5-1-68

Although the number-041 camshaft unquestionably debuted in the 1968½ Ram Air II when it was backed by a manual transmission (code-WU), many hobbyists disagree about which camshaft Pontiac used when the optional 400 was backed by an automatic (code-XT). Until I can find an unmolested example, we may never truly know. This Engine Identification Chart from a 1968 Pontiac Master Parts Catalog dated May 1, 1968, however, clearly specified the number-068 camshaft for the code-XT 400, highlighted in yellow here for easy recognition.

added airflow capacity of the new-for-1969 400 cylinder head, its valve lift was increased to .470-inch lift as measured with 1.5:1-ratio rocker arms. Boasting 87 degrees of valve overlap, which tends to favor improved cylinder fill at high RPM, the 041 was a rather radical grind for a 400-ci with a nasty idle, but it proved to be a solid performer and was pushed into production early for the Ram Air II.

The number-96 cylinder head was filled with large, tulip-shaped valves measuring 2.11-inch intake and 1.77-inch exhaust and were swirl-polished for improved durability. A special dual-valvespring package with increased

unmolested example with the 068 in place, one supporting document is a detailed Pontiac Engine Identification Chart printed on May 1, 1968. It clearly lists the number-068 for auto-backed Ram Air II engines and the 041 with the manual. It's further corroborated by vintage Master Parts Catalogs, which also list the 068 as the appropriate cam for automatic transmission applications.

Although others may disagree with this assessment, there's a very strong possibility that the 1968 Engine Identification Chart is accurate. With so few Ram Air II Firebirds (and GTOs) produced during the latter half of the 1968 model year, however, there's a chance that this theory could live on as conjecture until an original Ram Air II engine with its number-068 camshaft installed is located or an internal document detailing the factory assembly specifications of such an engine surfaces.

```
            1968½ PONTIAC FIREBIRD RAM AIR II ENGINE

Option may be ordered on the Firebird model by specifying code WV or XT on car order form.
Manual transmission order should specify 358 close-ratio 4-speed manual transmission (2.20 1st
gear) and 3.90 or 4.33 axle ratio.

                         ENGINE SPECIFICATIONS

400 Cubic Inch Displacement                          Valve in Head V-8

Bore 4.1200 - 4.1244                            Stroke 3.746 - 3.754

Compression Ratio :          Nominal 10.75:1         Maximum 11.4:1

Max. BHP 340 @ 5300                     Connecting Rods: Arma Steel

Max. Torque 430 @ 3600                     Bearings: Moraine 400A

Cylinder Head Volume 65.0 c.c. (Minimum)     Crankshaft:  Arma Steel

Deck Clearance 0 (0 to .034 Below)     Crankshaft Bearings:  Moraine 400A

Flat pistons with valve clearance notches     Hydraulic valve lifters

1 - 4-barrel Rochester Carburetor          Rocker Arm Ratio 1.5 to 1

9794041 Camshaft

         Intake opens 42 BTC closes 86 ABC:  Duration 308

         Exhaust opens 95 BBC closes 45 ATC:  Duration 320

         Lift:  Intake .480

              Exhaust .475


Standard Inner and Outer Valve Springs

                                      Dual Springs

    Total Spring Load Closed:          107 - 123

    Total Spring Load Open:            303 - 327

    Intake Valves
        GM-8440 Aluminum treatment on face - chrome plated stem
        5.198 Long    2.113 - 2.107 Head Diameter    .34 Stem Diameter

    Exhaust Valves
        21-2 Steel - Aluminum treatment on face - chrome plated stem
        5.212 Long    1.773 - 1.767 Head Diameter    .34 Stem Diameter



                              Product Information Section
                              June 5, 1968
```

Pontiac issued this bulletin outlining the specifications of its newly released Ram Air II engine in the 1968 Firebird on June 5, 1968. It infers that the number-041 camshaft was used with either transmission, but the minimum and maximum tolerances listed for various components, as well as mention of 4.33:1 rear axle gearing, makes this document appear as if it were some sort of technical document that Pontiac submitted to racing organizations to secure competition eligibility. An identical document for the GTO accompanied it.

The shape and size of the intake port in the Ram Air II cylinder head was identical to that of the D-port number-31 it replaced in midyear 1968. Airflow capacity of either casting peaks around 205 cfm at 28 inches of pressure, or about the same as virtually every other D-port cylinder head with an intake valve diameter of 2.11 inches from that era.

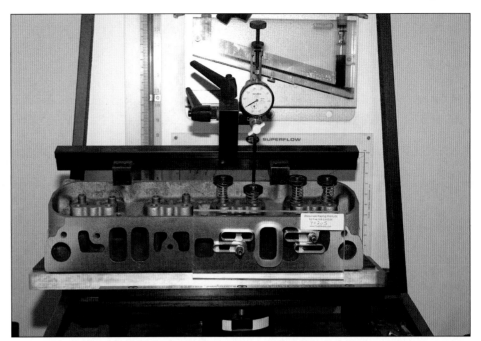

A Super Flow airflow bench allows operators to professionally measure the airflow capacity of a cylinder head. By comparing records, you can predict the performance effects a particular cylinder head can have over another. I have been testing Pontiac cylinder heads on my Super Flow 110 bench for years. I recently had the opportunity to test a Ram Air II casting. As expected, when compared to a D-port casting of the same vintage, its exhaust ports peaked some 35 cfm better than the Ram Air I, while its intake ports flowed identically.

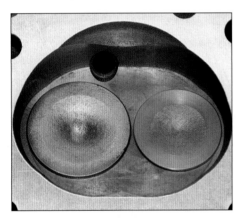

The Ram Air II cylinder head had a newly designed wedge-type combustion chamber whose shape and spark plug positioning enhanced flame propagation. Valve sizes remained 2.11/1.77 inches as with other 1968 400-ci 4-barrel engines, but the heads of the unique, tulip-shaped valves were each recessed to shed weight. That minutely increased overall chamber volume. With the stock valves in place, the chamber displaced 72 to 73 cc and yielded an actual compression ratio of 10:1 on a stock-bore 400-ci.

When the Ram Air II cylinder head was released, Pontiac equipped it with a special set of intake and exhaust valves (numbers 9794021 and 9794019) with diameters measuring 2.11 and 1.77 inches, respectively. The area where the stem transitions into the head is much wider, creating a pronounced tulip shape intended to enhance airflow. Although tulip-shaped valves are more common on the exhaust side of typical production engines, they can also be found on the intake side in various applications.

pressure was required to control the aggressive valve action of the radial number-041 cam. A standard hydraulic lifter (number-5232265) maintained quiet and consistent operation over the engine's lifetime and a 1.5:1 stamped-steel rocker arm provided valve lift of .470 inch. A thicker pushrod (number-9794043) measured 11/32 inch yet retained the standard overall length of 9.16 inches of limited deflection.

Buyers who wanted the latest technology in their Pontiac were rewarded with a 5-hp boost, taking the total to 340 at 5,300 rpm. Torque remained at 430 ft-lbs at 3,600 rpm. Pontiac expected buyers to pay a premium for it, too, however. The Ram Air II retained both the "L67" UPC code and "347" order form punch code. The option's retail cost increased by more than $115 when the Ram Air II superseded the Ram Air I in production.

The chamber side (or face) of a typical nailhead valve is generally flat, but the tulip-shaped intake valve for the Ram Air II contained a deep recess. Its intent was to reduce overall valve weight, which measures 136 grams, about the same as a similar size standard Pontiac intake valve. A physical measurement of the recess volume to accurately predict its effect on actual compression ratio revealed that it displaces exactly 1 cc. The volume of the slight recess present in the exhaust valve face is negligible.

The midyear addition of the Ram Air II is a relatively well-known fact among first-generation Firebird enthusiasts, but do you know exactly how it differs from the Ram Air I? Pontiac issued P&A Extra 68-13 on May 23, 1968, to provide dealership parts department staff with an equipment list for any owner who wanted to update a Ram Air I Firebird to Ram Air II status.

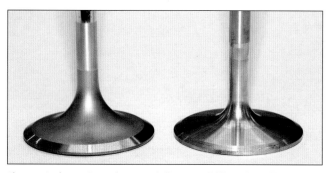

It's easy to see how the tulip-shaped intake valve used on the Ram Air II (left) differs from a typical nailhead valve such as an aftermarket unit from Ferrea (right). The tulip valve head generally works in conjunction with the port shape to enhance airflow at all lift points. The tulip shape also adds strength to the valve in the process. Knowing that the Ram Air II intake port was unmodified from the D-port it replaced, it's quite likely the valves were among the features designed to complement the 1969 Ram Air IV, but many of the components were ushered into early production to create the midyear 1968 Ram Air II.

PONTIAC
P&A EXTRA!

PONTIAC
PARTS AND ACCESSORIES

No. 68-13
May 23, 1968

Ram Air Two Engine

The Ram Air Two Engine released for the 1968 Firebird and G.T.O. is built up with some parts which are different from the earlier 1968 Ram Air Engine.

In order to update an early 1968 Ram Air Engine, all of the parts marked with an asterisk (*) must be used. They have not been released for, nor should they be used on the 1967 engines.

Prices will not appear in the Price Schedule until July, so we have included this information for your use in the meantime.

. . .

		Per Car	List	Dealer
*9793596	Cylinder Head	2	$ 75.00	$ 48.75
*9794042	Valve Guide	4	.60	.36
*9794044	Inner Spring	16	1.10	.66
*9794045	Outer Spring	16	1.30	.78
*9794019	Exhaust Valve	8	4.50	2.25
*9794021	Intake Valve	8	3.00	1.50
*9794058	Harmonic Balancer	1	13.75	8.25
*9794275	Oil Pump	1	21.00	12.60
*9794041	Camshaft	1	85.60	51.36
*9794325	Arm, Ball, & Rod Package	16	1.75	1.05
*5232265	Valve Lifters	16	3.30	1.98
9794054	Crankshaft	1	110.00	71.50
9794056	Piston	8	13.75	7.56
9794055	Exhaust Manifold Gasket	2	1.10	.55
9794033	R. H. Exhaust Manifold (42)	1	60.00	36.00
9794035	L. H. Exhaust Manifold (42)	1	50.00	30.00
9794036	R. H. Exhaust Manifold (23)	1	70.00	42.00
9794038	L. H. Exhaust Manifold (23)	1	60.00	36.00
1111941	Distributor	1	33.80	20.28
7036484	Carburetor A.T.	1	78.05	54.64
7036485	Carburetor M.T.	1	78.05	54.64

. . .

Engine assembly prices are available on written request to F. E. Barnard, Parts & Accessories Department.

PONTIAC MOTOR DIVISION ■ GENERAL MOTORS CORPORATION ■ PONTIAC, MICHIGAN

R/A I VERSUS R/A II

Pontiac introduced its high-performance Ram Air II in May 1968 and it superseded the Ram Air I, a carryover package for the 400-ci from 1967. Even though 5 hp separates the two on paper, the Ram Air II tends to overshadow the Ram Air I because of its technological enhancements and its potential to respond more favorably to modifications. So how do the two 400-inch V-8s compare on the dragstrip? That's a question few can accurately answer.

Jim Mino of Belle Vernon, Pennsylvania, has owned and drag raced a number of 1968 Ram Air Firebirds in various Pure Stock and Factory Stock class competitions over the past few decades. Using factory-issued equipment and reproductions of the original bias-ply tires, he and his Firebirds have gained the reputation of astounding performances that seemingly defy the laws of physics. Jim is quick to point out, however, that the key to his success is spend-

ing time tending to details while assembling the 400-inch mills Pontiac so expertly packaged.

Over the years, Jim has built and competed with Ram Air I and Ram Air II engines in his Firebirds. His racing experience makes him a qualified source to gauge the actual performance variance between the two. His current racer is an Autumn Bronze 1968 Firebird originally equipped with the Ram Air II engine and 4-speed manual transmission. Built to the limits of NHRA specifications for Factory Stock class racing, which basically allows a sizable compression boost and the use of some modern components, it has run a quarter-mile best of 11.75 at 118.90 mph while maintaining a factory-fresh appearance and show-ready detailing.

When asked to compare the performance of the two engines in stock form, Jim replied, "I have built both engines to factory tolerances using original components and believe

It's not uncommon to find Jim Mino and his 1968 Ram Air Firebird in the pits of a dragstrip in or around his home state of Pennsylvania on any given weekend. Not only is his Firebird maintained for action, it's minutely detailed. It could be considered a strong contender for any points-judged show he chose to enter. Autumn Bronze was a midyear exterior color addition and it's absolutely striking in the bright sun.

the quarter-mile difference between the Ram Air I and Ram Air II is about 0.10 to 0.15 in elapsed time and 1.5 to 2 mph in trap speed. When prepped similarly and on the same track, with my own Firebirds, I have run a best of 12.35 at 113.32 mph with the Ram Air I and 12.20 at 115.47 with the Ram Air II." Not only do Jim's results prove how potent Pontiac's Ram Air II engine is, they also reveal that the Ram Air I is nearly as capable as its successor.

The 1967–1968 Ram Air Firebirds were serious performance machines capable of competing handily with the top offerings of other makes. When the Ram Air II was introduced in midyear 1968, its round-port cylinder heads, aggressive camshaft, and special valvetrain components made it an even better performer than the already-potent Ram Air I. Jim's engines are generally completely stock. The only modification he allows during rebuilds is blueprinting to NHRA's maximum allowable technical specifications for the application.

Jim has been actively racing Ram Air I and Ram Air II Firebirds for decades. He currently pilots an Autumn Bronze 1968 Firebird with a Ram Air II and a 4-speed down the dragstrip. Although the Firebird typically runs in the very low 12-second range with trap speeds in excess of 116 mph, it has dipped into the 11.70s at nearly 119 mph with stock components. How's that for Pontiac engineering?

The 1968 Firebird was immensely popular; more than 112,000 units were sold. In less than two model years, Pontiac had created its own F-car that stood apart from Chevrolet's. By capitalizing on its performance image and injecting it with a stellar powertrain, the Firebird was not-so-coincidentally ranked among the hottest cars in America during the late 1960s. The venerable Ram Air II only helped bolster its reputation. This is one of 110 produced with the optional midyear mill.

The earliest correspondence pertaining to the Ram Air II is an internal bulletin issued to dealers on May 6, 1968. It detailed the unique components of the Ram Air II engine and announced engine codes "WU" for Firebirds equipped with a 4-speed manual transmission and "XT" when backed by the Turbo-400. It also revealed that the total cost increased from $631.12 to a whopping $747.77. Like the Ram Air I it replaced, $273.83 of that cost was for the Firebird's 400 Sport Option. This same bulletin may be the first instance where Pontiac actually referred to the preceding 400 as the Ram Air I.

The billing change was to occur internally in late April 1968 so that when Ram Air II production began a few weeks later, vehicles were billed correctly. However, in a few instances, Pontiac billed the first few cars equipped with the costlier Ram Air II at the Ram Air I price of $631.12. The division issued price adjustments in early July 1968 seeking to collect from dealers the $101.65 that had been under-billed for the Ram Air II Firebird. It's unclear what dealers actually charged the customer, or if they attempted to collect the additional money from previously filled Ram Air II orders.

The changeover to the Ram Air II in vehicle production has been difficult to document. Thanks to the efforts of Jim Mattison at PHS Automotive Services, we know from the billing history cards that the first 1968 Firebird with the Ram Air II was produced on May 20, 1968. It's a Cameo Ivory coupe complete with bench seat and column-shifted automatic transmission that was originally delivered to an Ohio-based Pontiac dealer who campaigned it that year as a dealer-sponsored racer.

Subsequent zone bulletins report that June 14, 1968, was the last day dealers could place orders for a Ram Air Firebird. From the information gathered from PHS Automotive Services, the last Ram Air II Firebird, a Nightshade Green coupe, was assembled on August 6, 1968, and shipped immediately. Typical 1968 Firebird production continued for a couple of weeks after that date.

Transmission Lineup

A column-shifted, Saginaw-built M12 3-speed manual was the standard transmission included with the OHC-6 (code-FY) and either 350-ci V-8s (code-RJ). A floor-mounted shifter was available with either engine for $42.13, and 2,711 buyers opted for it. A floor-shifted M12 (code-FK) was standard equipment with the Sprint-6.

For 1968, all floor-shifted V-8s required the Ford-built M13 heavy-duty 3-speed manual with 2.42:1 first-gear ratio (code-DB). Although the M13 was included in the cost of the Firebird 400, any 350-ci buyer who wanted a floor-mounted shifter was required to purchase the M13 at $84.26. A total of 6,841 M13 3-speeds were installed that model year; just 754 were used in Firebird 400 applications. The remaining 6,087 were teamed up with the 350 2-barrel and 350 H.O. engines.

An M20 floor-shifted 4-speed manual was available with all engines for $184.31. A Saginaw-built gearbox with a 3.11:1 first-gear ratio (code-FH) was used with either 6-cylinder. A Muncie-built transmission with a 2.52:1 first-gear ratio (code-FF) was used behind 6,506 vehicles, either 350-ci or Firebird 400. A special-order

Firebird transmission choices for 1968 were numerous, with 3- and 4-speed manuals as well as 2- and 3-speed automatics. A factory-installed Hurst shifter replaced the low-quality ITM unit from 1967 with the manual transmission. A round knob was standard; the simulated woodgrain M09 Custom Gear Shift Knob debuted midyear. The optional U35 Electric Clock was mounted on the transmission tunnel unless the D55 Front Console was specified, in which case it was console-mounted.

M20 Muncie 4-speed with a 2.20:1 first-gear ratio (code-FX) was required with the Ram Air engine and wherever a special-order axle ratio was ordered. A total of 8,210 M20 Muncie 4-speeds were installed into Firebird 400s, but there's no known breakdown to differentiate 2.52:1 first-gear units from special-order 2.20:1 units.

A 2-speed automatic transmission remained a $194.84 option with the 6-cylinder and either 350-ci V-8. The M30 air-cooled variant from 1967 was dropped from the 1968 lineup, suggesting reliability issues. Instead, the typical radiator-cooled M31 was specified for those applications to increase overall service life. Firebird 400 buyers who opted for an automatic transmission received the highly durable M40 Turbo-400 3-speed at $236.97 extra.

Rear Axle

The Firebird rear axle was a carryover design for 1968 and used the same 8.2-inch ring gear diameter and 10-bolt retention method. Gear ratios ranged from 2.56 to 4.33:1 depending on the application, and axle identification was made in the same manner as in 1967.

Although a single-track axle remained standard equipment with ratios up to and including 3.55:1, the G80 Safe-T-Track Differential was a $42.13 option for drivers who

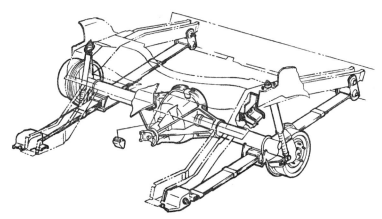

Pontiac engineers found that the Chevrolet-designed mono-leaf rear springs and shock absorber arrangement lacked the stability required during hard acceleration or braking for the 1967 Firebird. A radius rod proved to be an effective temporary solution until a new multi-leaf assembly and staggered shock absorbers were developed for 1968. The revised rear suspension not only provided a permanent solution, it improved Firebird's ride and handling qualities to boot. (Photo Courtesy General Motors)

wanted improved traction. Just as in 1967, a heavy-duty axle (G83) was automatically included wherever G80 was combined with a gear ratio of 3.36:1 and numerically higher, taking the total cost of the option to $63.19. Again, 3.90:1 was the only axle ratio available with the Ram Air engines. It could also be had with the 350 H.O. and a 4-speed manual, and the 400 4-barrel and 400 H.O. regardless of transmission choice. Availability of the 4.33:1 axle ratios was limited to the 400 4-barrel and 400 H.O., and only when backed by the M20 4-speed manual.

Suspension and Steering

Although Firebird's front suspension was a carryover for 1968, the rear suspension was significantly modified. The mono-leaf spring on each side was replaced with a multi-leaf unit for a softer and smoother ride that was also more predictable. The shock absorbers, which had been mounted ahead of the axle for 1967, were staggered for 1968. By relocating the left shock behind the axle, engineers found that, when combined with multi-leaf springs, the entire suspension assembly allowed for even better handling and stability. Axle windup was controlled so well that the radius rod(s) were eliminated from all applications.

The Y96 Ride and Handling package was offered for 1968, but it was no longer included in the W66 400 Sport Option. Although a document containing official reasoning has yet to surface, internal information shows that

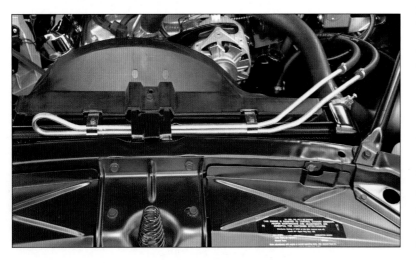

Pontiac Sales Promotion BLUEPRINT

March 11, 1968   P.S.B. 68-38

VARIABLE RATIO POWER STEERING - FIREBIRD

Variable Ratio Power Steering, Code 511, has been released and is immediately available on all Firebird models.

Variable Ratio Power Steering automatically employs a lower steering ratio reducing the steering wheel turning distance by about 30%. You have less effort in parking with the same precise highway control as always.

This new feature is standard on Firebird 400 with optional power steering. All other Firebird models require ordering Code 501, Power Steering, and adding Code 511 in the Other Accessories Section. Prices are as follows:

	LIST
Firebird - Exc. 400 with 501/511	$100.00
Firebird 400 - with 501	$100.00

This luxury car option is available on Firebird now for only $5.21 more than the standard power steering option.

Please make certain your salesmen are fully informed on this new Firebird feature.

C. L. Copeland
C. L. Copeland
Sales Promotion Manager

CLC:Bc

PONTIAC MOTOR DIVISION ▼ GENERAL MOTORS CORPORATION

Although power-assisted steering was available in 1968, Pontiac announced the release of a variable-ratio option with Pontiac Sales Blueprint 68-38 issued on March 11, 1968. The new option provided slower-ratio steering on center for precise control at speed and a quicker turn ratio driver ease. Upon its release, Firebird 400s equipped with N40 Power Steering automatically received the variable-ratio unit for $100. It was a $5.21 upcharge with other engine packages.

the Firebird 400 sold even better than Pontiac had anticipated for 1967. Based on the bulletin (see Chapter 2) where customers commented on Firebird's harsh ride, the division recognized that the Firebird 400 was quite popular with average customers who simply wanted a powerful-yet-comfortable sports car and softened its ride for 1968. The Firebird 400 still received up-level springs and shocks for a slightly firmer ride when compared to the entry-level Firebird, but devout buyers who sought an even tauter ride could add Y96 to their Firebird 400 order for $4.21. The option was $9.48 on other models.

Although quietly available for 1967, FG1 Adjustable Shocks Front and Rear were newly listed in 1968 Firebird sales material. Available with or without Y96, the $52.66 option equipped buyers seeking the ultimate in handling with a set of fully adjustable Koni shock absorbers in place of the non-adjustable Delco units. Savvy owners could then tailor the shock's effect on ride and handling to suit their needs. Just 695 buyers did so.

A power-assisted steering gear had been a Firebird option in 1967, and it continued to be offered in 1968. Whereas the manual steering gear consisted of a constant ratio of 24:1 (or 28:1 with V-8 and C60 Air Conditioning), the optional N40 Wonder Touch Power Steering provided a belt-driven pump that pressurized a steering gear with a reduced ratio of 17.5:1, which might otherwise be difficult to maneuver when parking without power assist.

In March 1968, Pontiac employed technology developed in conjunction with Saginaw for its full-size models and released a variable-ratio power steering option for the Firebird. With a varying ratio of 16 to 12.2:1, the new gear provided precise on-center driving at speed and good maneuverability when parking. Constant-ratio N40 Wonder Touch Power Steering

To promote maximum power steering pump and gearbox life of the variable-ratio power steering system, Pontiac developed an external cooling pipe to reduce the operating temperature, thereby increasing service life. It routed low-pressure fluid passing from the steering gearbox to the pump reservoir across the radiator support, where it radiated heat and received airflow wash created by the moving vehicle and engine cooling fan.

Not all 1968–1969 Firebirds were equipped with a power steering oil cooler and you may be wondering just which ones were. Pontiac issued Service Information Bulletin 68-I-76 on June 7, 1968, explaining to dealership service staff exactly that. This image depicts the portion of that bulletin where Pontiac clearly identified the criteria and applications.

(order code 501) remained a Firebird option at $94.79, but selecting order code 511 along with 501 netted the variable-ratio steering gear, which increased the cost of N40 by $10.53 to a total of $105.32.

Although power-assist and variable-ratio steering options were available on other Firebirds, effective March 1, 1968, Pontiac limited Firebird 400 buyers to the variable-ratio steering gear only. Any Firebird 400 ordered after that date and equipped with N40 Wonder Touch Power Steering received the variable-ratio box at a cost of $105.32.

When variable-ratio power steering made its way into the 1968 Firebird model line, Pontiac incorporated an integral oil cooler for maximum effectiveness in certain instances. It was automatically included on Firebird V-8s equipped with C60 Air Conditioning and an axle ratio of 2.93:1 and higher (numerically); any 6-cylinder Firebird with C60; and any Firebird equipped with an axle ratio of 3.36:1 and higher (numerically), regardless of engine size and C60 option. These same options and restrictions carried over to 1969.

Wheels and Tires

A 14 x 6–inch steel wheel with chrome-plated hubcap was again standard equipment on the Firebird and wheel color was coordinated with body finish in some instances. Full wheel cover options included P01 Deluxe Wheel Cover for $21.06, P02 Custom Wheel Cover with eight larger holes for $41.07, and N95 Wire Wheel Cover for $73.72. Because P01 Deluxe Wheel Cover was included in the cost of the W54 Custom Trim option, buyers who elected to equip their Custom Option Firebird with P02 or N95 could purchase either option for $21.06 less.

Although the Rally I wheel remained available on the Tempest model line for 1968, it was eliminated from the Firebird option list. An internal Pontiac Engineering manual states that the addition of F70 x 14 tires on most Firebirds required a wheel offset of .26 inch for maximum brake clearance. The Rally I offset measured .60 inch, making it incompatible with the new tire. N98 Rally II Wheel in 14 x 6–inch continued to be available for 1968, however. The styled wheel option was priced at $84.26 on standard Firebirds and $63.19 on Custom Option vehicles.

A 14 x 6–inch steel wheel adorned with a small hubcap was standard equipment on basic Firebird models. An E70-14 Firestone Wide Oval tire with black sidewall was included with the Firebird when powered by the OHC-6 with a 1-barrel carburetor. An F70-14 was included with all other engines. Sidewalls trimmed with white or red lines were available at extra cost.

Eight large cooling holes gave the 1968 P02 Custom Wheel Disc a very distinctive appearance. With a satin finish and red center, it was an available option on the Firebird at every level as well as on the Tempest model line. It proved to be a rather unpopular option with Firebird buyers, however. Just 4,300 vehicles were equipped with it.

The N95 Wire Wheel Disc (an intricately designed wheel cover that simulated the appearance of an aftermarket wire-spoked wheel typically popular with customizers) was available for 1968. It was teamed with a standard 14 x 6–inch rim and was offered for all tire options. A total of 2,932 Firebird buyers added the extra-cost option to their order.

Suspension enhancements for 1968 were limited to multi-leaf rear springs and staggered shock absorbers. The Firestone F70-14 Wide Oval tire was popular with Firebird buyers and both white and red sidewall treatments were available. The attractive 14 x 7–inch Rally II wheel released in 1967 was equally as popular for 1968. The Verdoro Green exterior finish was almost dropped for 1968, but it remained available and virtually defined Pontiac during the late 1960s.

Pontiac Sales Promotion BLUEPRINT

May 10, 1968   P.S.B. 68-55

NEW POLYGLAS TIRE AVAILABILITY

"Polyglas" tires are now available on all Firebirds in both the red stripe and white stripe F70 x 14's as an extra-cost option.

This newly designed tire has the unique combination of two fiberglass tread ply and two polyester cord body ply that give the advantages of increased tire life and road hazard resistance. The application of fiberglass in the tread ply restricts the movement of the tread and keeps it more firmly on the road. This increases tread life while the sidewalls remain flexible to better absorb road shock and the leaning action in turns.

This revolutionary tire was developed by Pontiac's engineers and their tire suppliers, and is presently available from Goodyear only -- and is advertised by that company as the "Polyglas" tire.

The "Polyglas" tire may be ordered on Firebird by placing Sales Code MT (white stripe) or Sales Code MR (red stripe) in the 'Other Accessories' Section of the Wholesale Car Order.

Prices for Code MT or MR tires on Firebird are:

	Dealer Net	Factory D & H	List	Label
1 Bbl. 6 Cyl. (Code 341)	$52.44	$3.67	$69.00	$72.67
4 Bbl. 6 Cyl. (Code 342) and 350 V-8's (Code 343-344)	$41.80	$2.93	$55.00	$57.93
4 Bbl. 400's (Codes 345-347-348)	$19.00	$1.33	$25.00	$26.33

This is another example of the flexibility in available options. Please make certain your sales team is aware of the selling features of "Polyglas" tires.

C. L. Copeland
C. L. Copeland
Sales Promotion Manager

CLC:Gc

PONTIAC MOTOR DIVISION ▼ GENERAL MOTORS CORPORATION

A black sidewall Firestone Wide Oval in F70 x 14 sizing (code-ME) became the standard tire on the Firebird Sprint, Firebird 350, and Firebird H.O. It increased overall track width by about 1 inch and lent a sportier appearance and slightly improved handling capability. A white-line (MC) or red-line (MD) version of the same tire was available for $31.60. The red-line F70 x 14 tire was included in Firebird 400 package content and the white-line variant was available as a no-cost option.

Firestone's E70 x 14 Wide Oval tire with black sidewall (HE) remained standard equipment on the base-model Firebird with OHC-6. White-line (HD) or red-line (HC) versions were available in identical sizing for $31.60 extra. Buyers could opt to equip their 6-cylinder Firebird with the white-line (ME) or red-line (MC) tire in F70 x 14 sizing for $46.34.

A 195R x 14 white sidewall radial tire (KM) replaced 1967's 185R x 14 unit. Available on all

Pontiac engineers worked directly with Goodyear to develop a new fiberglass-reinforced bias-ply tire marketed as the Polyglas, which boasted extended tread life plus improved ride, handling, and durability. Pontiac issued Sales Blueprint 68-55 on May 10, 1968, outlining its advantages and pricing of the red- or white-lined offerings. The Polyglas and the variants it spawned soon found their way onto other makes.

Firebirds, the tire was priced at $56.87 on the base model; $42.13 on Sprint, 350, and H.O. applications; and $10.53 on the Firebird 400.

During the 1968 model year, Pontiac Engineering worked with Goodyear to develop a fiberglass-reinforced tire that offered improved traction and additional protection against road hazards when compared to the Wide Oval. The Polyglas tire was introduced into the Firebird line around May 1968 and was available in F70 x 14 sizing with white-line (code-MR) or red-line (MT) sidewalls. The new tire option cost $72.67 on the base-model Firebird; $57.93 on Firebird Sprint, 350, and H.O.; and $26.33 on Firebird 400. According to production records, only 77 Firebird buyers elected to buy the new technology.

Production and Options

When introducing the 1967 Firebird to consumers, Pontiac General Manager John DeLorean predicted that Firebird sales would reach 100,000 units in its first year (12 calendar months). When the count was taken in February 1968, more than 115,000 had been sold. Some interesting facts he revealed in a 1968 press release include: 71 percent of all Firebird sales were new customers to Pontiac; more than 6 percent of total trade-ins were foreign cars; Firebird represented 30 percent of all new Pontiacs sold on the West Coast; and the median Firebird buyer age was 31.5 years, or 8 years younger than that of the average Pontiac buyer.

When 1968 model year production ceased in late August 1968, Pontiac had produced 107,112 Firebirds and the Lordstown, Ohio, assembly plant (code-U) had assembled 94,892 of them. To satisfy production demands as Firebird's popularity overtaxed the Lordstown line, the existing GM plant in Van Nuys, California (code-L), was brought online in March 1968. Another 12,148 Firebirds were assembled there. Pontiac reported that the addition of Van Nuys took daily production from 480 units to 576.

The remaining 72 Firebirds were part of the CKD ("Completely Knocked Down") program, which were partially assembled stateside and finished overseas. It's unclear where any ultimately landed, but coincidentally, all CKD cars were Firebird Sprints equipped with the L72 4-barrel engine. Forty-eight were equipped with the Saginaw M20 4-speed manual transmission and the remaining 24 were equipped with the M31 automatic.

I located a Pontiac production report that details Firebird volume for 1968 and it includes some optional equipment combinations. This book is the first time most of it has ever been presented to Firebird enthusiasts. Appendix B details known engine and transmission combinations as well as a complete breakdown for most Firebird levels.

Firebird H.O. production totaled 6,423 and the M31 2-speed automatic went into 2,640 of them. A manual transmission, whether 3-speed or 4-speed, accounted for 3,783 units, 2,497 base-model Firebirds and 1,286 Custom Option Firebirds.

Despite small revisions required for new model year compliance, the exterior appointments of the 1968 Firebird 400 carried over from 1967 without any changes. The 1968 model year went on to be the most popular ever for the first-generation Firebird. Beautiful examples like this leave little doubt about why consumers felt that way. Meridian Turquoise was a new selection in Firebird's lengthy color lineup that year. (Photo Courtesy David Belz)

A total of 21,316 Firebirds were equipped with W66 400 Sport Option. The M40 Turbo-400 was installed into 11,933; 9,383 were backed by a manual transmission. The standard M13 heavy-duty 3-speed went into 754 cars; the remaining 8,629 Firebird 400s were equipped with a Muncie M20 4-speed.

The D55 Front Console was installed in 17,264 units, of which 6,363 were equipped with a manual transmission. Records show that 387 Firebird 400s were ordered with N33 Tilt Steering Wheel and a manual transmission, 18 of which with the M13. Firebird 400s equipped with J52/JL2 Power Front Disc Brakes numbered 3,820. And 4,262 received the N64 Conventional Spare Tire.

According to Pontiac production records, the L74 400 H.O. was installed into 2,087 Firebird 400s during the 1968 model year. Of these, 1,411 were backed by a manual transmission. The remaining 676 were equipped with an automatic transmission, and 81 of them were

The 400 Ram Air carried over to 1968 with only a few changes. Its stellar performance was largely unaffected. The Ram Air Firebird remained the ultimate F-car for 1968 and several hundred buyers were willing to pay a premium for it. This Primavera Beige example was originally exported to Australia and professionally converted to right-hand drive to comply with vehicle laws in that country. (Photo Courtesy Don Keefe)

The Firebird convertible was rather popular for 1968 with nearly 17,000 produced, but the droptop represented only about 15 percent of the total Firebirds produced that model year. Despite the vast number of hardtops that Pontiac produced, convertibles remain quite popular with enthusiasts today and examples like this Firebird 400 in Flambeau Burgundy are excellent candidates for restoration projects.

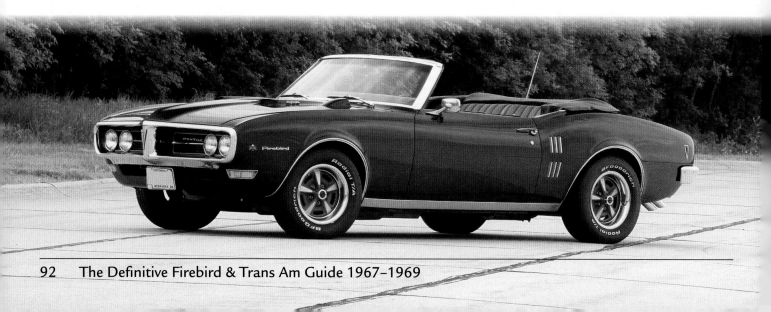

Pontiac found great success marketing its performance image to consumers. The flash of chrome accents proved to be an ideal way to call attention toward the components responsible for it. To accentuate N10 Dual Exhaust, Pontiac offered chrome-plated exhaust tips that contained split outlets. These "splitters" were available as UPC N25 on 1967 and 1968 Firebird H.O.s and 400s for $21.06. A total of 1,733 were installed during the 1968 model year.

```
P&A EXTRA 67-27              Page 2           December 6, 1967


WALNUT GEARSHIFT KNOB USAGE

#984989   3 Speed Manual Transmission (Floor Shift)  1967 Firebird only.

#984700   4 Speed Manual Transmission (Floor Shift)  1966-68 Pontiac and
          Tempest   1968 Firebird

#984848   3 Speed Manual Transmission (Floor Shift)  1966-68 Pontiac and
          Tempest   1968 Firebird
```

If you have ever wondered if Pontiac's Custom Gear Shift Knob differed from year to year, P&A Extra 67-27 issued on December 6, 1967, contains the part numbers for various 1966 to 1968 applications. Interestingly, the Firebird's 3-speed simulated wood-grain knob was changed from 1967 to 1968.

column-shifted. Just 355 Firebirds with the 400 H.O. were fitted with emissions equipment for California registration.

Ram Air Firebird production (Ram Air I and Ram Air II) totaled 523 units. A total of 419 were equipped with the M20 4-speed manual; the remaining 104 received the M40 Turbo-400. Most Ram Air Firebirds were built at Lordstown, but Van Nuys assembled 46 (41 with M20 and 5 with M40). N40 Power Steering was installed in 68 Ram Air Firebirds with M40 and 128 with M20 transmission. The K45 Heavy Duty Air Cleaner was installed into 33 Ram Air Firebirds; 51 received N25 Exhaust Extensions.

C60 Custom Air Conditioning was a $370 option that was growing in popularity with consumers. Planned availability for the 1968 model year included all Firebirds except those equipped with Sprint-6 or 400-inch Ram Air engines. In a recent conversation with Jim Mattison, he noted that he'd not yet found a 1968 Firebird equipped with both a manual transmission and air conditioning. That prompted further investigation, which resulted in uncovering the following.

Preliminary sales information showed no restriction beyond the aforementioned applications. Subsequent printings of the Pontiac Price Schedule and Accessorizer booklets simply reflected that C60 wasn't available when combined with V-8 or manual transmission. A zone bulletin dated November 3, 1967, clearly stated the combination, previously on tentative hold, had been placed indefinitely on extended hold. No reason was given, but it was likely the result of some type of chronic cooling-related issue.

C60 Air Conditioning was installed into 24,826 Firebirds during the 1968 model year. (Appendix B contains a breakdown by level.) The only 1968 Firebirds with manual transmission to receive air conditioning were 126 base-model cars powered by the OHC-6. All V-8 applications with C60 were backed by an automatic transmission, and that includes 17,021 L30 350 2-barrels, 934 with the 350 H.O., and 6,127 Firebird 400s. C60 was installed on 618 Firebirds with the OHC-6 and automatic transmission.

Only 6 1968 Firebird H.O.s were equipped with K82 Heavy-Duty Alternator. Only 15 Firebirds received U15 Safeguard Speedometer and U30 Rally Gauge Cluster together. UB5 Hood-Mounted Tachometers were installed on 6,780 units; a 6-cylinder engine represented 631 of that total while Firebird 400s made up the remaining 4,685.

D55 Front Console Sales

Combination	Quantity
With automatic transmission and D55	59,540
With M20 4-speed manual and D55	12,204
With M13 3-speed manual and D55	3,340
With M12 3-speed manual and D55	1,692
Firebird Sprint with D55	2,227
Firebird Sprint with manual transmission and D55	1,500
CKD Firebirds with D55	72

CHAPTER FOUR

1969 FIREBIRD

The 1969 Firebirds went on sale September 26, 1968. At model year startup, the base price was $2,831 for hardtops and $3,045 for convertibles. Competition was fierce and nearly every manufacturer was in the pony car game. Early in the model year, Pontiac tried very hard to justify Firebird's greater cost over Camaro, Mustang, Cougar, and AMC's Javelin by listing standard equipment not supplied by the competitors. Marketing material was filled with the benefits and features that put the Firebird ahead of its peers, and new styling was among them.

Safety and comfort were also on the forefront of Firebird's enhancements for 1969. Most notably, the ignition switch was relocated from the instrument panel to the steering column, and it became an integral component in the anti-theft ignition lock system, a feature that required the gear selector be placed in Park (automatic) or Reverse (manual) to lock the column and remove the key.

On February 15, 1969, John DeLorean was promoted to general manager of the Chevrolet division and future General Motors President F. James McDonald was appointed to the general manager's position at Pontiac. Pet performance projects that DeLorean felt were critical to Pontiac's success were sidetracked or shelved upon McDonald's arrival as he assessed the division's position

A mild refresh for the 1969 model year rewarded Pontiac with the opportunity to inject its own flavor into the F-car. Virtually every side panel was new and none of it was interchangeable with the Camaro. Despite the beautiful exterior styling and an extended model year to cover for the delayed 1970 F-car, the 1969 Firebird was a sales underachiever. That was most likely the result of tougher competition from other manufacturers as well as news of the completely redesigned 1970 F-car circulating around the industry. By today's standards, examples like this 1969 Firebird in Matador Red are highly coveted by Pontiac enthusiasts.

After posting stellar sales volume in 1968, Pontiac had positioned the 1969 Firebird as a rising star in a field of hot-running late-1960s performance cars. To maintain exclusivity, a handful of special-order exterior colors were limited to the Firebird line. Code-72 Carousel Red (an eye-popping shade of orange most commonly associated with the 1969 GTO Judge) was among them at model year startup.

PRODUCT ENGINEERING INFORMATION

Bulletin #69-29
April 15, 1969

Changes in 1969 Firebird

The following changes have been made in the
1969 Firebird:

On 6 Cylinder: 7.35 tire instead of E70

On 350 V-8 Options: 7.75 tire instead of
    F70, 6" rim wheel replaces 7" rim.
    F70 remains part of W-66 400 option.

Standard spare replaces Space Saver Spare.
    Space Saver Spare is optional on all
    models.

Bright drip scalp exterior moldings cancelled
    as standard. Included as part of Y81
    decor group and part of W66 400 option.

Courtesy lamp cancelled as standard on all
    except convertible. Available as U29
    courtesy lamp option, and as part of
    W66 option. Retained as standard on
    convertible.

Glove box lamp cancelled as standard. Release
    available as an option in U27, and part
    of W66 400 option.

C. G. Carlson

JWB:yc

Ref. RCA 69-255

ENGINEERING DEPARTMENT
PONTIAC MOTOR DIVISION
GENERAL MOTORS CORPORATION, PONTIAC, MICHIGAN

against the competition and prioritized developmental concepts. Performance purists might immediately recognize the tunnel-port Ram Air V (or R/A V) as one such example.

Conscious of Pontiac's price points in a highly competitive market, reviewing the standard content list of each model line and removing inconsequential items to reduce base costs was among McDonald's first objectives as general manager. The Firebird was one of the first where McDonald's efforts were realized.

On March 17, 1969, Pontiac reduced the cost of its Firebird hardtop by $72 and the convertible by $56, taking them to $2,759 and $2,989, respectively. Wide Oval tires, the Space Saver spare tire, roof drip moldings, and various interior lights were removed as standard equipment and made available at extra cost. When 1970 Pontiacs went on sale and pricing was announced on

Pontiac made a number of changes to the Firebird's standard features in midyear 1969. Pontiac's newest general manager, F. James McDonald, wanted to make its base pricing more competitive. The additions and deletions are best outlined in Product Engineering Bulletin 69-29, dated April 15, 1969. These types of internal correspondence are extremely helpful when attempting to document changes.

A new rear body panel housed taillights similar to 1967–1968, but the 1969 units tapered toward the top and were consistent with the overall theme of the tail panel shape. A strong side crease is visible over each wheelwell, which was now flat on top, instead of completely round. Simulated air louvers were added behind the front wheel and the fuel filler was moved to behind the rear license plate.

The Space Saver spare tire remained standard equipment on the 1969 Firebird at model year startup. As F. James McDonald reviewed Firebird's standard features list, he dropped the collapsible spare as a basic feature to reduce the Firebird's base price. The full-size spare took its place and N65 Space Saver became an extra-cost option for $15.80.

September 18, 1969, the base cost of the carryover 1969 Firebird increased by $94, where it remained until production ceased in November.

The Firebird Lineup

The Magnificent Five marketing theme carried over to 1969. Beyond the new external appearance, the package was virtually identical to that of 1968. At model year startup, pricing of the W53 Firebird Sprint was $121.44 and the L30 Firebird 350 was $110.88. The L76 Firebird 350 H.O. (no longer adorned with external striping) was priced at $185.86; the W66 Firebird 400 was available for $358.09 with the standard 3-speed manual. An automatic or 4-speed manual transmission cost $273.83 above that.

Pontiac Sales Blueprint 69-27 was issued on November 22, 1968, announcing a price adjustment of the Firebird Sport Options effective December 1. W53 increased by $8.10 to $129.54. L30 actually dropped a few cents to $110.59. L76 increased by $13.19 to $199.05. W66 jumped by $18.96 to $377.05 for the standard 3-speed manual, and $292.79 for the automatic or 4-speed.

One final price change occurred on April 28, 1969, when PSB 69-61 was issued announcing another adjustment to W66 pricing directly related to Firebird's McDonald-driven midyear base-cost reduction. W66 included some previously standard equipment on the base Firebird that was made extra cost on March 17. This resulted in Pontiac adjusting some pricing. The standard 3-speed manual increased to $431.81, and the automatic and 4-speed increased to $347.56. W66 pricing for a Firebird convertible was now listed separately, and was $15.80 less than either above price because U29 Courtesy Lamps included with W66 remained standard equipment on the convertible.

The pinnacle of the 1969 Firebird model year was the all-new Trans Am. Introduced at the Chicago Auto Show on March 8, 1969, it was a complete performance package that transformed the already-potent Firebird 400 into a corner carver. The rather costly WS4 Trans Am Option gave consumers a uniquely equipped Firebird. Pontiac marketed it as the ultimate Firebird in the lineup and

The 350 H.O. was a high-performance small-cube engine package that delivered a good-running Firebird without elevated insurance premiums associated with the 400-ci. Included with the Firebird H.O., the package included side accent striping in the two previous model years, but the Firebird H.O. was more subdued for 1969, lending a sleeper look. Nothing immediately visible separated the Firebird 350 from the Firebird H.O. that model year, but in timed acceleration events, the Firebird was roughly a second quicker in every respect. (Photo Courtesy Barry Kluczyk)

Although consumers had little trouble distinguishing the final iteration of the first-generation F-car as Pontiac's Firebird, it was subjected to a number of exterior revisions for 1969 that many enthusiasts believe enhanced its appearance. As the division's four-seat sports car, everything about its styling was aimed at portraying that image. The C08 Cordova Roof option was quite popular and worked well with the semi-fastback design. (Photo Courtesy Barry Kluczyk)

In addition to The Magnificent Five campaign where buyers selected a Firebird from a lineup equipped with preselected features, Pontiac also offered a host of performance options that allowed consumers to expand on that at every level. The Firebird 400 was at the top and its available 400 H.O. could be had with and without Ram Air to create the ultimate street machine. This beautiful example in Crystal Turquoise with a black Cordova top, Rally II wheels, and red-line tires exemplifies the Firebird's sporty appearance. (Photo Courtesy Tina M. Campbell)

FIREBIRD OF TOMORROW SHOW CAR

Pontiac had a rich history of creating exciting one-off show cars that it showed in divisional displays at various new-car expos throughout the country. The jet age was in full swing in the late 1960s and aerodynamic styling was a hot selling point. Combine them all and what's the result? The Firebird of Tomorrow!

Beginning with a typical 1968 Firebird as its base, Pontiac designers created a unique convertible by draping fiberglass over the Firebird's stock body panels to create a fluid exterior shape free from airflow disruptions. Door handles were shaved and name badging was replaced by flush-mounted accents. A roll bar located where the rear seat would otherwise sit was added to increase passenger safety while doubling as an airfoil that added stability in high-speed conditions.

Overall length of the Firebird concept car measured nearly 200 inches, or about a foot longer than a production example. Its wraparound glass featured a chopped windshield that measured 15 inches shorter than a production version and that contributed to an overall vehicle height of 38 inches, which enhanced its low-slung speedster attitude. The exterior was finished in pearlescent orange paint with solid orange accents. The two-passenger interior featured black seats and paneling and was accented by orange floor carpeting. Power was provided by a potent 400-ci V-8.

The Firebird of Tomorrow made its debut at the 1968 New York International Auto Show that began on March 30, 1968. According to a transcript from its introduction at that show it was also billed as the Firebird 400X. The Firebird of Tomorrow then made the new-car expo circuit in its original configuration throughout the remainder of the 1968 model year.

It was updated for 1969 and received a white exterior finish with red and orange accents while the interior went largely unchanged. It was renamed the Firebird Fiero and at some point was even referred to as the Banshee II.

To draw excitement toward the Firebird line, Pontiac created a sleek show car that promoted aerodynamic styling. It featured a slick body shape and a rear bumper that tucked beneath the body. Dual exhaust outlets exited in the center of the body. Introduced at the 1968 New York International Auto Show and billed as the Firebird of Tomorrow, it made the new-car show circuit during the latter half of the 1968 model year. It sported a pearlescent orange exterior finish. (Photo Courtesy General Motors)

The Firebird of Tomorrow was renamed the Firebird Fiero for 1969 and the orange exterior gave way to a white finish trimmed in red and orange. The Endura front bumper was carried over with twin grilles that served as engine cooling ducts. Side scoops provided cool air to the rear brakes. Headlights were hidden units that folded down when not in use. It's unclear what became of the vehicle after its tenure as a concept car, but rumors of its existence have continued for years. (Photo Courtesy General Motors)

A 160-mph speedometer continued for 1969. It was relocated to the right-hand pod in Firebird's instrument cluster and its font was revised for greater legibility. Standard features in the left pod were a fuel gauge and warning lamps. A Carpathian Burl overlay trimmed the instrument panel on Firebirds equipped with W54 Custom Interior.

Pontiac's General Manager John DeLorean was hired as an engineer during the 1950s. He was directly involved with many of the division's performance innovations, such as the 1964 GTO, as well as approving the creation of the ultimate Firebird, the Trans Am. Although it wasn't the hottest seller in 1969, the Trans Am was practically race-ready. It further bolstered the Firebird's performance image and garnered copious amounts of media attention and showroom traffic.

one sure to generate showroom traffic. (Because of its significance to Pontiac hobbyists, the Trans Am has its own chapter in this book.)

Exterior and Interior

The Firebird received its first refresh for 1969 with an entirely new appearance. Pontiac emphasized its trademark "split grille" theme up front, with a small chrome bumper at center. It was flanked on each side by molded plastic trim that was painted to match the body color and housed four round headlights deeply recessed in square openings. The grille texture was of a tight "egg crate" pattern that was painted silver. The Firebird 400 featured chrome surrounds for added flair. A new stamped-steel front valance panel housed the combination parking lights and turn signals.

"I remember we wanted a one-piece bumper in Endura for the 1969 Firebird," says Bill Porter, who was promoted to design chief at Pontiac Studio in February 1968 and oversaw the finalization of the facelift. "The flexible bumper would have eliminated a number of gaps that simply wasn't possible with molded plastic while eliminating the need for a chrome bumper, just as we

did with the 1968 GTO. Bill Mitchell was fond of having chrome on the front end, however, so we kept it."

The front fenders were slightly restyled and contained a small circular marker lamp on the leading edge and simulated air vents behind each wheelwell. The rear quarter panel was also restyled and its wheelwell was not totally radiused as in years past. The rear marker light was shaped like the Firebird logo and though similar in appearance to previous units, the rear bumper was also new for 1969. The tail panel was redesigned to accommodate a concealed fuel filler neck located behind the rear license plate. Overall vehicle length increased to 191.1 inches and ride height was reduced by about a half inch.

Exterior color choices were plentiful for 1969 and a total of 15 were available at model year startup. Pontiac announced on September 6, 1968, in Car Distribution Bulletin (CDB) 69-15, that Carousel Red, Goldenrod Yellow, and Windward Blue would be new special Firebird colors available for $12.64 extra, taking the palette to a total of 18. Other GM colors were available under SPS Special Solid Paint for $115.85 but it required prior approval before production. If equipped with a Cordova or convertible top, SPS cost dropped by $15.80 to $100.05.

BOLD DECORATION FOR 1969

Pontiac covertly developed many interesting vehicles and concepts during the late 1960s. The redesigned Grand Prix proved to be an industry bombshell when it debuted in 1969, and the midyear 1969 additions of the GTO Judge and Firebird Trans Am generated a frenzy of media attention. But did you know that Pontiac Styling also worked with 3M to develop large Firebird decals to decorate its 1969 Sprint and 400 models?

My literature collection contains a number of Master Parts Catalogs, which Pontiac printed sporadically throughout a given model year. Containing thousands of pages, sometimes with exploded diagrams, copies were distributed to dealership parts departments so staff could obtain the part number(s) of the appropriate component(s) required for servicing and/or warranty repairing a specific application, no matter how obscure.

To keep parts departments apprised of product updates between major catalog printings, small revision packets were issued piecemeal and I happen to have several. Comparing the 1969 Firebird 400 ornamentation from several 1969 revision packets, I noticed a peculiarity in Revision 7. Among the typical brightwork and common emblems, the rear perspective showed a large Firebird decal emblazoned on the deck lid. The accompanying part number key described it as "Decal - Compartment Lid," but there wasn't any mention as to whether it was planned as an option or to be made part of the standard W66 400 Sport Option package. Its absence in Revisions 6 and 8 indicates that the concept went just as quickly as it came.

In the Firebird 400 rendering in Revision 7, the deck lid bird shares a similar overall shape to a unique Firebird illustration in my collection drawn by Pontiac stylist Norm Inouye. "Firebird of the Future" is handwritten on it and determining its origin had been impossible until now. With some diligent research and lots of luck, I recently uncovered a copy of the

**1969 FIREBIRD 2-DOOR COUPE
REAR END VIEW—2337
(WITH 400 SPORT OPTION)**

Searching for part numbers in my collection of vintage Pontiac Parts Manuals while writing this book, I happened across a diagram that left me absolutely stunned. This drawing of an otherwise typical 1969 Firebird 400 appeared in dozens of printings and/or supplements when these cars were new or commonly roaming the streets. I had seen this particular diagram only once. It depicts a large Firebird-shaped decal on the Firebird 400 deck lid and provides a Pontiac part number for it. Did you know it existed?

This image of a unique Firebird emblem is part of my literature collection. Handwritten at the bottom is "Firebird of the Future by Norm Inouye." Inouye was a designer at GM Styling and Bill Porter credits him with drawing the second-generation Firebird under Porter's direction. Although this rendering certainly looks similar to the later bird, its original intent could never be determined. We now know of at least one usage! Porter redesigned the bird for the 1970 Firebird upon his arrival at Pontiac Studio in 1968. This rendition of it was developed by Inouye for the Firebird of the Future show car, which was redecorated for its tour during the 1969 model year. (Photo Courtesy General Motors)

original 1969 Firebird 400 deck lid decal drawing, a document that probably hasn't seen the light of day since 1969. I now know that Inouye's illustration and the Firebird 400 deck lid decal are identical.

Further investigation of the drawing reveals that developmental efforts began in June 1969 and that the finished component was released to production on August 27, 1969. The bird's overall dimensions measured 16 inches wide and just over 8 inches tall. Planned availability was limited to a single color combination predominantly of light and dark oranges. To experience its visual impact, the Firebird was digitally re-created by a professional graphics artist for this project and I am extremely excited to bring this new 1969 Firebird information to hobbyists for the first time!

No other production vehicle from any make during the era had a decal on its deck lid only. Having placed a diagram of this Firebird on a first-generation vehicle, it's unclear just how visually appealing this feature would have been then or now. Pontiac may have shared a similar sentiment, which could have been a driving force behind its quick cancellation. The large hood-mounted Firebird introduced in 1973 had many naysayers, too, but its popularity was overwhelming, so there's no telling how a deck lid decal would have been received by consumers.

Revision 7 also reveals that Pontiac planned to accentuate the raised portion of the Firebird Sprint hood with a slightly smaller bird decal shaped and colored similarly to that of the Firebird 400's deck lid. The body measured 11 inches wide and was flanked by a feather-shaped accent streamer extending rearward 24 inches from each wing. The attractively designed and tastefully located decals were also limited to Revision 7.

When considering the time frame and how quickly the Firebird Sprint and 400 decorations disappeared, you wonder why Pontiac added the bold accents so late in the 1969 Firebird production run. Since uncovering the revelations, the search was on to learn more about them and that included speaking with former Pontiac engineers and designers who would have likely been involved in some way, but none were able to recall any detail of it. The answer may be lost to history, but we now know how close both decals came to production.

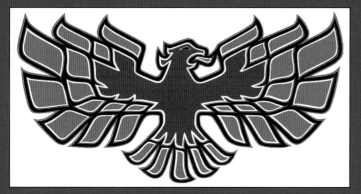

I was able to uncover a source that revealed the dimensions and coloration of the decal destined for the 1969 Firebird 400 deck lid and digitally re-created its appearance for this book. The bird takes on the shape of the new-for-1970 styling, and was vividly colored for maximum visual impact. It's quite likely that Pontiac dropped the feature after determining that the average Firebird 400 consumer may not have been prepared for such a bold statement, particularly on their vehicle's deck lid.

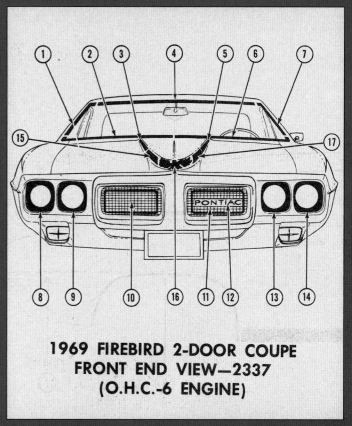

1969 FIREBIRD 2-DOOR COUPE FRONT END VIEW—2337 (O.H.C.-6 ENGINE)

Pontiac had also intended to offer a smaller, but similar bird to adorn the plateau on the Sprint-6 hood. Separate decals extended its outstretched wings to create a decorative statement that traveled nearly 3 feet rearward from the point of the hood's spine. Coloration was to be identical to the Firebird 400 bird.

Although the 1967–1968 Firebird shared most of its exterior sheet metal with Chevrolet's Camaro, the 1969 Firebird was Pontiac's first chance at giving its F-car its own look from practically every angle. The front-end treatment was completely new with body-colored trim panels and a small chrome bumper in the center. The dual-scooped hood was a feature carried over for the Firebird 400.

Firebird's front styling was all-new for 1969. Initial plans included the soft Endura nose from the GTO, but Bill Mitchell, who headed GM Styling, pushed for a chromed bumper instead. To accommodate that, engineers were forced to surround the headlights with several small panels constructed of hard plastic, much to the dismay of the designers who wanted to create a fluid appearance. Despite the added steps required for assembly on the production line, the result was stunning. (Photo Courtesy Larry DeLay)

Although Pontiac coyly disguised the newly required rear side marker as an arrowhead logo on the 1968 Firebird, it was even better integrated for 1969 with the appearance of a typical die-cast Firebird emblem. The body was filled with reflective and transparent plastic that illuminated whenever the parking lamps were on.

Firebird's standard interior was largely unchanged for 1969; only minor changes were implemented. The front bucket seats were wider and the decorative pattern on the Morrokide cover was revised slightly and carried over onto the door panels. Front-seat headrests were made standard equipment to increase passenger safety.

During the 1968 model year, the Firebird's standard steering wheel was a hard-rimmed unit that contained three spokes. For 1969, Pontiac released a two-spoke unit that retained its hard rim but featured a new contoured center. It went on to be Pontiac's basic wheel through the mid-1970s.

The instrument panel was handsomely restyled and thoroughly padded for 1969, and was no longer directly influenced by the Camaro. The instrument pod and switch layout was revised for improved appearance and accessibility. On Firebirds with standard interior, the plastic instrument trim panel was matte black. The simulated woodgrain N34 Custom Steering Wheel was an extra-cost option.

A two-tone exterior paint treatment was also available for $31.60 with standard Firebird colors (code-RTT) and for $147.45 with special paint colors (code-STT). C08 Cordova Top was available for $89.52 in White, Black, Dark Blue, Parchment, Dark Brown, and Dark Green. Convertible top choices included White, Black, Dark Blue, and Dark Green.

The Firebird's standard interior was made even more plush and occupant friendly. The seats and door panels received additional padding to improve comfort. Front headrests became standard equipment. A new, one-piece dash panel replaced the multi-unit design, and woodgrain was removed from the standard interior and a new texturized plastic panel provided added appeal. The accessory controls were made larger for easier operation and the speedometer moved from the large pod left of the steering wheel to its right. Interior door locks were moved forward for easier occupant access.

W54 Custom Interior again transformed the basic Firebird into a Custom Option Firebird at an added cost of $78.99. Knit Morrokide seating surfaces remained. Door panels were an essential carryover, trimmed with brightwork, and contained an attractive Firebird emblem. Carpathian Burl graining adorned the dash panel and the passenger-side assist grip remained. Although a shallow-dish two-spoke steering wheel was standard on base-model Firebirds, W54 included N30 Deluxe Steering Wheel, which was all-new for 1969 and featured a soft center and a molded color rim.

Standard interior colors were Blue, Gold, Green, Parchment, and Black. Custom interiors with knit vinyl were available in Blue, Gold, Red, Green, Parchment, and Black.

Firebird's interior was as inviting as ever for 1969. The standard interior remained plush, but the W54 Custom Interior option took passenger comfort to the next level. Seats were slightly wider than in previous years and woodgrain increased the appearance of luxuriousness. Several color choices were available for every level.

Although the seat covers and door panels of 1969's W54 Custom Interior were essentially identical to those of 1968, the use of Carpathian Burl woodgrain trim expanded from the console onto the dash panel and made the interior even more luxurious and attractive. The N34 Custom Steering Wheel option was an extra cost. The A39 Custom Seat Belts Front and Rear option most often color-matched the strap with the interior and always included brushed-chrome buckles.

In addition to Morrokide, genuine leather seat covering was an available option with W54 Custom Interior. Color choice was limited to Gold, which wasn't a huge departure from Saddle that was used previously. N30 Deluxe Steering Wheel remained part of the W54 package and a mandatory option with the Firebird 400. It was redesigned for 1969 and featured a soft center and firm molded rim. (Photo Courtesy Christopher Phillip)

Dash-mounted twist and/or pull switches controlled the accessories of 1967 and 1968 Firebirds. Pontiac injected a touch of modernization to its Firebird instrument panel for 1969 with the addition of low-profile rocker switches or most accessories. Not only did it increase visual appeal, the rocker switches improved reliability as well.

The front bench seat was available only with W54 Custom Interior and offered in Parchment or Black. It added $31.60 to the package cost, taking it to a total of $110.59. Genuine leather returned for 1969 and was limited to Gold and included W54 appointments for $199.05.

Engine Lineup

The Firebird's 1969 base engine remained the OHC-6 complete with 1-barrel carburetor, 240-degree camshaft, and an advertised compression ratio of 9.0:1. As a carryover from 1968, the 250-ci's output was identical at 175 hp at 4,800 rpm and 240 ft-lbs at 2,600 rpm. Within a few weeks of production startup, Pontiac revised the intake and exhaust valveseat angles in the cylinder head of its OHC-6 engines from 30 to 45 degrees to accentuate airflow, but no changes were made to casting part numbers.

When teamed with an automatic transmission for 1969, the L72 Sprint-6 with 4-barrel carburetor, 244-degree camshaft, and 10.5:1 compression ratio was basically identical to the 1968 model, and subsequently rated identically at 215 hp at 5,200 rpm and 255 ft-lbs at 3,800 rpm. However, to bolster the performance of cars with a manual transmission, Pontiac developed a new 260-degree camshaft that increased output to 230 hp at 5,400 rpm and 260 ft-lbs at 3,600. DeLorean's team charged hard to make the 6-cylinder more appealing to consumers wary of overhead cam technology by offering increased output that rivaled the performance of competitors' small eights.

The L30 350 2-barrel remained virtually unchanged for 1969. Equipped with the 269/277-degree number-254 camshaft and an advertised compression ratio of 9.2:1, the small-cube V-8 was rated at 265 hp at 4,600 rpm and 355 ft-lbs at 2,800 rpm. Its number-17 cylinder head with

The basic 250-ci OHC-6 with 1-barrel carburetor was unchanged for 1969, and retained its output rating of 175 hp at 4,800 rpm and 240 ft-lbs at 2,600 rpm from the previous year. Although the Sprint-6 with automatic transmission was rated at 215 hp at 5,200 rpm and 255 ft-lbs at 3,800 rpm, a new camshaft for the Sprint-6 (when backed by a manual transmission) increased the output of that application to 230 hp at 5,400 rpm and 260 ft-lbs at 3,600 rpm. Availability of C60 Air Conditioning was limited to the 1-barrel application. The 1969 model year marked the last time until 1975 that air conditioning was available with a 6-cylinder.

Despite the fact that the Quadrajet's secondary action on the 1969 Firebird 400 was no longer restricted, its standard 400-ci engine, which included D-port cylinder heads and the 273/289-degree number-067 camshaft, was still rated at 330 hp at 4,800 rpm and 430 ft-lbs at 3,300 rpm. The Firebird 400 remained an excellent performer capable of running the timed quarter-mile in the 14-second range in stock trim.

The L74 400 H.O. was available on the Firebird 400 from 1969 model year startup and gave buyers a horsepower boost over the standard 400-inch V-8. Availability of the T42 Hood Ram Air Inlet option was limited to the L74, and it didn't reach production until February 1969. When the 400 H.O. was combined with Ram Air, the engine was renamed Ram Air III. Very few 1969 Firebirds were equipped with functional Ram Air that model year. (Photo Courtesy Tina M. Campbell)

1969 400-INCH D-PORT CYLINDER HEAD

Over the years, there have been a number of theories about the cylinder heads that Pontiac used on its 400-ci during the 1969 model year. Many references have stated that 4-barrel applications could be fitted with casting numbers-16, -48, or -62, but that seems to be erroneous. Much of the confusion may lie in the fact that Pontiac carried over some of its small-valve cylinder heads (number-17, for instance) into 1969. They were quickly replaced when valveseat angles went from 30 to 45 degrees early in the model year.

Whether GTO or Firebird, a 400-ci originally equipped with large-valve number-16 heads after the 1968 model year remains undocumented. Although it's certainly possible that a handful of leftover 1968 castings were used on early 1969 400 4-barrel applications, there's been no evidence of that. It doesn't appear that Pontiac ever installed number-16 cylinder heads on any 1969 400, and that numbers-48 and -62 were the only D-port castings used on Firebird 400s that model year.

A 1969 Pontiac product information sheet confirms that the numbers-62 and -48 cylinder head assemblies found on Firebird's 400-ci engines included identical components with the exception of valvesprings. Whereas the number-62 was fitted with typical production springs, the number-48 received slightly stiffer units. That was likely because the number-48 was pirated from the GTO, which received the rather radical number-744 cam with aggressive lobe design. The Firebird used the number-068 camshaft in similar applications.

The general belief is that numbers-48 and -62 cylinder heads shared an identical combustion chamber volume nominally stated at 72 cc. This thought likely comes from the fact that Pontiac advertised in its 1969 Firebird sales literature an identical compression ratio of 10.75:1 for all 400-inch V-8s. Physical measurements have proven, however, a wide variance in the actual volume of the two castings, and that directly relates to a difference in the true static compression ratio of the 1969 Firebird's 400 engines.

It is my experience that the combustion chamber of a virgin number-62 measures approximately 77 cc and that of a number-48 measures about 66 cc. A copy of the original drawing for each confirms the accuracy of my physical measurements. There is the strong possibility of unique number-48s displacing 72 to 74 cc, however. I have visually verified actual

Pontiac's number-48 cylinder head is best known as the large-valve D-port casting for the 1969 Ram Air III. Although that may be true of GTO applications, the number-48 was limited to 1969 Firebirds with the optional L74 400 H.O. engine when backed by a manual transmission (code-WQ), regardless of Ram Air inclusion. Unique characteristics include minimal combustion and specific valvesprings intended for high-RPM operation. This same casting was also found on the 1969 350 H.O.

Most regard the number-62 cylinder head as the casting intended for the standard-performance 400 in the 1969 Firebird, but that's not totally true. Although it was the D-port casting found on all basic Firebird 400s, it was also used in 1969 Firebird applications equipped with the optional L74 400 H.O. backed by an automatic transmission, regardless of Ram Air inclusion. Technically speaking, the number-62 can be considered a Ram Air III casting in certain auto-transmission Firebird applications. It differs from the number-48 in combustion chamber volume and valvesprings only.

differences in number-48 chambers, but have yet to find a way that Pontiac distinguished them, visually or on paper.

When factoring the chamber volume variances into a compression ratio calculator, where all other values are equal, the actual compression ratio of a typical 400 with number-62 cylinder heads is approximately 9.8:1. Only when using a measured volume of 66 cc for the number-48 does the static compression ratio approach the advertised rating of 10.75:1. I am confident that at least some 1969 400s had a compression ratio that high.

The reason that Pontiac used two cylinder head castings (numbers-62 and -48) that generated actual compression ratios that deviate so far has yet to be uncovered. It's quite possible that, from the combined effects that camshaft timing and compression ratio can have on performance, Pontiac carefully assembled its Firebird engine packages to remain compliant with the corporate horsepower-to-weight policy without the need for a special carburetor linkage, allowing the elimination of the feature for 1969. Regardless of the reasoning, you're likely to find that the numbers-62 and -48 were the only D-port cylinder heads used on Firebird 400s that model year.

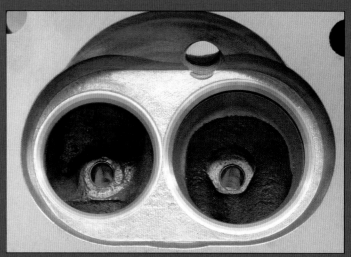

I have measured the combustion chamber volume of a virgin number-48 cylinder head from a 1969 350 H.O. and found that it displaced exactly 66 cc. I have seen others with a slightly larger combustion chamber shape, and suspect that those were originally intended for 400-ci engines. I inspected every inch of the 66-cc unit, searching for any identifiers that might denote it as a casting of lesser volume, but I found nothing. Research continues to determine if and how Pontiac actually differentiated the castings.

1.96/1.66-inch valves was carried over from 1968 for the first few weeks of 1969 model year engine production. It was replaced by the number-47, which featured 45-degree valveseat angles that improved airflow compared to the 30-degree seats of the number-17.

The 350 H.O. introduced in 1968 was the result of Pontiac's decision to enlarge its 326-ci. The high-performance small-cube engine was carried over into 1969 but not without some rather significant changes. Whereas the 1968 350 H.O. was equipped with 1.96/1.66-inch valves, the 1969 engine received the larger-valve number-48 cylinder head directly from the 400 H.O. The 2.11/1.77-inch valves were so large that additional cylinder wall relieving was required to ensure that airflow wasn't limited by shrouding. The number-48 combustion chamber displaced 66 cc, which produced an actual compression ratio of 10:1 despite the 350 H.O.'s advertised rating of 10.5:1.

Although Pontiac was somewhat conservative when selecting camshafts for its 1967 326 H.O. and 1968 350 H.O., engineers sought to increase the high-end performance of the 1969 engine, and pushed the valve timing envelope. The 273/289-degree number-067 camshaft

was specified for automatic transmission applications (code-XC). Manual transmission applications (code-WN) received the 288/302-degree number-068. Originally intended for larger-cube engines, both could be considered fairly radical for the 350-ci. The changes boosted the 350 H.O. output to 325 hp at 5,100 rpm and 380 ft-lbs at 3,200 rpm.

Despite the fact that the 350 H.O. was dropped from the 1970 model year engine lineup, monthly production records indicate that Pontiac continued producing Firebird H.O.s until the cessation of the extended 1969 Firebird model year with 32 units in November 1969. It's unknown if engines and/or components were stockpiled at the end of the traditional 1969 model year, but it's certain that 1969 Firebirds produced during the extended model year were equipped with 1969-spec engines.

The basic L78 400-ci 4-barrel included with W66 400 Sport Option was rated at 330 hp at 4,800 rpm and 430 ft-lbs at 3,300 rpm. The number-9790071 block with two-bolt main caps was carried over from 1968 and it was teamed with cast pistons and connecting rods, and a new, number-9795480 crankshaft constructed of

611/T42 HOOD RAM AIR INLET OPTION

If 1969 Firebirds hold your interest, you're likely familiar with the T42 Hood Ram Air Inlet package introduced that year. Rather than making the driver replace parts for inclement weather operation, the 1969 Ram Air assembly featured a cable-actuated baffle that allowed the driver to manually seal the air scoops from outside air. Although standard equipment to maximize the performance of its L67 Ram Air IV, making the Ram Air system more practical for daily use allowed Pontiac to expand availability to other engines such as the L74 400 H.O. According to one source, it was even considered for the L76 350 H.O., but that never materialized.

Pontiac may have considered making T42 standard equipment with the L74 400 H.O. for 1969. Over the years, I have painstakingly gathered dealer invoices of Firebirds originally equipped with L74 (order code 348) and/or T42 (order code 611). I have also collected factory documents specifically discussing either option. After having pored over these materials, I am absolutely certain that Pontiac made it quite difficult to understand the availability of T42 Hood

Ram Air Inlet on the 1969 Firebird, particularly early in the model year.

In reviewing sales literature, certain materials Pontiac distributed for the 1969 model year startup denote the L74 engine as "400 H.O." while others name it "400 Ram Air." The 1969 Pontiac Sales Manual describes L74 as "400 H.O." and clearly shows T42 Hood Ram Air Inlet as a separate option available on all Firebirds equipped with a 400-inch engine, not just L74. The September 1968 and January 1969 printings of the Dealer Price Schedules list L74 as "400 Ram Air" yet neither makes any reference to T42 Hood Ram Air Inlet even being available for separate purchase.

Firebird's 1969 Ram Air system was redesigned for greater versatility in adverse weather conditions, and that increased its complexity. The driver could select between cooler outside air through the hood scoops for maximum performance in clear conditions, or underhood air in extreme cold weather or to prevent ingesting precipitation. The lower Ram Air pan constructed of stamped steel was mounted to the carburetor; an upper pan, which housed a round air filter, was bolted to the hood. The entire unit was sealed by large foam gaskets.

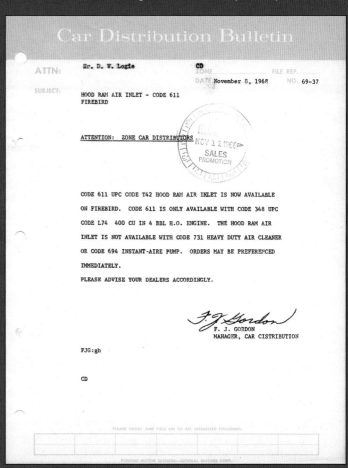

Although the T42 Hood Ram Air Inlet option was listed in Firebird sales material early in the 1969 model year, it remained on hold status for unknown reasons. Pontiac announced its availability for immediate ordering to dealership sales staffs with Car Distribution Bulletin 69-37 on November 8, 1968. None were produced and the option returned to hold status shortly thereafter with the issuance of CDB 69-45.

Actually ordering T42 was made even more difficult. The September 3, 1968, printing of the 1969 Firebird order form doesn't contain an appropriate punch code for ordering the option. Subsequent printings do, however, contain code-611 and list it as "T42 Hood Ram Air Inlet - Opt 348 Only." Worth noting, all order form printings, regardless of date, refer to punch code-348 as "L74 400 H.O." engine and Ram Air is never associated with it.

Where pricing is concerned, the September 26, 1968, printing of the 1969 Pontiac Accessorizer is the earliest publication I've located where Pontiac specifically mentions T42 Hood Ram Air Inlet and lists an option cost. At $84.26, availability was limited to L74 400 H.O. To accommodate the extended 1969 Firebird production run, T42 remained

in the Pontiac Accessorizer through at least the first 1970 model year printing in September 1969.

Lack of production detail about T42 has plagued the hobby for years. The earliest 1969 Firebird equipped with the 400 H.O. I have documented thus far was shipped October 28, 1968, but monthly production totals reveal that Pontiac produced 40 in September. Code-348 is described on its dealer invoice as "F/B 400 R/A," and that remained consistent through early December 1968, at which point Pontiac revised it to read "F/B 400 HO."

Does the lack of T42 information and an invoice descriptor from the early 1969 model year suggest that Pontiac

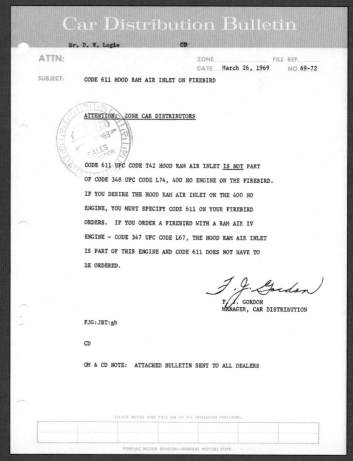

With Car Distribution Bulletin 69-60 dated January 21, 1969, Pontiac notified its dealers that the T42 Hood Ram Air Inlet option was immediately available. Based on 1969 model year production records that denote monthly totals, the T42 option reached production just days after the issuance of this bulletin.

Although Pontiac clearly stated that T42 Hood Ram Air Inlet was available with the 400 H.O. only, much confusion surrounded the package's automatic inclusion with the engine. Shortly after actually reaching production in February 1969, Pontiac issued this Car Distribution Bulletin clarifying that, although included with the Ram Air IV, it was optional at extra cost with the 400 H.O.

611/T42 HOOD RAM AIR INLET OPTION CONTINUED

planned to equip the 400 H.O. with Ram Air? The 1969 Firebird Engineering Information manual holds the answer. The internal resource, which was printed prior to model year

The Ram Air system's cable-operated baffle was controlled by a push-pull knob mounted beneath the steering column. Pushing it inward sealed the scoops from outside air and opened the air filter to typical underhood air. Pulling the knob, as shown, opened the scoops to fresh air and sealed the air filter from warmer underhood air, maximizing engine output.

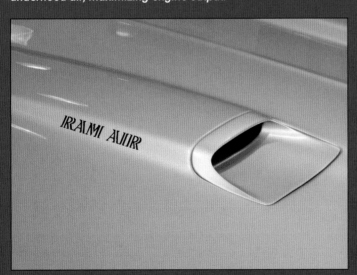

When equipped with the T42 Hood Ram Air Inlet option, the hood was unique to the application. Otherwise equipped with piercings to accept the "400" badges, the raised hood scoop on Ram Air Firebirds was unpierced and adorned with "Ram Air" decals. An original Ram Air hood is quite rare in today's restoration market.

startup and updated accordingly throughout the year, details content and associated changes for all aspects of the model line. Page FA-16 of the manual is dated August 23, 1968, and clearly states that the 400 H.O. engine "includes Hood Ram Air."

The source refers to the optional 400-inch Firebird engine in at least two other locations as "400 Ram Air" and the Horsepower and Torque Curve chart reveals that its power ratings of 335 hp and 430 ft-lbs were obtained "with Ram Air Induction System" installed. So what prevented Ram Air from being included with L74 400 H.O. as seemingly planned and prompted Pontiac to make the T42 Hood Ram Air Inlet available as a separate option shortly thereafter?

That answer is contained in a series of CDBs printed sporadically throughout the 1969 model year. CDB 69-37 was issued to dealers on November 8, 1968, formally announcing T42 and its immediate availability on L74-equipped Firebirds. CDB 69-45 was issued on November 23, placing the Ram Air option on hold status for approximately three weeks. On January 21, 1969, CDB 69-60 again announced the immediate availability of T42, and on March 26, 1969, Pontiac issued CDB 69-72 clarifying that T42 was a separate option available with L74, and not automatically included.

Research indicates that T42 Hood Ram Air Inlet reached production during February 1969, and this not-so-coincidently coincides with the release of L67 Ram Air IV. Pontiac production records indicate that T42 was installed onto 877 Firebirds during the 1969 model year. A note accompanying the total says that L67 R/A IV and WS4 Trans Am, both of which received Ram Air as standard equipment, were included in that total. That means just 78 1969 Firebird 400s were equipped with options L74 400 H.O. and T42 Hood Ram Air Inlet, but the accuracy of that breakdown remains unproven.

An interesting point to note while discussing T42 Hood Ram Air Inlet option is Firebird 400's stamped sheet-metal hood. When fitted with T42, "Ram Air" decals replaced the die-cast "400" emblems adorning each raised air scoop, and a specific hood lacking the emblem-retention piercings and with modified internal bracing to accommodate the Ram Air assembly was developed for T42. Part number 9793430 is the standard Firebird 400 hood; 9797763 is specified for those equipped with functional Ram Air.

cast-nodular iron. Whether backed by an automatic (code-YT) or manual (code-WZ) transmission, the 400-ci was fitted with number-62 cylinder heads and 067 camshaft with 273/289 degrees of duration. Advertised compression ratio was rated at 10.75:1, but actual compression was much lower.

The L74 400 H.O. remained the optional performance mill for 1969. It included high-flow exhaust manifolds that boosted output 5 hp over the standard 400 to a total of 335 at 5,000 rpm. When teamed with functional Ram Air that reached production in midyear 1969, the horsepower rating was unchanged, but it was named Ram Air III in those instances. A total of 1,509 Firebirds were built with the optional L74 400 during the 1969 model year.

The Ram Air IV was Pontiac's newest high-output engine for 1969. Conservatively rated at 340 hp at 5,400 rpm and 430 ft-lbs at 3,700 rpm, the round-port mill proved to be the ultimate in first-generation Firebird performance, delivering timed quarter-mile acceleration in the 12-second range with proper traction. Functional Ram Air was standard. Production delays forced a mid-model-year release. Just 157 Firebird 400s were equipped with the optional L67 engine that year.

For $76.88 over the cost of W66 400 Sport Option, buyers could equip their Firebird with the L74 400 H.O. rated at 335 at 5,000 rpm and 430 ft-lbs at 3,400 rpm. Using the same number-9790071 block as the basic L78 400 4-barrel, the 400 H.O. was equipped with the number-62 cylinder head and the 273/289-degree number-067 camshaft in automatic applications (code-YW) and the number-48 cylinder head and 288/302-degree number-068 with the manual (code-WQ). Its 5-hp boost is attributed to the high-flow exhaust manifolds, as in the preceding year. Whenever it was equipped with the optional T42 Hood Ram Air Inlet, the 400 H.O. was named Ram Air III.

There's been debate whether L74 production was available immediately upon 1969 model year startup or if it was delayed several weeks. The confusion surrounding the engine is most likely caused by the T42 Hood Ram Air Inlet option, which many associate with it, but in actuality, is a separate option. A total of 1,509 Firebirds (including Trans Am) were equipped with the L74 engine and Pontiac's monthly production figures (see Appendix C) for L74-equipped Firebirds erases any questions about the production rates or time frame.

1969 Ram Air IV

The 1969 model year ushered in a new high-performance 400-ci capable of effectively operating up to 6,000 rpm. A portion of its technology was ushered into engine design to create the Ram Air II, which was released in midyear 1968. The new-for-1969 Ram Air 400-ci further boasted high-flow cylinder heads, a new 4-barrel intake manifold, a high-lift camshaft, and a valvetrain suited for the extended operating range.

Assigned UPC L67 and selling for $558.20, Pontiac slated the new engine to include cold-air induction that drew from two sets of dual scoops. One set was traditionally located on the hood and the second set was located behind the grilles within the front bumper. A vintage report from Pontiac explains that its engineers determined that the Firebird and GTO's dual-scooped hood didn't lend much "ramming" effect. By adding frontal ducts, the incoming air at high speed was slightly pressurized, thereby providing a true ramming effect and increasing engine output.

With four points in which to ingest outside air, the division marketed the mill as the Ram Air IV. As it went to production, however, the grille-mounted air ducts were eliminated, and the traditional hood-mounted Ram Air scoop setup was the sole source of cold-air induction.

The Ram Air IV (or R/A IV) used the same number-9792506 block with four-bolt main cap as the Ram Air 400 from 1968. Its cylinders were filled with forged aluminum pistons for improved durability though cast connecting rods remained. At some point during the 1969 model year, Pontiac stopped casting the number-9792506 block and began machining typical number-9790071

units to accept four-bolt caps. In these instances, the "9790071" casting number was partially or fully removed and "9792506" was hand-stamped into place.

The Ram Air IV received a specific cast nodular iron crankshaft (number-9795481). According to its original drawing, it differed from the standard 400 unit in two ways. Its counterweights were balanced for use with forged pistons and its main bearing journals included .001-inch greater clearance, which increased oiling for added protection during high-RPM operation. The bottom end was assembled using a "select fit" process, described in Pontiac engineering information as "selecting pistons and bearings that possess the closest tolerances during engine assembly." In essence, the Ram Air IV was mildly "blueprinted" right from the factory.

Pontiac began creating an entirely new cylinder head for its 1969 Ram Air IV as early as December 1967. Whereas volume of a typical Pontiac intake port measured about 153 cc and airflow capacity with a 2.11-inch valve peaked around 210 cfm at 28 inches of pressure,

Pontiac's cast crankshafts were quite beefy and rarely problematic. When assembling the Ram Air IV for 1969, engineers began with a typical 400 crank constructed of cast nodular iron with 3-inch main journals and a stroke length of 3.75 inches. They modified it only slightly. The main journals received an additional .001 inch of oil clearance and the counterweights were uniquely balanced to accommodate the forged pistons. Although reconstructing Pontiac's original intent with a standard crank is easily done today, an authentic number-9795481 is quite desirable among hobbyists who seek maximum correctness for a restoration.

The foundation of the Ram Air IV was the number-9792506 400-ci block equipped with 3-inch-diameter main journals and four-bolt main caps. When compared to a typical two-bolt cap, the extra material associated with the four-bolt unit increased the rigidity of the main journal bulkhead, which improved high-RPM durability. Pontiac considered it added insurance with the Ram Air IV's 6,000-rpm capability.

A new cylinder head with enlarged intake ports that peaked at about 235 cfm at 28 inches of pressure and included round exhaust outlets capable of increased airflow was paramount in allowing the Ram Air IV to produce maximum horsepower at high RPM. The 1969 Ram Air IV casting is identifiable by "722" cast into the far-left exhaust port. Unmolested examples can command a few thousand dollars from restorers.

The round exhaust port outlet developed for the Ram Air IV was pushed into production in 1968 with the midyear introduction of the Ram Air II. The revised intake port with added airflow capacity was, however, held off until the Ram Air IV's 1969 release. The capacity increase was the result of boosting port volume by 10 percent, achieved by raising port height by .125 inch compared to the typical D-port cylinder head.

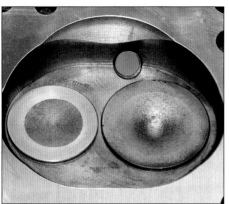

The number-722 casting was fitted with the same tulip-shaped 2.11/1.77-inch intake and exhaust valves as those introduced with the Ram Air II from the previous year. Combustion chamber shape and spark plug location in relation to the scallop was specific to that cylinder head during the 1969 model year. The chamber displaced 71 to 72 cc. That allowed for an actual compression about a half point lower than the advertised ratio of 10.75:1.

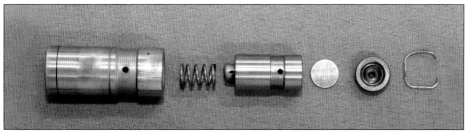

Hydraulic valve lifters use an internal plunger and pressurized engine oil to take up valve lash and provide quiet operation in all driving conditions. The rate at which a lifter bleeds off that pressure can limit its effectiveness at certain engine speeds. Pontiac developed a new lifter for its Ram Air IV that featured a high bleed rate and limited internal plunger travel. The result was a hydraulic camshaft that operated quietly but offered performance similar to that of a solid lifter cam.

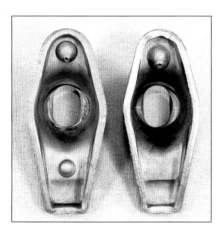

To take advantage of the added intake and exhaust airflow capacity of the new round-port cylinder head, Pontiacs equipped with Ram Air IV with the high-lift 041 that was released early and teamed with a 1.65:1 ratio rocker arm, took gross valve lift to nearly .520 inch. First used to increase valve lift on the Super Duty 421, the stamped-steel unit created for the Ram Air IV (right) was identical to the 1.5:1 unit (left) found on all other engines. The increased ratio was achieved by moving the pushrod cup closer to the rocker stud (fulcrum).

the intake ports of the new number-9796722 (or 722) cylinder head were made .125-inch taller, which effectively added volume and airflow capacity. Displacing about 180 cc, peak airflow jumped roughly 10 percent to 235 cfm. The exhaust port featured the round outlet shape that debuted with the 1968½ Ram Air II, and internal port work and resultant airflow capacity was very similar to that of the Ram Air II.

The number-722 cylinder head was filled with tulip-shaped valves measuring 2.11-inch intake and 1.77-inch exhaust that were swirl-polished for greater durability. A revised set of high-rate valvesprings complemented them. Despite the Ram Air IV's advertised compression ratio of 10.75:1, the number-722 drawing reveals that the target volume of its spherized wedge-shaped combustion chamber was 71 cc, two of which were achieved by the cupped head of the tulip-shaped valve. Using a compression calculator, actual compression ratio is closer to 10.2:1 on a standard-bore 400-ci.

With a planned maximum operating speed of 6,000 rpm and cylinder heads to support it, Pontiac engineers developed an all-new high-performance hydraulic camshaft for the Ram Air IV. The number-9794041 (or 041) featured 308/320 degrees of duration with an aggressive lobe profile. Lobe lift had been previously limited to roughly .271 inch (about .407 inch at the valve), the point where typical Pontiac D-port cylinder heads begin to reach peak flow. To complement the added airflow capacity of the Ram Air IV's number-722 casting, lobe lift of the number-041 was increased to .313 inch; when combined with 1.65:1 ratio rocker arms, gross valve lift measured .516 inch.

During the late 1960s, the oil pump in low-performance V-8s pressurized the lubrication system to approximately 40 psi. V-8s with increased performance were equipped with a unit that boosted output to 60 psi. The L74 400 H.O. used the same 60-psi pump (number-9787518) as standard 400-ci applications, but number-9794275 was specified for the Ram Air IV. Making its first appearance in the Ram Air II in midyear 1968, the new pump delivered 60 psi but included a thicker bottom plate to resist flexing at high RPM.

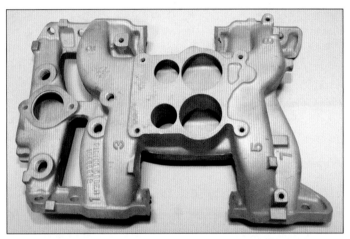

With its ability to dissipate heat and its lightweight characteristics, cast aluminum technology became increasingly popular during the 1960s. Pontiac wanted to construct its standard 4-barrel intake from cast aluminum. Durability concerns and cold-weather operation prevented the idea from moving forward in typical passenger car applications, but cast aluminum was ideal for constructing the Ram Air IV's high-flow unit. Runners were enlarged to match the intake port dimensions of the number-722 cylinder head. A separate exhaust crossover (not shown) limited the amount of heat the carburetor was exposed to. The Ram Air IV manifold proved to be an excellent design that remains highly coveted by Pontiac performance enthusiasts and restorers alike.

To provide consistent high-RPM operation, Pontiac developed an entirely new hydraulic valve lifter specifically for the Ram Air IV. In general, a hydraulic lifter provides quiet and consistent valvetrain operation that's virtually maintenance free. It consists of an internal plunger that floats within the lifter body. During normal operation plunger travel is taken up by pressurized engine oil to minimize valve lash. When exposed to valvespring pressure, oil trapped beneath the plunger bleeds off at a specific rate during each lift cycle so that the valve can properly return to its seat.

Although that hydraulic actuation is ideal for typical passenger cars that are driven daily (and it accounts for the typical wear that occurs as miles increase), the continuous bleed-down function can soften the aggressive lobe action of a high-performance camshaft. That limits its effectiveness, particularly at high RPM where there's less time between lift cycles to bleed off pressure. For this reason many manufacturers during the 1950s and 1960s chose a solid lifter for maximum performance engines. It made for noisier operation and routine manual valve lash checks and/or adjustments.

Pontiac created a new hydraulic lifter that offered the operational benefits of a hydraulic lifter but possessed the performance benefits of a solid lifter for its number-041 camshaft. The special hydraulic lifter (number-5232675) had an internal plunger. Its travel was limited from the typical .125 inch of standard lifters to a maximum of just .050 inch. The result was a lifter that provided minimal hydraulic cushion for quiet operation but followed the lobe much more precisely once its internal pressure bled off. The lifter was popular with racers who recognized its capability and the design remains in production today.

A new intake manifold constructed of cast aluminum was developed for the Ram Air IV. The drawing for number-9796614 was initiated in December 1967 and released for production in midyear 1968. When compared to a cast-iron unit, aluminum better dissipated heat and shed about 15 pounds. Its runners were made taller to accommodate the added cylinder head intake port height, and that subsequently increased airflow capacity of the manifold. Like many GM divisions at that time, Pontiac's foundry specialized in iron and simply wasn't capable of pouring molten aluminum in high volume, so production was outsourced to Winters Foundry and Machine of Canton, Ohio.

A separate cast-iron exhaust crossover located beneath the cast aluminum manifold warmed the divorced choke coil and minimized the amount of heat to which the manifold and carburetor were exposed. Dual heat stoves provided the carburetor with warm air during cold startup and drive-away. It was teamed with

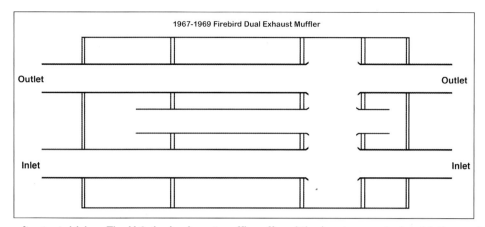

1967-1969 Firebird Dual Exhaust Muffler

Outlet

Outlet

Inlet

Inlet

The N10 Dual Exhaust system of every 1967–1969 Firebird H.O. and Firebird 400 originally consisted of a pair of small, 12-inch resonators beneath each rear seat and a 19-inch muffler mounted transversely above the rear axle. A resonator typically attenuates certain frequencies without grossly restricting airflow and works in concert with the muffler to achieve a desired tone and eliminate resonance (or drone) at the frequency engineers deemed offensive or annoying after test driving. The V-8 dual exhaust muffler offered the least amount of restriction and muffling as any transverse muffler could. Based on its internal pipe style and configuration, it's clear that Pontiac deliberately engineered a crackly and powerful exhaust note for Firebird that was intended to further bolster its image as a dominating performance vehicle.

COMPUTER-DESIGNED 041 CAM

Pontiac advertised "Cams by Computer" in vintage sales literature during the late 1960s and early 1970s. That has led many to believe that Pontiac's camshafts were computer designed and/or optimized. Many modern references often tout the high-performance number-041 as the first time such technology was used.

Retired Pontiac engineer Malcolm "Mac" McKellar was instrumental in designing the number-041 and he told me before his passing that its design was very much a manual process. In fact, its valve events are identical to the number-10 mechanical grind developed for the early-1960s Super Duty 421, but with greater valve lift, though the lobe shapes are quite different.

In contrast to computer-assisted design, once optimal specifications were determined from actual engine performance testing, Pontiac used computerized equipment to measure the lobe profile instead of an otherwise tedious manual process. The computer recorded exact lobe lift for each degree to one-millionth of an inch. That information was used to populate the Cam Contour Data chart found on the blueprint of a given camshaft, which was an important portion of creating accurate copies for production.

The 041 was likely the first camshaft to use Pontiac's new computerized measuring equipment. McKellar said that computers were new technology at the time and that Pontiac's marketing department hoped to capitalize on the fact that computers had a part in the production of its cams. He admitted, however, that it's very unlikely that the computerized process had any effect on actual engine performance. At the time, determining the best-suited grind remained a manual function of the engineering team.

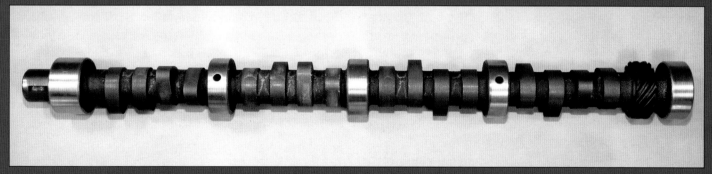

Pontiac's number-041 may be the most popular camshaft the division ever produced. The design of the hydraulic flat-tappet grind was marketed in vintage Pontiac sales literature as "computer assisted." That's been interpreted a number of ways by automotive writers and hobbyists. In fact, the camshaft was designed manually using traditional methods, but its valve events were computer recorded.

a Rochester Quadrajet carburetor with a capacity of 750 cfm to feed the hungry 400-ci. It proved to be an excellent performance combination.

To adhere to GM's policy of limiting a vehicle's horsepower-to-weight ratio, Pontiac rated the Firebird's Ram Air IV at 340 hp at 5,400 rpm and 430 ft-lbs at 3,700 rpm. However, the same engine used in the GTO (but with A-body–spec exhaust manifolds) was rated at 366 hp at 5,500 rpm and 445 ft-lbs at 3,900 rpm. The latter lends clear insight to the Ram Air IV's true capabilities. Racers who campaigned these vehicles can attest to the fact that the Firebird and GTO ratings were grossly understated and that actual output is closer to 400 hp in both applications.

Although the Ram Air IV was announced in preliminary material that predated 1969 model year startup, actual production was delayed several months. Ram Air was a standard feature with this engine, so its delayed release was directly related to the issues that prevented the release of the T42 Hood Ram Air Inlet package for the L74 400 H.O. until midyear 1969. We know for certain that Pontiac planned its release immediately after 1969 model year startup and this can be corroborated with the September 13, 1968 (I138), cast date on at least two pair of number-722 cylinder heads that have surfaced over the years.

Pontiac built 157 Firebirds (including Trans Am) with the L67 Ram Air IV engine during the 1969 model year. Pontiac's monthly production records numbers reveal that the Ram Air IV didn't enter production until February 1969 and it continued through the extended model year.

Transmission Lineup

Understanding Pontiac's transmission usage for 1969 can be quite confusing. As in previous years, 3- and 4-speed manuals, and 2- and 3-speed automatics were standard equipment and/or available options, but when considering internal gear ratios and calibrations, a total of 19 different automatic and manual transmissions were used, depending on application, during the 1969 model year.

A Saginaw-built M12 3-speed manual with a 2.85:1 first-gear ratio was used with 6-cylinder (code-FK) engines; the same manufacturer's 2.54:1 variant was used behind any 350-ci V-8 (code-RJ). Both were column-shifted. A floor-shifted M12 was standard equipment with the Sprint-6 (code-FY) and available on the OHC-6 for $42.13.

Ford Motor Company supplied Pontiac with its heavy-duty 3-speed manual transmission for M13 applications. Coded "DB" and with a first-gear ratio of 2.42:1, the top-loading design was available with floor-mounted shifter only. It was standard equipment on the Firebird 400 and available for $84.26 with the 350-ci 2-barrel and 350 H.O.

An M20 4-speed with floor-mounted shifter was available with all engines at an extra cost of $195.36. A Saginaw-built M20 with a first-gear ratio of 3.11:1 was used with the 6-cylinder (code-FH). Most V-8s received a Muncie-built M20 with a 2.52:1 first-gear ratio (code-FF); it was used with rear axle gearing through 3.55:1. The close-ratio M21 Muncie with a first-gear ratio of 2.20:1 (code-FX) was specified whenever the Firebird was equipped with a 3.90 or 4.33:1 axle ratio. Because the L67 Ram Air IV was only available with 3.90:1 gearing in the Firebird, the M21 was the only manual transmission available with it.

The M31 Super Turbine-300 (or ST-300) 2-speed and M40 Turbo-400 3-speed were virtual carryovers from the 1968 model year, but the M38 Turbo-350 3-speed was all new. Originally developed for light-duty use with smaller displacement engines, its intent was to provide the smooth operation, improved efficiency, and performance associated with the Turbo-400 but in a smaller package. The Turbo-350 went on to become one of GM's most versatile automatic transmissions and was used well into the 1980s.

The M31 ST-300 2-speed automatic was available for $174.24 with the OHC-6 1-barrel (code-LH with C60 Air Conditioning and code-LF without). It cost $184.80 when combined with the L30 350 2-barrel (code-MC with C60 Air Conditioning and code-MA without).

The M38 Turbo-350 was available with the OHC-6 (code-JB) for $195.36. It was also the only automatic transmission available with the Sprint-6 (code-JD) and was priced identically. The M38 was also available with the L30 350 2-barrel, but only if C60 Air Conditioning was also ordered (code-JF) for $205.92. It's not clear why Pontiac specified the M38 with this particular combination and not with others. Axle ratios called for when cars were equipped with air conditioning may have been rather tall, and the new 3-speed automatic provided good acceleration.

The M40 Turbo-400 was optional at an extra cost of $227.04. Availability wasn't limited to the Firebird 400 as in years past, however. It was optional with the L30 350 2-barrel when equipped with C60 Air Conditioning (code-PV) and was the only automatic available with the L76 350 H.O. (code-PS). An identically calibrated M40 was used in L78 and L74 400 4-barrel (code-PX)

The 1969 model year may be the most confusing as to Firebird transmissions. Saginaw, Ford, and Muncie provided 3- and/or 4-speed units for specific applications. A column-mounted shifter was available only with the Saginaw 3-speed and a floor-mounted shifter was required with the rest. A Hurst shifter was included only with premium transmissions.

The T-shaped automatic transmission shifter carried over from 1968 and was used as the floor-mounted option with the 2-speed. The transmission was limited to 6-cylinder engines and the 350-ci 2-barrel. Compared to the 3-speed M38 Turbo-350 and M40 Turbo-400, the 2-speed automatic wasn't nearly as popular in years past.

A new feature for Firebirds with Turbo-350 and -400 transmissions equipped with a floor-mounted shifter was the new Rally Sports Speed Shifter. By pushing the selector toward the right, manual upshifts could be made in quick succession without the fear of overriding the intended gear. Pontiac used the dual-gate feature on most of its performance cars throughout the 1970s.

The optional M09 Custom Gear Shift Knob was available for an upcharge of $5.27. The sculpted knob had an attractive simulated walnut-grain appearance. The clear plastic center contained a Pontiac arrowhead logo with a 3-speed transmission; it had the gear pattern with a 4-speed.

applications, and a unique Turbo-400 with increased full-throttle up-shift speed was used with the L67 Ram Air IV (code-PQ).

A round-ball shifter knob constructed of black plastic was standard with a manual transmission. M09 Custom Gear Shift Knob of simulated wood construction was optional for $5.27 and 1,673 were ordered. When floor-shifted, the M31 2-speed automatic reused the "T" shaped shifter handle from 1968, while floor-shifted 3-speed automatics received an all-new Rally Sports Speed Shifter featuring a dual-gate design. When placed in manual gear selection mode, it would allow only a single upshift to prevent unintentional over-shifting. It was accented by a new plastic knob with a simulated woodgrain appearance and a Firebird emblem in the shift button.

Rear Axle

For 1969, Firebird again used the Pontiac-built rear axle featuring an 8.2-inch-diameter ring gear and 10-bolt retention with a few minor revisions. Most notably, its rear axle tubes were flattened on the outer edges to allow for a reduced ride height. When combined with new spring rates, the 1969 Firebird sat lower than earlier examples, but maintained the same amount of compression travel.

Rear axle gearing ranged from 2.56 to 4.33:1 depending on the application; an open differential remained standard equipment. The G80 Safe-T-Track option rewarded buyers with a limited-slip differential for $42.13. When combined with a rear axle ratio of 3.36:1 or greater (numerically), the G80 cost increased to $63.19 and a four-pinion heavy-duty differential with forged steel axle shafts was specified.

G80/G93 Special Axle Ratio, G90/G92 Performance Axle Ratio, and G95/G97 Economy Axle Ratio, all available for an upcharge of $2.11, were ways buyers could uniquely equip their Firebirds to match their driving style.

Parts & Accessories Extra 69-16 was issued on July 21, 1969, and stated that from June 26, 1969, onward, the 10 3/8-inch-diameter ring gear retaining bolts had been replaced by larger 7/16-inch units with left-hand threads to further improve durability of the Pontiac-built axle. The bulletin added that the early and late ring gears and differentials were not interchangeable.

If you have any question about the components a particular 1969 Firebird is equipped with today and it appears to remain completely unmodified, the easiest way to determine that is by removing the differential cover. An "L" was stamped into the head of the original ring gear bolts signifying left-hand thread.

Suspension and Steering

Although Pontiac reduced the Firebird's ride height by about .5 inch from 1968, it was accomplished using different front coil and rear leaf springs, but the compression rate was designed so that ride quality wasn't affected by less suspension travel. Y96 Ride and Handling package delivered the sportiest ride with its high-rate springs and shock absorbers. Because the Firebird 400 had increased rate springs as standard equipment, the jump to Y96 was only $4.21. It was, however, a $9.48 upcharge on others models.

FG1 Adjustable Shock Absorbers Front and Rear supplied by Koni remained on the option list for 1969 at $52.66. According to CDB 69-26, availability was delayed until October 18, 1968. Pontiac production records reveal that 232 were installed before the option was officially canceled on January 28, 1969, with the issuance of CDB 69-64. No reason was provided. Detailed production records reveal that 149 of that total were combined with Y96, and the Firebird Sprint accounted for 14 of them.

A manual steering gearbox with a ratio of 24:1 was standard in all Firebird applications for 1969. That was, however, reduced to 28:1 whenever a V-8 was equipped with air conditioning. The constant-ratio power-steering box from 1967 and 1968 was eliminated and N41 Variable-Ratio Power Steering ranging from 16 to 12.4:1 was available on all Firebirds at an extra cost of $105.32.

Wheels and Tires

The 14-inch stamped-steel wheel remained standard on the 1969 Firebird. Rim width, however, increased to 7 inches on all but the entry-level Firebird equipped with the OHC-6 1-barrel. The wider wheel lent an appearance of greater aggressiveness and improved stability and load-carrying capacity. By adjusting wheel offset, Pontiac increased the Firebird's footprint without affecting tread width. The base-model Firebird retained its 6-inch-wide wheel.

A black or body-colored wheel with small hub was standard, and P01 Deluxe Wheel Discs for $21.06, P02 Custom Wheel Discs for $41.07, and N95 Wire Wheel Discs for $73.72 were extra-cost full-wheel cover options. N98 Rally II wheels in 14 x 6–inch (code-JC) or 14 x 7–inch (code JK) sizes were also available for $84.26. Because P01 was included with W54 Custom Trim Group, P02, N95, and N98 could be had on Custom Option Firebirds for $21.06 less than the corresponding price previously stated above.

At the beginning of the model year, the E70-14 Wide Oval tire with black sidewall was standard equipment on the entry-level Firebird with OHC-6 1-barrel. A white-line (PX2) or red-line (PX3) sidewall was available for $31.60. An F70-14 with

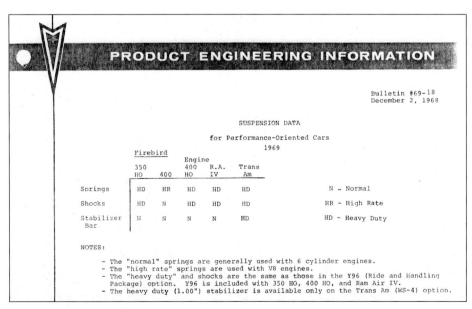

	Firebird		**Engine**				
	350 HO	**400**	**400 HO**	**R.A. IV**	**Trans Am**		
Springs	HD	HR	HD	HD	HD	N – Normal	
Shocks	HD	N	HD	HD	HD	HR – High Rate	
Stabilizer Bar	N	N	N	N	HD	HD – Heavy Duty	

Bulletin #69-18
December 2, 1968

SUSPENSION DATA

for Performance-Oriented Cars
1969

NOTES:
- The "normal" springs are generally used with 6 cylinder engines.
- The "high rate" springs are used with V8 engines.
- The "heavy duty" and shocks are the same as those in the Y96 (Ride and Handling Package) option. Y96 is included with 350 HO, 400 HO, and Ram Air IV.
- The heavy duty (1.00") stabilizer is available only on the Trans Am (WS-4) option.

Understanding 1969 Firebird suspension systems can be a daunting task for even the staunchest enthusiast. Some were tauter than others, but very little has been written about the components. Pontiac Engineering Information bulletin 69-18 dated December 2, 1968, summarizes it better than any resource. And it even includes Trans Am.

Pontiac increased the size of the Firebird's footprint with the addition of 7-inch-wide wheels on all examples except the entry-level model powered by the OHC-6 with 1-barrel carburetor. The stamped-steel wheel with small hubcap remained standard and about 8,000 1969 Firebirds were equipped with it. The restyled PO1 Deluxe Wheel Discs that featured six stamped spokes was, however, the most popular wheel accessory that model year, with installation onto 49,145 Firebirds during the 1969 model year.

The restyled PO2 Custom Wheel Discs was Pontiac's 1969 attempt to simulate the appearance of a mag-type wheel without the added cost. The rather attractive wheel covering wasn't popular with Firebird buyers, however, as just 1,379 opted for the up-level option. The design lasted only one model year; finding examples in good condition can be a difficult task.

Although N95 Wire Wheel Disc remained on the list of options without change for 1969, its popularity waned as Pontiac's first-generation F-car closed out its final model year. Just 1,334 Firebirds were equipped with the $73 option that year, making it quite rare today.

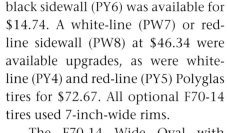

black sidewall (PY6) was available for $14.74. A white-line (PW7) or red-line sidewall (PW8) at $46.34 were available upgrades, as were white-line (PY4) and red-line (PY5) Polyglas tires for $72.67. All optional F70-14 tires used 7-inch-wide rims.

The F70-14 Wide Oval with black sidewall (PY6) was standard with the Sprint, 350, and 350 H.O. Sport Options. White-line (PW7) or red-line (PW8) sidewalls were available for $31.60 extra. The F70-14 Polyglas tire with white-line (PY4) or red-line (PY5) sidewalls was $57.93 extra. Firebird 400 buyers had the choice to equip their car with F70-14 Wide Oval tires with white-line (PW7) or red-line (PW8) sidewalls at no charge; the charge for white-line (PY4) or red-line (PY5) Polyglas tires was $26.33.

Tire options grew very convoluted in mid-March 1969 when Pontiac reduced the Firebird base cost. The E70-14 Wide Oval tire was replaced by a 7.35 x 14 bias-ply with black sidewall on entry-level Firebirds. The 7.75 x 14 tires became standard on Firebird Sprint, 350, and 350 H.O. The E70 x 14, E78 x 14, F70-14, and F78-14 with black, white, or red sidewalls were all available at slightly higher costs depending on the application. Tire size availability on the Firebird 400 went unchanged.

Precipitating this was a division-wide change to fiberglass-belted tires. Touted benefits when compared to

Firestone Wide Oval tires in F70-14 sizing gave Firebird a wide footprint and an aggressive stance. Included with the Firebird 400 (and available on others), white- and red-line sidewall treatment was popular with consumers, as was Pontiac's attractively styled Rally II. The 14 x 7–inch stamped-steel wheel was a premium option that simulated the appearance of an aftermarket mag-type unit. The fender-mounted simulated air vents were a new feature for 1969.

Push-button radio options included U63 AM-band, U69 AM/FM, and U58 AM/FM Stereo. Although the U35 Electric Clock option was previously mounted on the transmission tunnel (or console if so equipped), it was relocated to the instrument panel in 1969 and available separately or with the Rally Gauge cluster as part of W63.

C60 Air Conditioning was a popular Pontiac option. It was installed in nearly 40 percent of all 1969 Firebirds. That was up approximately 20 percent in the two preceding model years. Round vents at each corner of the dash were standard. The "Firebird" emblem in the center of the instrument panel was replaced by a rectangular ventilation outlet on vehicles equipped with air conditioning.

bias-ply tires included improved traction, greater tread life, and increased durability. Fiberglass tires added about $25 to the costs shown above, and Pontiac urged dealership sales staffs to upsell based on the noted advantages.

Fiberglass tires reached the Firebird assembly plants in limited quantities during the week of April 21, 1969. By mid-June, all Firebirds were equipped with fiberglass tires, which made it a mandatory option through the remainder of the traditional 1969 model year. It's possible that McDonald's base price review and option changes were also in part to offset the pending price increase associated with new tires. Upon startup of the 1970 model year, the cost of the fiberglass tire was included in the $94 base cost increase of the carryover 1969 Firebird.

The Firebird's spare tire changed in mid-March. Previously, the Space Saver was standard equipment and N64 Conventional Spare was available at no extra charge. Beginning midyear, N64 became standard equipment and N65 Space Saver was made available at $15.80. It's unclear if the change was mandated by McDonald's base price revision or the move to fiberglass tires, but it was likely a combination of the two.

Options

Optional equipment on the 1969 Firebird was much the same as in the preceding years. A variety of appearance, convenience, and/or performance options were available. As noted previously, some otherwise standard items were made optional in March 1969 to allow for a slight reduction in base pricing.

C60 Air Conditioning was available for $375.99 with all engines and transmission combinations with the exception of the Sprint-6 and Ram Air IV. A total of 28,091 Firebirds were equipped with it. Engine wiring was much less complex than in the previous year, however. Where it was once a separate harness, for 1969, functionality was controlled by a single jumper wire that originated from the main engine harness. It was much simpler and just as effective.

A new option available on all 1969 Pontiacs was C57 Power Flow Ventilation. Consisting of a pair of small, dash-mounted blower motors controlled by a single three-position toggle switch, the system provided forced airflow from the dash-mounted vent outlets. The added circulation was a reasonable solution in conditions such as stop-and-go traffic where normal airflow may be limited.

CDB 69-4 was issued on August 2, 1968. It notified dealers that C57 wouldn't be available on the Firebird at 1969 model year startup, but no details of the delay were provided. Its immediate availability was announced on January 9, 1969, with the issuance of CDB 69-53. Availability included any Firebird hardtop or convertible not equipped with C60 Air Conditioning. Just 54 Power Flow Ventilation systems were installed on Firebirds during the 1969 model year, and that includes at least one Trans Am.

Although UB5 Hood-Mounted Tachometer remained an available option for $63.19, U30 Rally Gauge

The Firebird was recognized as an excellent grand-touring vehicle and some dealers created their own customized packages to expand on it. Canadian dealer Grant Hamilton Pontiac created the Comanche package that added a host of suspension upgrades and exterior appointments. Only a handful were produced during 1968 and 1969. This Espresso Brown 1969 Firebird convertible may be the only of its kind that exists today. (Photo Courtesy Christopher Phillip)

Cluster with Instrument Panel Tachometer was a new $84.26 option. It positioned the tachometer in the large pod just left of the steering wheel and relocated the analog gauges to the right of the speedometer in a vertically stacked arrangement. CDB 69-16 was issued on September 13, 1968, stating that U30 wouldn't be available until mid-December 1968. On January 9, 1969, CDB 69-54 stated that U30 was immediately available. A total of 881 Firebirds received it that model year.

For owners less interested in watching engine revs, or for those who wanted a hood-mounted tachometer, Pontiac offered W63 Rally Gauge Cluster and Electric Clock for $47.39. The package was very similar to U30, but a set of sweeping gauges replaced the warning lamps in the left pod, and an electric clock was located just right of the speedometer. W63 was the choice of 6,313 buyers that model year. The U35 electric clock was also available as a standalone option for $15.80 and 19,166 added it to their order.

Deluxe seat belts (front and rear) were optional on all 1969 Firebirds regardless of hardtop or convertible styling. Although the straps most often color-matched the interior, black units were included with Parchment seats. Although the A39 option, which consisted of deluxe-level lap belts for convertibles only was the most common upgrade, a handful were fitted with WS1, which added deluxe-level shoulder straps to increase front-seat passenger safety.

The front shoulder strap feature included in WS1 Deluxe Seat Belts Front and Rear was an increasingly popular Pontiac option during the late 1960s that improved front passenger safety. A relatively unknown option for 1969 was WS2, which added deluxe-level rear seat shoulder straps to the WS1 option. Only 233 were produced with that option during the 1969 model year.

Pontiac heavily marketed A67 Fold Down Rear Seat as a way to increase the storage capacity of its first-generation Firebird. Nearly 10,000 Firebirds received the option in 1967, but its popularity had waned by 1969. Only 2,527 were equipped with it that model year, which makes it a relatively rare option. Just 6 of those were Trans Ams. (Photo Courtesy Greg Dilbert)

Drum brakes remained standard for Firebirds for 1969, and front disc brakes were an available option. Where JL2 Front Disc Brakes previously included bulky four-piston calipers, the $64.26 option now consisted of a much simpler, single-piston caliper that was equally as effective, cheaper to produce and maintain, and a much smaller package overall. Delco-Moraine's latest technology was used on 21,080 Firebirds.

The M21 close-ratio 4-speed manual transmission was included wherever a rear axle ratio of 3.90 or 4.33:1

was specified. Pontiac installed 535 M21s into Firebirds during the 1969 model year; 116 were combined with the L67 Ram Air IV where a 3.90:1 ratio was standard. Apparently 113 buyers of 400 H.O. Firebirds opted for G92 Performance Axle Ratio and chose a 3.90 or 4.33:1 ratio, as production records reveal that many M21s were installed with that engine. The remaining 306 units were used behind L76 350 H.O. and L78 400 4-barrel engines with the G92 axle option.

Tailpipe emissions were a growing concern by 1969 and pollution controls were not far off. To reduce emissions of vehicles continually operating at high altitude (above 4,000 feet), Pontiac created WT5 Mountain Performance Option, which it introduced with CDB 69-47 issued on December 6, 1968. Firebird availability was limited to the L30 350 2-barrels with automatic

U80 Rear Speaker was a relatively popular Firebird option with AM and AM/FM radios. In those instances, it was a single unit typically fixed-mounted to the right-hand side of the rear package shelf on hardtop models; it was fastened to the flexible trim sash behind the rear seat on convertibles. Dual rear speakers were included with the AM/FM stereo and/or eight-track tape player.

transmission, and the option package included a specially calibrated carburetor, a 2.93 or 3.08:1 rear axle ratio, and a heavy-duty radiator. Only 147 Firebirds received the option during the 1969 model year.

Production Notes

At the beginning of the 1969 model year, Firebirds were being built at General Motors' Lordstown, Ohio (code-U), and Van Nuys, California (code-L), assembly plants. Lordstown built full-size Chevrolets alongside the Firebird and the growing popularity of each taxed the plant's capacity. GM's plant in nearby Norwood, Ohio (code-N), was producing Camaros only, and it was capable of producing a greater volume of cars than the 1969 Camaro was selling. General Motors decided to consolidate F-car production to Norwood, which allowed Lordstown to produce full-size models at a greater rate. The Firebird volume took all of Norwood's available capacity. The move effectively satisfied the consumer demand for all three vehicles.

After producing 42,826 Firebirds, production at the Lordstown plant was stopped for several days beginning on March 27, 1969, so Pontiac's tooling could be removed for

Pontiac changed the Firebird's fuel tank during the 1969 model year. On March 7, 1969, Pontiac issued P&A Extra 69-7, which explained that a revision to the Firebird's fuel vapor venting system occurred in production and that new components were introduced at the assembly plants and superseded the originals in the parts system as well.

Handsomely styled and highly refined, the 1969 Firebird is revered by enthusiasts as one of the best-looking F-cars. Its impact with consumers, particularly as the model year progressed, may have been compromised by the pending release of the 1970 Firebird that was in development and being reported by media outlets. The 1969 Firebird is hugely popular with hobbyists today.

transport to Norwood. Production at the Norwood plant was then stopped on April 7, halting Camaro production to accommodate the installation of Pontiac's equipment that was removed from Lordstown. When production resumed at Norwood on April 14, it produced F-cars for both divisions, and 23,516 Firebirds were built there over the following several months.

Van Nuys produced a number of GM vehicles during the 1969 model year and its Firebird capacity was unaffected by the changes in Ohio. A labor strike brought the Van Nuys plant to a halt on April 28, 1969. When work resumed on June 19, one vintage newspaper report claimed that vehicles in process at the time of the stoppage would be finished before production at the plant was stopped in July (and before 1970 model year production began). Just 21,366 Firebirds rolled off the Van Nuys assembly line during the extended 1969 model year.

A redesigned F-car was slated for 1970 model year introduction along with all other new vehicles, but production delays forced Chevrolet and Pontiac to extend the 1969 F-car model year for several months. "The delay was because of wrinkles and splits that occurred when stamping the 1970 Camaro quarter panels," John Hinckley, a senior process engineer for Chevrolet Pilot Line, explained. "I don't know if Pontiac's Firebird was affected similarly, but the draw dies and draw rings in the press that Fisher Body was using to stamp our quarter panels had to be completely rebuilt, and that delayed the 1970 F-car launch until February 1970."

The delayed introduction and resultant model year extension was certainly a nightmare for General Motors' suppliers. "We planned to launch the new F-car with all the other 1970 models in September 1969 when our suppliers were travnsitioning to 1970 model year production. They had to unexpectedly drag out 1969 model year production until November 1969. That also made the 1970 F-car launch quite difficult," Hinckley said.

Pontiac General Manager James McDonald reported at a 1970 Pontiac new-car preview in September 1969 that the re-styled Firebird's delayed introduction was planned. The rationale given was that midyear introductions were exciting and stimulated showroom traffic in a sales season that was historically slow. Nothing was mentioned about body production issues. "It was certainly very embarrassing to Fisher Body. To my knowledge that was the first time they were ever responsible for a production loss and public relations departments covered it up with some clever wording," added Hinckley.

As other 1970 Pontiacs hit dealer lots in September 1969, the 1969 Firebird production continued at Norwood only. Pontiac used the 1969 Firebird, billing it as a 1969 model year vehicle, to fill the void, but knew going in that production couldn't continue past December 31, 1969. Any vehicle produced on or after January 1, 1970, had to be considered a 1970 model year vehicle and had to adhere to all new safety and/or emissions standards. According to information General Motors distributed at the time, November 10, 1969, was the final day of F-car production at Norwood.

The long and sleek profile of the restyled 1969 Firebird works in concert with the convertible top in the down position. The lines of the new body panels are quite apparent from a side perspective. Unlike in 1967–1968, which borrowed Camaro's exterior sheet metal, the Pontiac had a distinct personality that shared nothing with the Camaro.

There's no denying that Pontiac was on its game during the late 1960s. Output from its V-8 was at record levels and the engineering team had a host of exciting engine projects in development. Its stylists had abandoned any visual commonality between the Firebird and the Camaro. The Trans Am was a midyear introduction intended for consumers who wanted to compete on the racetrack, or simply experience the feel of a real race car on the street. Production of the 1969 Firebird began in September 1968 and build out would have typically occurred in about July 1969. Due to the delayed completion of the newly redesigned 1970 Firebird, however, Pontiac elected to extend the 1969 Firebird into the 1970 model year. The last 1969 Firebirds were produced in November 1969. A total of 87,708 were produced during its 14-month run.

During its lengthened 1969 model year, Pontiac built a total of 87,708 Firebirds. Assembly plant and build date information from original cars agrees with the production time frames noted above. Any Lordstown-built Firebird with a cowl-tag date past 03D has yet to be found. Although completion and ship dates may postdate the Van Nuys strike, no Van Nuys–built Firebirds with an initial build date past 05A have surfaced. And 04C is the earliest date for a Norwood-built Firebird, with 11A the absolute latest so far.

According to Pontiac production records, the total number of basic and Sport Option Firebirds is listed as 9,052 entry-level units with the OHC-6 1-barrel, 1,979 Firebird Sprints, 59,280 Firebird 350s, 4,466 Firebird 350 H.O.s, and 12,968 Firebird 400s. That equals 87,745 units, or 37 more than the stated production total of 87,708. Where the discrepancy lies is anyone's guess.

Although some books and articles printed over the years list 1969 W66 Firebird 400 production at 11,522, it isn't supported by Pontiac-printed documents. Instead, Pontiac clearly stated in two separate production reports that 1969 W66 volume was 11,302 units. A total of 4,769 Firebird 400s produced with the L78 400 4-barrel engine

were equipped with a manual transmission. (See Appendix C for a detailed production breakdown of L74 and L67 engines.)

Additional production figures for the 1969 model year are rather sketchy. It's not that the division didn't keep accurate records; it seems that the detailed reports the hobby has become accustomed to haven't yet surfaced. Based on current information, hardtop and convertible sales were 76,059 and 11,649, respectively. The base-model Firebird with the OHC-6 1-barrel accounted for 932 of the total convertibles produced. Convertibles equipped with a manual transmission numbered 2,558, and the OHC-6 engine was installed in 261 of them. The L67 Ram Air IV was installed into 17 Firebird convertibles, and 12 were equipped with a manual transmission.

Production totals for 1969 reveal some interesting equipment combinations of the 11,649 Firebird convertibles assembled that model year. Only 209 were equipped with a manual transmission and C60 Air Conditioning. Just 151 were equipped with A31 Power Windows, C06 Power Top, and UB5 Hood-Mounted Tachometer. Just 64 Firebird Sprint convertibles were equipped with the Y96 Ride and Handling package.

1969 Firebird Production

Firebirds sold in Canada	5,198
Firebirds with M38 Turbo-350 and Y96 Ride and Handling package	1,320
Firebirds equipped with A31 Power Windows and A46 Power Bucket Seat	632
Custom Option Firebirds equipped with the 400 H.O. and M40 Turbo-400	122
6-cylinder Firebirds equipped with the M12 3-speed manual and M09 Custom Gear Shift Knob	109
Firebird 350 H.O.s fitted with K96 Cruise Control	34
350 H.O. Firebirds equipped with V01 Heavy-Duty Radiator	11

WHERE IS THE RAM AIR III?

In today's Pontiac hobby market, most early-Firebird enthusiasts are familiar with the Ram Air III from 1969 and 1970. As a hot 400 boasting a 4-barrel carburetor, extended RPM camshaft, large valve heads, and increased-flow exhaust manifolds, it was among Pontiac's most well-balanced performance engines of the era.

In preceding years, Pontiac typically used "Super Duty" or "Ram Air" to signify its hottest competition engine for a given model year. Often, a "High Output" (or H.O.) variant was built with similar equipment but included provisions to improve street manners for more practical use. The Ram Air IV was Firebird's top engine option in 1969.

The Ram Air III was also available in 1969, but the engine is a bit of an anomaly. Why, you might ask? That's because the equipment Pontiac used to create the Ram Air III is more closely associated with the H.O. series.

How did the 400 H.O. and Ram Air III truly differ? The two engines were, in fact, identical in every respect. They not only shared UPC L74 and punch code 348, they also shared code-YW (auto) and code-WQ (manual) Firebird engine application identifiers. The terminology that appeared on certain pieces of 1969 Pontiac sales material has spurred the confusion among owners and hobbyists.

Would you be surprised to learn that Pontiac never initially referred to the 400 H.O. as "Ram Air III" or even intended it to carry that name? When the 400 Ram Air was replaced by the Ram Air II in midyear 1968, Pontiac began referring to its predecessor as Ram Air I. It apparently skipped over Ram Air III; the new-for-1969 Ram Air IV was aptly named because Engineering planned to include four air inlets, a feature that never reached production.

Whether derived internally from dealership sales staffs, the media, Firebird owners, or anywhere else, the L74 400 H.O. was quickly dubbed "Ram Air III" (T42 Hood Ram Air Inlet was an option with it). The name filled the natural void in Pontiac's Ram Air series lineup. The nickname created issues when attempting to order replacement components for a Firebird supposedly equipped with a Ram Air engine, however. Pontiac parts catalogs listed engine components intended for R/A IV as "Ram Air," whereas those for the 400 H.O. read "Except Ram Air."

Pontiac took notice and issued *P&A Extra* 69-11 on April 23, 1969, explaining to parts department personnel that with the May 1, 1969, printing, components intended for the Ram Air IV would be clearly identified in the parts catalog,

Would you believe that the 400 H.O. and Ram Air III for 1969 are identical? Pontiac didn't initially refer to the optional 400 and the Ram Air III until it issued this bulletin clarifying the equipment package (highlighted in yellow) to parts department personnel on April 23, 1969. The pages that followed contained the part numbers of every component for both engines, verifying their uniformity.

and that 400 H.O. components would note "Ram Air III or H.O." The bulletin even listed the proper engine codes and appropriate terminology for each.

Clarifying the matter even further, Pontiac issued Pontiac Sales Promotion Blueprint 69-61 on April 28, 1969 to dealership sales staffs. In addition to outlining several changes from the January 1969 Pontiac Accessorizer, the note defined the separation between 400 H.O. and Ram Air III. It stated, "H.O. nomenclature becomes 'Ram Air' when 611/T42 Hood Ram Air Inlet is ordered." There's no doubt that the 1969 400 H.O. and Ram Air III engines were identical. The only difference between them, which earns Ram Air status, was the addition of the T42 Hood-Ram Air Inlet option.

When considering the number of Firebirds equipped with T42 during the 1969 model year, 720 Ram Air III engines were produced. Of that total, 642 were used in the Trans Am. From simple subtraction, it appears that just 78 Firebird 400s were produced with the Ram Air III in 1969, but there's presently no way to determine that accurately.

Pontiac Sales Promotion Blueprint 69-61 was issued on April 28, 1969, and provided official notification to dealership sales staffs that the 400 H.O. was named Ram Air whenever T42 was added to the list of optional equipment. Thus, the 400 H.O. and Ram Air III technically describe the same basic engine. The Ram Air III is only so named when actually equipped with Ram Air.

Pontiac
Sales
Promotion
BLUEPRINT

April 28, 1969   P.S.B. 69-61
1969 PONTIAC ACCESSORIZER CHANGES

The following price and equipment changes have been made since the January printing of the 1969 Pontiac Accessorizer. These changes are the result of the recent equipment adjustment on Firebirds produced on or after March 17, 1969 -- the base MSRP for the Firebird Hardtop Coupe decreased from $2831 to $2759 -- and the Firebird Convertible base MSRP decreased from $3045 to $2989. The changes are as follows:

Page 1   Under the Decor Group, Roof Drip Scalp Moldings for Hardtop Coupes are now <u>included</u> at no extra cost.

Page 2   Under Sport Options, <u>change copy and prices</u> to read:

     345 W66 Firebird 400 w/std. 3-spd. H.D. Man. Trans.
               -2337 . . . . $431.81
               -2367 . . . . 416.01
           w/4-spd. Man. or H.M. Trans.
               -2337 . . . . $347.56
               -2367 . . . . 331.76

Page 2   Under Engine Options, <u>change copy</u> to read:

     348 L74 400, 4 Bbl. HO*
               (Available w/345 only) . . . . . . $ 76.88
     (*"HO" nomenclature becomes "Ram Air" when Sales Code 611, Hood Ram Air Inlet, is ordered)

Page 4   Under Appearance/Convenience Options, <u>add</u> the following:

     661 U29 Lamps, Courtesy - 2337 . . . . . $ 4.21
     664 U27 Lamp, Glove Box 3.16
     708 N65 Space Saver Spare Tire-w/o 454 . 15.80
                            -w/454 . . N/C

Page 13   Under Heavy-Duty Performance Options, <u>delete</u> the following:

     634 G66 Shocks, Superlift - Rear only. . .$ 42.13

Also, the suggested retail prices of the new fiberglass belted tire options are listed on the attached schedules.

<u>Please inform your salesmen of these additions and changes</u> as there will not be a revised printing of the Accessorizer; however, each dealership will receive, in the near future, revised wall price charts.

C. L. Copeland

CLC:Rc   C. L. Copeland
Attachment   Sales Promotion Manager

PONTIAC MOTOR DIVISION ▼ GENERAL MOTORS CORPORATION

CHAPTER FIVE

1969 TRANS AM

GTO loyalists carry a strong argument when claiming it among the industry's most influential vehicles. As the first entry into the "muscle car" category, Pontiac coyly created a hot performance package for 1964 that married the intermediate-size A-car with a large-cube V-8 from the full-size lineup. The concept initiated a generational craze that spawned countless imitators. Unfortunately, Pontiac cannot be credited with similar innovation with its 1967 F-car. However, no one can refute the lasting effects that the Firebird, and particularly the Trans Am, had upon the industry as the years passed.

As Pontiac's performance flagship for three decades, Trans Am's reputation propelled the Firebird into an iconic symbol of 1970s and 1980s Americana. Its origin dates to 1969. That's when Pontiac introduced WS4 Trans Am Option for the Firebird 400, a low-volume package aimed at giving racers a factory-built race car that was capable of running with the likes of the Camaro Z28 and Boss Mustang on Sports Car Club of America (SCCA) road courses with minimal modification. Better yet, it was available from their nearest Pontiac dealer!

Developed and introduced concurrently with the GTO "The Judge" package with its eye-popping orange finish, wild graphics, and 60-inch rear air spoiler, the Trans Am was another attention-getting specialty vehicle. The division hoped to garner even more media attention in a fiercely competitive 1969 performance car market.

The sporty Firebird was among the many 1969 four-passenger vehicles raced competitively in such venues as the SCCA Trans-Am series. Although other manufacturers had developed and were offering race-oriented packages for their pony car entries, Pontiac's process was a bit more arduous. But the result was astounding. Although general appearance was similar, the new Trans Am differed from the basic 1969 Firebird 400 in many ways.

A rear air spoiler that spanned the width of the body and blue accents went a long way in visually separating the 1969 Trans Am from other Firebirds. The Trans Am's appearance was DeLorean's attempt to create a hip, customized Pontiac to compete with Shelby's successful efforts with the Ford Mustang. Pontiac developed the entire appearance package and sent the prototype Firebird to the designers at GM Styling for finishing. The team at Pontiac Studio had to pull away from 1970 Firebird development to complete it.

When the Firebird was introduced in 1967, it used Camaro suspension designed by Chevrolet Engineering. Pontiac's engineers felt its handling was lax and immediately initiated a program to improve it. The Pontiac Firebird Sprint Turismo (or PFST) program was the division's first attempt to create a good-handling Firebird capable of adhering to SCCA's Trans-Am series rules. The first PFSTs were equipped with the Sprint-6 engine, purposely selected for its small-displacement and high-RPM capability, but at least one 1968 PFST was equipped with a Ram Air 400. Automotive writer Joe Oldham road-tested this particular PFST and was astounded with its improved handling capability. Practically all of its chassis enhancements were included in the production Trans Am. (Photo Courtesy Joe Oldham)

Although the uniquely equipped Firebird Trans Am certainly had many fathers and a countless number of Pontiac engineers and many GM Styling designers had lent some degree of input into its creation, the two most often credited with key roles in its development are Bill Collins and Herb Adams. These men took the input gleaned from a unique Firebird exercise where Special Projects maximized handling and, with John DeLorean's backing, transformed it into an optional performance package that eventually catapulted the Firebird to supercar status. With so few produced, the 1969 Trans Am is highly coveted by the Firebird faithful. It is most deserving of its own chapter.

Pontiac Firebird Sprint Turismo

As quickly as Pontiac began working on Firebird development in 1966, the division felt the need to create a special example of some sort, but exactly what was anyone's guess. All the while, John DeLorean and his engineers conjured up ways to improve Firebird's handling and performance to distance it from Chevrolet's Camaro in every way possible. The first Ram Air Firebirds were stout performers on the dragstrip, but Pontiac's 1967 F-car wasn't generally regarded as an exceptional handler. That's mostly because its suspension was comprised of unmodified Camaro underpinnings and there really wasn't sufficient developmental time for Pontiac's engineers to improve on that before production startup.

The SCCA Trans-Am racing series was a professional road-race circuit where factory-backed and high-end private teams competed with the four-passenger sports cars of the pony car category. By limiting maximum displacement to 305 ci, the SCCA could keep peak horsepower in check and limit top speeds to a moderate level. Manufacturers that wanted to capitalize on the series' popularity developed hot, factory-available packages compliant with SCCA rules. One example is Camaro's Z28, which included up-level suspension components and a high-performance 302-inch V-8.

Magazines regularly covered Trans-Am series events and the cars running in the races. Although other manufacturers were basking in the publicity, Pontiac and its Firebird were noticeably absent. Under DeLorean's direction, Collins and Adams initiated the Pontiac Firebird Sprint Turismo (PFST) project. Its intent was to create a hot Firebird that proved to be a formidable on-track contender fully compliant with SCCA rules. "We were basically handed Chevrolet's Camaro in 1967 and were limited with what we had to work with. We tried to do the best we could with it. Our ultimate goal was to create a Firebird that outperformed the Z28 in all areas," Adams said.

The PFST project consisted of a handful of 1967 and/or 1968 Firebirds, and all were painted in typical American racing fashion, white with a single blue stripe running the length of the body. It seems that 1967 was limited to a single PFST and it was equipped with an OHC-6 engine topped by a trio of Weber carburetors and a machined-aluminum hood scoop peering through the hood. DeLorean was proud of his 6-cylinder and felt its high-winding capability could make it competitive with the small-cube V-8s from other makes yet keep insurance ratings manageable. Although the Firebird suspension was crafted by Chevrolet, Adams' efforts to improve on it were quite noticeable.

No one can recall exactly when the project was initiated, but the PFST first appeared in the July 1967 issue of *Motor Trend* magazine. Considering publishing lead time, the Detroit-based photo session likely occurred at least three months prior to the issue date. Considering the lack of snow or foliage in the background of the photos, March 1967 seems quite likely. Further corroborating this is the April 1967 processing date found tied to the original photos. All of this suggests that the PFST project was well underway by the time the 1967 Firebird was made available to the public.

Six additional PFSTs powered by the new 350-ci V-8 were purportedly built for promotional use in 1968, but not a single photo has surfaced that proves their existence. Instead, photos accompanying vintage magazine reports clearly indicate that Pontiac built at least one OHC-6 and one 400-powered PFST that year. Author Joe Oldham

Not only did the PFST project pioneer the Trans Am package, it literally served as a test mule for various engineering assignments related to the new option package. Pontiac engineer Dan Hardin snapped this photo of a 1968 PFST as it was being modified for a controlled test in Pontiac's Engineering garage.

road-tested the 400-ci PFST for the December 1968 issue of *Speed and Supercar* magazine. Many of the mechanical features Oldham describes were used on the 1969 Trans Am, which reached production just months later.

Reminiscing about his experience of driving a PFST that seemingly doubled as a Trans Am prototype, Joe said, "Typically, car companies present finished, ready-to-sell product to both the press and public. They are reluctant to even talk about future products much less show it in public. So it was a rare privilege to be allowed to drive the Pontiac Firebird Sprint Turismo, an engineering test mule that allowed me a glimpse into the future."

Attempts were made to determine how many vehicles were built under the PFST project, but no one connected with it can recall a specific number or even what became of the cars. Unfortunately, because PFST was an engineering exercise and not an actual program, GM Heritage Center has no information on them, either. Presumably, all of the cars were destroyed. Based on its origin and intended purpose, however, there's no denying that the PFST project greatly influenced the WS4 Trans Am Option for 1969. The 1967 and 1968 cars served as test beds to determine effectiveness of the modifications. Herb Adams agrees. "In my opinion, the PFST *was* the forerunner to the Trans Am," he said.

Fitch Firebirds

John Fitch was a successful racer and savvy innovator. His connection to General Motors dates back to at least the mid-1950s. He spent most of the 1960s starting John Fitch & Company, where he modified the body, suspension,

John Fitch was an automotive racer who enjoyed creating innovative vehicle packages that improved handling without compromising ride quality, and Pontiac's John DeLorean had taken notice. Seeking ways to elevate the Firebird above the Camaro, DeLorean sent Fitch & Company two 1967 Firebirds for evaluation. Fitch's external modifications included sail panel extensions with faux ducting and a lower baffle to direct greater airflow toward the radiator for improved cooling capacity. The OHC-6 prototype is in private hands today. (Photo Courtesy Rick Salzillo)

and drivetrain of select GM models at his Falls Village, Connecticut, facility. There he churned out vehicles including the Fitch Corvair Sprint, which transformed the otherwise unassuming passenger vehicle into a worthy competitor in the emerging sports car racing scene.

Fitch's contribution, where Pontiacs are concerned, was creating what some argue as another Firebird Trans Am forebear. Recognizing the F-car's potential as a grand-touring vehicle, Fitch used his association with John DeLorean to acquire two 1967 Firebirds (OHC-6 and 400 V-8) to modify and to return to Pontiac for evaluation. DeLorean likely viewed it as a potential opportunity to secure a relationship with an outside source to draw interest toward the division and its performance model, much like the arrangement that Ford had with Carroll Shelby and the very successful Shelby Mustang program it created.

Fitch felt his Firebird should perform smoothly and exceptionally well in every aspect, and that also meant in normal conditions associated with daily driving. Standard features included many new mechanical components as well as winged panels that extended rearward from the Firebird's roof and above each quarter. The Fitch trademark was intended to gather air at speed and duct it to the rear brakes as well as ventilate the interior. The panels were purely cosmetic in standard form, but they could be made functional if a buyer desired.

A private individual in Connecticut owns what's believed to be Fitch's OHC-6 prototype. Its build sheet denotes "Tag Fitch & Co" and the vehicle's data tag reveals that the Firebird was produced during the first week of June 1967 (or 06A) and the 400 V-8 prototype was probably built concurrently. In addition to sending the prototypes back to Pontiac for review, Fitch also sold his modified Firebird to consumers, offering a host of optional equipment. Including the prototypes, it's believed that as many as seven 1967 and 1968 Firebirds were modified by Fitch, and each was uniquely equipped.

Pontiac also provided John Fitch with a 1967 Firebird 400 to modify. The Fitch Firebird was treated to the basic Fitch equipment and was given a two-tone paint treatment. The extra grille meshing to prevent headlight damage from debris is quite visible in this photo. Its potential to obstruct forward lighting caused many to question its legality. (Photo Courtesy The Revs Institute for Automotive Research, Inc.)

Fitch & Company created a number of enhancements to expand on Firebird's image as a grand-touring vehicle and outlined them in a three-page informational report distributed to media outlets. The undated document explains the intent of the Fitch Firebird and details package content. It's very unlikely that many copies of this report exist today, but it lends clear insight into the potential John Fitch saw in the Firebird.

```
                    FITCH FIREBIRD

        That elusive ideal of a 4 seater touring sports car with
European handling qualities and American car serviceability
has been achieved in the Fitch Firebird.  Eschewing the
standard Detroit route toward this objective of hard suspen-
sion, raucous exhaust and engine output stretched to shrill
impracticality, Fitch has drawn on his unmatched experience in
taming the domestic beast to create a comfortable, controllable
automobile of a very high level of refinement.

        The result is a tidy package with that tight, all-of-a-
piece feel that pleases experienced drivers of the likes of
Mercedes 250 SL, Rover 2000, Lancia and Porsche.  You are
invited to shoot down these broad claims by a road test.

                    Mechanical Description:

Rally Steering.  Heretofore, drivers of American cars have
had the choice of an unmanagable 5 turn lock-to-lock manual
arm twister or the erie-light, directionally unstable faster
ratio traditionally supplied with power steering.  The Fitch
version has a high ratio (15 to 1) with a judicious revalving of the
power unit and geometry settings which give the road feel of
a light and accurate manual steering (This must be experienced
to be believed).

Rally Brakes.  Similarly, the American car owner's choice has
been a heavy manual pedal or a hypersensitive, low-pressure
control which puts passengers into the windshield at the
slightest touch.  The Fitch brake can be applied both quickly
and progressively to meet any road situation.

G. T. Suspension.  The key to this comfortable and controllable
suspension is the auxilliary rubber springs (as used by
Ferrari & Lotus) which introduce into the system a progressive
wheel rate so essential for confident and predictable handling
on roads at sustained high average speeds.  The progressive
feature permits comfortable wheel control with driver alone
without inducing the loss of roadholding inevitable when
suspensions bottom.  Wheel travel and roadholding are retained
with a full load.

Englebert Radial Tires.  Supporting the excellent G. T.
suspension are a superior steel belt radial tire of long
life.  No aquaplaning with excellent block tread water drainage.
No self-steering on cambered roads and no necessity for snow
tires.

Positive Throttle Control.  A repositioning of the lever
angle provides the controlled part throttle operation so often
missing on high performance American cars.
```

Racer John Fitch was pleased with the results of the effort he spent transforming Pontiac's Firebird into what he believed was a capable handler. Fitch & Company distributed photos of the modified Firebird to media outlets and interested parties seeking additional information. How about this vintage photo of John Fitch behind the wheel of his 400-ci creation?

The Fitch Firebirds were met with mixed reviews by magazine writers. Many lauded the performance enhancements despite expressing disdain toward the quarter panel extensions and the visual impact they created. In its April 1968 issue, *Car Life* magazine directly compared the 6-cylinder Fitch Firebird to the PFST and found that Fitch's iteration rode better in typical conditions, but Pontiac's PFST was much more purposely equipped and better suited for racing applications.

Not surprisingly, Pontiac felt that Fitch's car was good, but the division's iteration was better. "Our PFST project was running parallel to Fitch's efforts," Herb Adams recently said. "We each had ideas on how to make the Firebird better. John was a good friend and his Firebird was great, but we felt ours was better aimed in the direction we were looking to take it. When John found out we were working on the PFST project, he was supportive of our efforts." Not long after that Pontiac formally decided Firebird's direction and the evolution of Fitch's Firebird, at least at the divisional level, ceased.

WS4 Trans Am Option

Despite internal criticism about its marketability, Pontiac decided during the summer of 1968 that it needed a special-edition Firebird that exuded performance to draw attention and set it apart from typical Firebirds. DeLorean had his engineering team take all it learned from the PFST project, create a complete race-oriented package, and apply it to a production Firebird.

	Kit	Installed
Firm Response Brakes (with HD lining - for disc brake cars only)	$39.50	$48.00
GT Suspension (4 Konis, 4 Aux. springs & brackets)	145.00	178.00
GT Suspension (Soft Ride) (2 Konis, 4 Aux. Springs and brackets)	95.00	128.00
Positive Throttle Control Linkage (400 only)	5.00	8.50
Gear Shift Boot	7.50	12.00
Low Pressure Exhaust ('67 400 cnly)		34.00
Englebert Radial Tires (185 x 14 Rallye) ($57 each x 5)		285.00
Tubes ($6 each x 5)	30.00	30.00
Uniroyal MAX Radial 205R14 ($54 each x 5)	270.00	270.00
Essential Light Monitor	24.50	29.50
Formula 1 Steering Wheel Leather Rim, Long Reach	54.95	59.95
Formula 1 Steering Wheel Same with Matte Black Spokes	59.95	64.95
Electronic Magnets Transistor Ignition	49.50	53.00
Air Horn	22.00	29.00
Long Range Driving Light (replacing left high sealed beam)	8.75	10.95
Headlight Flasher	4.95	9.50
One-Time Windshield Wiper	4.95	9.50
Gear Shift Boot	3.95	6.50
Fitch Metallic Brake Lining (for drum brake cars only)	42.00	59.00
Steering Wheel Glove	7.50	10.00
Air Scoops (non functional)	210.00	270.00
(a) With operating passenger compartment air exhaust	235.00	350.00
(b) Plus operating brake ducts	285.00	450.00

Although Pontiac decided to not move forward with John Fitch's modified Firebird, what might it have cost to upgrade your own Firebird with Fitch & Company components? This copy of an April 11, 1968, price list reveals the available options as well as kit costs and fully installed costs. At the top is a hand-written note from John Fitch to the original recipient.

This inter-organization letter is the earliest official correspondence to specifically discuss the 1969 Trans Am. Issued on November 11, 1968, it called for a meeting of departmental heads just days later to introduce the new GTO Judge and Firebird Trans Am. Signed by Bill Collins, he copied many individuals who are likely responsible for the Trans Am's existence, and whose names Pontiac fans likely immediately recognize.

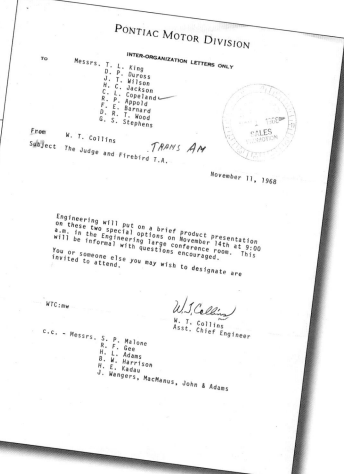

Remaining true to its performance image, Pontiac named its vehicles after popular racing venues such as Bonneville, Grand Prix, and Le Mans. The same approach was taken with the new Firebird package.

Aimed at competing in the SCCA Trans-Am racing series, Pontiac considered names such as Daytona and Sebring, but found other manufacturers had already used them. After much consideration of proposed names, including a marketing survey with consumers, many close to the project claim it was DeLorean who ultimately coined "Trans Am" in tribute to the Trans-Am racing series in which the Firebird was intended to compete. Thus, the Firebird Trans Am was born.

The earliest official document that refers to the "Firebird Trans Am" by name is an internal document from Bill Collins dated November 11, 1968. It invites Pontiac departmental heads and other key individuals to a high-level meeting on November 14 to introduce

PALADIUM SILVER PROTOTYPES

Although Pontiac was developing its WS4 Trans Am Option for the 1969 Firebird (the underpinnings were very much complete), decisions were needed on how to handle the exterior appearance. Initial plans called for availability in regular-production Firebird colors; accent stripes were not included. At least two Trans Am prototypes painted code-69 Paladium Silver were created for internal review. Upon program acceptance, Pontiac made the pair available to magazines for coverage about its new Firebird Trans Am. Both cars can be found in vintage road tests and both have unique stories.

The first Trans Am prototype was apparently modified by noted customizer Gene Winfield in advance of 1969 model year production, based on his proposal for the concept. John DeLorean had been interested in creating a customized Firebird using aftermarket components to partake in the success Ford was having with its Mustang and Shelby's bolt-on scoops and spoilers. It was a covert endeavor that DeLorean embarked upon to gain project momentum; and very likely a way to sidestep initial influence and/or protest from GM Styling.

In DeLorean's quest to secure a partnership with an outside company, he approached John Fitch in 1967. That resulted in the Fitch Firebird concept, which Pontiac compared internally against its own PFST. He reportedly sent California car customizer George Barris a pair of Firebirds to customize; the result is unknown. Cognizant of Gene Winfield's customizing skills, DeLorean commissioned him to tart-up a 1969 Firebird. That proposal eventually evolved into the 1969 Trans Am.

To conceptualize his ideas, Winfield relied on the talents of automotive designer Harry Bradley, a former employee at GM Styling during the mid-1960s who had spent time at Pontiac Studio. Bradley eventually left General Motors and Detroit to seek an independent venture in California and had worked with both Barris and Winfield in that capacity.

"Shelby was having great success installing its line of aftermarket components on Ford Mustangs," Bradley told me. "Gene was working with the AMT model kit company, designing customized parts for its scale model kits. Based on Shelby's success, AMT was considering expanding its line of customized kits to real cars as well. Gene hired me to develop design ideas for AMT and the Firebird was one of them. I developed hood scoops, air scoops, and a rear spoiler. He presumably presented them to Pontiac when they contacted him."

The components that Bradley created were dated May 1968, and Winfield shared the ideas with Pontiac immediately after that. DeLorean was pleased with Winfield's efforts and in June 1968, hired him to create fiberglass prototypes of the components that Bradley rendered. DeLorean flew Winfield to Pontiac in July to install the hand-crafted dual-scooped hood, front brake ducts, fender-mounted air extractors, and a large rear air spoiler onto a silver-painted pre-production 1969 Firebird 400 at the division's Engineering garage.

DeLorean was very pleased with the customized Firebird that Winfield presented. The prototype components were given to Pontiac Studio at GM Styling with

Special editions of a manufacturer's top performance cars were quite common during the late 1960s. Chevrolet's Z28 Camaro, Ford's Boss 302 Mustang, and Mercury's Cougar Eliminator were among the Firebird's competitors. When John DeLorean approved a special-model Firebird for 1969, he contracted customizer Gene Winfield to create an appearance package. Winfield's proposal strongly influenced the Firebird that became the Trans Am.

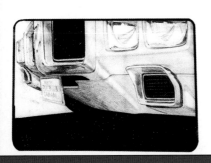

ADDITIONAL OPTIONS...
TOP LEFT: FIBERGLAS HOOD SWEEPS UP TO WINDSHIELD AREA & INCLUDES ~~NUMBER SHROUD~~ OUTSIDE TACH & FUNCTIONAL SCOOPS MOULDED INTO HOOD. BOTTOM LEFT AIR INTAKES COOL FRONT BRAKES. PARKING LAMPS HIDDEN BEHIND GRILL. ABOVE: STONE-THROW SHIELDS PROTECT LOWER BODY & MAKE SUPER WIDE OVALS ON REVERSED WHEELS LEGAL TOP RIGHT: NEAR CAR SHOWS 3-PIECE RING SPOILER—CENTER PART RISES WITH DECK LID & OUT-PORTIONS BOLT TO REAR FENDERS. FAR CAR SHOWS 1-PIECE RING SPOILER ON FIBER-GLAS DECK LID. NOTE THAT TAILLIGHTS ARE STACKED ONTOP OF EACH OTHER IN LARGE OPENINGS WHOSE SHAPE RE-FLECTS SPOILER. BOTTOM RIGHT: VARIOUS SCOOP THEMES ACCENTUATE BODY RECESSIONS, BLEND WITH THEM, OR COMPLETELY COVER THEM UP. ALL ITEMS ARE BOLT-ON & CAN BE FUNCTIONAL. FAR RIGHT TOP INTAKE HAS SAME READING AROUND OPENING AS SEEN AROUND REAR WHEEL OPENING. BOTTOM) INTAKE SEATBELTS HIGH VELOCITY BODY SHAPE BOTH INTAKES BOLT-ON & CAN BE FUNCTIONAL

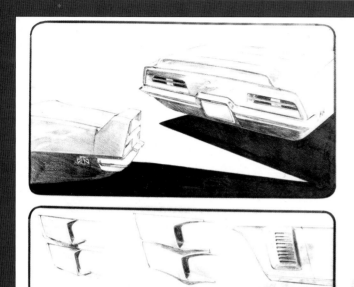

Gene Winfield asked former Pontiac designer Harry Bradley to sketch a host of add-on components and create storyboards for him in May 1968. Winfield presented them to Pontiac that summer. You can recognize the kinship of Winfield's concept to the Firebird that became the Trans Am. He told me he was asked to prepare a price quote should Pontiac choose to outsource production of the specialty equipment. Ultimately, production remained an internal process.

the request that designers ready them for in-house production to complete the visual cues of the Trans Am. The Firebird that Winfield modified appeared in at least two vintage magazine articles where it was presented as the new Trans Am. At that time, the silver coupe was equipped with black interior, 400-ci engine with Ram Air, and 4-speed manual transmission. No additional documentation has surfaced that suggests it survived. I presume that it was eventually destroyed.

When asked what influenced his ideas for the Firebird components, Bradley explained, "For a designer, influence is very broad. Scoops, spoilers, and ducts were typical of customized cars of that era, so using them on a customized Firebird wasn't really anything earth-shattering. I had previously worked on a Firebird project with George Barris and used those features on his car, and then Gene asked me to create a customized Firebird for him. It was only natural that I included all of the features you'd expect on a customized car."

The Barris Firebird that Bradley designed in December 1967 was for Peterson Publication's 1968 Super Teen promotion. In typical Barris fashion, practically each body panel of the giveaway 1968 Firebird was wildly customized and brightly painted and/or trimmed for maximum visual impact. Barris later offered the components from the Super Teen Firebird as a complete kit for dealership installation. Winfield's creation centered on aesthetics and functionality. With Bradley's background at GM Styling, it comes as no

surprise that his component ideas were tastefully designed and required only slight refining to reach production.

The second Paladium Silver prototype was modified by Pontiac and its Trans Am–specific components were

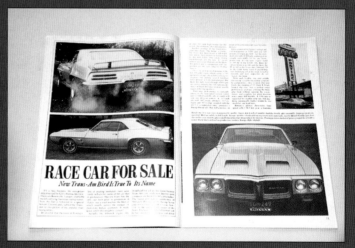

John DeLorean invited Gene Winfield to Pontiac's Engineering garage during the summer of 1968 and provided him with a silver 1969 Firebird 400 on which to install formed fiberglass panels based on his proposed body modifications. After the components were approved, the modified Winfield vehicle was presented to at least two magazines to road test as the new 1969 Firebird Trans Am. Car Craft *wrote about it and the GTO Judge in its March 1969 issue. The April 1969 issue of* Dragstrip *magazine (shown) contains several clear and detailed photos of that car.*

PALADIUM SILVER PROTOTYPES CONTINUED

Pontiac assembled a second Firebird with productionized Trans Am Option components that was campaigned as a Trans Am prototype and was made available to magazine writers. It was on hand at the December 8, 1968, press preview at Riverside International Raceway. The whereabouts of the Winfield-modified Firebird is unknown and it was presumably destroyed, but the second Trans Am prototype was discovered and restored. It remains in private hands today.

practically identical to those released for production. Uncirculated press photos from the GTO Judge and Firebird Trans Am media preview that occurred in Riverside, California, in December 1968, confirm that it and at least one other Trans Am in a traditional paint scheme were present. The Paladium Silver Trans Am appeared in several magazines after that day, and reports indicate that it was equipped with black interior, Ram Air IV engine, and automatic transmission.

There had been no trace of the second prototype for more than 40 years until hobbyist Curt Richards spied an interesting 1969 Firebird on eBay while searching for a suitable candidate to build as a race car in 2010. "The car was located in Kentucky but had spent at least 30 years in California," he told me. "It was advertised as a loaded 1969 Firebird used in the L.A. Auto Show. Although in rough shape, it was rather complete and had many of the unique Trans Am components, so I began researching the car and ordered a copy of its invoice from PHS Automotive Services. I noticed the handwritten notes and recognized its similarity to the silver test car in vintage articles. That's when I began piecing it all together."

With painstaking research and the help of Jim Mattison at PHS Automotive Services, Curt confirmed the Firebird's

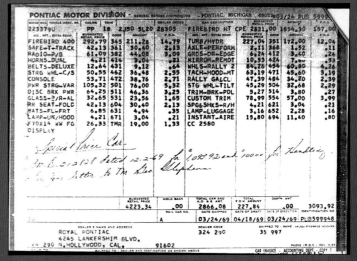

The dealer invoice for the second Trans Am prototype reveals that it began life as a fully loaded Firebird 400 designated for display. The handwritten note confirms that it was sold at a discounted price to Royal Pontiac in the Los Angeles, California, area. The presence of Trans Am–specific body equipment led Pontiac enthusiast Curt Richards to question its possible authenticity as a genuine Trans Am. After diligent detective work, I can state that it indeed is the second prototype. The VIN was digitally removed from the photo for security purposes.

authenticity as a Trans Am prototype. Its cowl-mounted data tag states that it was produced in late October 1968 at the Lordstown plant and its invoice reveals that it was originally built as a Firebird 400 coupe loaded with options. After its tenure as a press vehicle, Royal Pontiac in Hollywood, California, sold it on December 2, 1969, for the discounted sum of $2,000. Curt reports that noted SCCA racer Jerry Titus was the Firebird's original owner and he used it not only as a racer but also a mule for testing. His family sold the Firebird a short time later and it remained in obscurity until Curt located it.

I am able to further confirm the authenticity of the Palladium Silver Firebird as the second Trans Am prototype. One of the aforementioned uncirculated photos lends a clear view of the test car's data tag. Comparing it to that of Curt's Firebird, the two cars undeniably share the identical body number. The prototype car was expertly restored by Supercar Specialties in Portland, Michigan, in 2014 and was reintroduced to Pontiac hobbyists at the Muscle Car and Corvette National show held in Chicago, Illinois, in November of that year.

	THE JUDGE WT-1	TRANS AM WS-4
Suspension	Standard GTO	HD Springs & Shocks
Stabilizer Bar	Standard GTO	Heavy 1" with High Density Bushings
Axle	Standard Axle - 3.55 Ratio	Standard Axle - 3.55 Ratio
Brakes	Standard GTO	High Effort Power Disc
Brake Scoops		Fiberglass on Front Fenders
Engine	'69 Ram Air - 400 CID 366 HP	'69 Ram Air - 400 CID 335 HP
Opt. Engine	'69 Ram Air IV 400 CID 370 HP	'69 Ram Air IV 400 CID 345 HP
Transmission	3 Speed H.D. Standard With Hurst Tee Handle 4 Speed THM with 5200 rpm Shifts	3 Speed H.D. Standard 4 Speed THM with 4800 rpm Shifts THM with 5200 rpm Shifts with Ram Air IV
Steering	Standard GTO	High Effort Variable Ratio Power
Steering Wheel	Standard GTO	Simulated Leather (Vinyl)
Wheels	Rally II - No Trim Rings	Standard Firebird
Tires	G70 Polyglas (Black)	Standard Firebird
Hood	Standard GTO Ram Air	Aluminum with Longer Scoops
Grille	Black	Standard Firebird (Consider Black)
Air Foil	Floating Rear Deck	Floating Rear Deck
Identification	Ram Air Decal on Side of Hood Scoops "The Judge" on Front Fenders Three Color Vinyl Stripe on Upper Edge of Front Fender Door and Quarter	"Trans Am" Fender Name Plates Ram Air Decal on Side of Hood Scoops
Exterior Colors	Standard GTO	Standard Firebird
	DEC 15TH	JAN 30 11-14-68

At the introductory meeting that Bill Collins held on November 14, 1968, to discuss the WT1 GTO Judge and WS4 Firebird Trans Am option packages, this list containing the major components of each option was distributed to the attendees. Although equipment for the Judge had been sorted out, the list included several production variances from those listed for the Trans Am. Handwritten dates at the bottom suggested anticipated production startup.

the Division's newest options: GTO Judge and Firebird Trans Am. On that day, Collins outlined the equipment included in each package and its anticipated release date. An accompanying information sheet reveals that the Trans Am's basic content was very much defined by that point and its anticipated release date was January 30, 1969.

At the time of Collins' memo, Pontiac assigned UPC WS4 to the Trans Am Option and planned to offer it in any of the Firebird's 18 regular-production colors, and it even went so far as to issue 18 individual part numbers for the Trans Am's colored rear air spoiler. At least two Palladium Silver prototypes were built for testing, but Herb Adams also pushed for a scheme consisting of traditional American racing colors (white with blue accents) like the mules of the PFST project. "We were trying to inject racing flavor into the Trans Am model, and I always felt the white and blue combination went well together. I used it on a lot of my own cars and figured, 'Why not?' on the Trans Am, too," he said.

Pontiac sent GM Styling several prototype exterior components that it envisioned for its 1969 Trans Am that were presumably hand-crafted by customizer Gene Winfield. It was Pontiac Studio's job to design the components for production in a manner that would satisfy Pontiac and receive approval from Bill Mitchell, who headed GM Styling. "I wish I could say I was more involved, but my assistant, Wayne Vieira, was very much on top of the Trans Am project, and unfortunately he's no longer with us," said Bill Porter, who was promoted to chief designer at

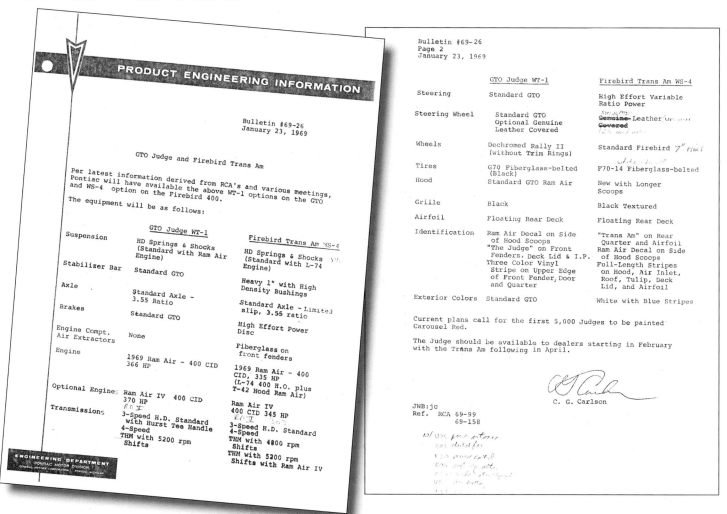

With the GTO Judge just reaching production, Pontiac released Product Engineering Bulletin 69-26 on January 23, 1969. The two-page document was an internal resource simplifying the details of the standard WT1 GTO Judge and WS4 Firebird Trans Am packages as well as major options. Handwritten notes were made as the packages were revised after the print date. One references the Ram Air V and 303 as optional Trans Am engines.

Pontiac Studio in February 1968. He oversaw finalization of the exterior features of the Trans Am Option. "I do recall making some contributions to the fender-mounted air extractors and forming the rear spoiler some to better integrate them. It was relatively minor, however."

As the Trans Am raced toward production, Adams persevered with his rendition, which included a white body with a pair of blue accent stripes that spanned across the body and ended with a blue-painted tail panel. Pontiac Studio recognized the color scheme's racing connection, took Adams' lead, and styled it for production so that each 5.25-inch blue stripe was accented with a .125-inch blue pinstripe on each side. Making it the only available treatment with the Trans Am Option not only aided production in the assembly plants, it also allowed consumers to immediately identify the racy, low-volume Firebird on the road.

The original drawing that details the exterior ornamentation of the 1969 Trans Am Option was dated January 16, 1969, and it clearly indicates that the decision had been made for a Cameo White body trimmed with Tyrol Blue. Pontiac issued internal Product Engineering Information Bulletin 69-26 on January 23, 1969, which outlined the near-finalized contents of the new GTO Judge and Firebird Trans Am packages. The bulletin points out that Trans Am color choice had been changed to include a white body with blue accent striping and tail panel. It also noted that planned availability had been pushed back to April 1969.

WS4 Trans Am Option was available only on the Firebird 400, and Pontiac went to great lengths to further improve on its ride and handling to give Trans Am buyers the feel of driving a real race car. In addition to the Firebird 400's already heavy-duty springs and shocks, and F70-14 tires with 7-inch-wide rims, engineers added a number of special components unique to the Trans Am. They have direct lineage to the 400-powered PFST built in midyear 1968.

To limit roll control in the turns, Pontiac pirated a 1-inch-diameter front sway bar (number-3958466) from Chevrolet's parts system. According to the description in internal information, it was accompanied by "high-density" bushings. I scoured through a number of factory sources to determine exactly what "high-density" meant and how such bushings differed from the standard production piece. The drawings for each component that I discovered explain the term.

The Trans Am sway bar frame bushing (number-3994335) was constructed of SAE J200–spec rubber. It was common to many non–F-car applications wherever a 1-inch bar was available, not only Trans Am. The control arm shaft bushings were also standard Firebird equipment. Unique for the 1969 Trans Am, however, was its sway bar end link grommet (number-9794854).

Developed in June 1968, the off-white bushing was constructed of cast urethane, which more than doubled the tensile strength of the standard rubber grommet found on all other Firebirds. It worked in concert to maximize the effectiveness of steering wheel input and reduce oversteer, particularly when cornering on rough pavement. The urethane bushing was a Trans Am exclusive for 1969, but vintage parts manuals reveal that it was also used in certain GTO applications in subsequent years.

Although rear sway bars have been available from the aftermarket for several years, Pontiac never factory-installed a rear sway bar onto the first-generation Firebird. According to former Pontiac engineer Herb Adams, it was certainly a detriment. "The Trans Am was a car designed to maximize handling but no one at Pontiac would buy into the idea of giving it a rear bar. We got it to corner as best as we could, but it really needed a rear sway bar to make it an exceptional handler," he explained.

High-effort power steering was among the many standard features noted in Trans Am marketing materials. Although the power steering pump assembly was common to all 1969 Firebirds equipped with the N41 Power Steering option, the actual Saginaw 800-series power steering gear was unique. Beginning with the Firebird's standard unit equipped with a variable ratio ranging from 16.1 to 12.4:1, Pontiac

Pontiac engineers worked hard to give the Trans Am a handling package of its own. In addition to a high-effort steering box, heavy-duty springs and shocks, and a 1-inch-thick front sway bar, Pontiac specified a hard nylon sway bar end link grommet in place of the standard rubber piece. Whereas the rubber deflected under load, the nylon's resistance to deflection allowed the Trans Am to respond quicker to driver input.

The Trans Am Option included power brakes with front discs as standard equipment. Although its master cylinder is the same as any other similarly equipped Firebird, its unique power brake booster offered high pedal effort much like that associated with a real race car. Pontiac was certainly ahead of its time in making its Trans Am look and feel as authentic as possible.

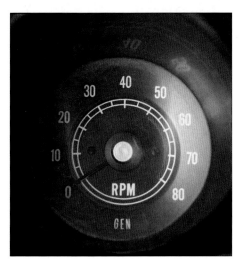

Although UB5 Hood-Mounted Tachometer had been a popular option with buyers in previous years, Pontiac realized that its location (where the delicate electronics were subjected to engine vibrations and harsh operating conditions) wasn't ideal for longevity and began developing an instrument package mounted within the dash. About the same time as the Trans Am Option was released for production, U30 Rally Gauge Cluster with Instrument Panel Tachometer was also released. It featured an 8,000-rpm tachometer with 5,100-rpm redline in the left gauge pod.

engineers worked with Saginaw to add high-effort valving, which increased road feel and added stability during high-speed conditions. The box (number-7807056) was limited to the Trans Am and included the heavy-duty cooling pipe regardless of rear axle ratio.

Certain documents reveal that the Trans Am was equipped with front disc brakes and high-effort power

Preliminary information on WS4 Trans Am Option makes reference to its scooped hood being made of stamped aluminum. It's unclear if that statement was correct, and Pontiac initially planned to give the Trans Am a lightweight hood, or if it was a simple mistake. Regardless, the unique production hood was constructed of stamped steel. It featured wide air scoops on the leading edge, which were fully functional and more efficient than those of the standard 400 hood. The scoops had no effect on horsepower ratings, however.

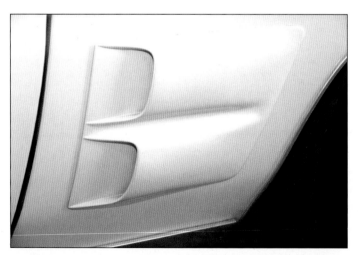

The Trans Am Option included a pair of functional side scoops referred to as "air extractors" that were mounted behind the front tire on each fender. Beneath each attractively sculpted duct is a corresponding hole in the fender that actually relieves the engine compartment of air trapped at speed to reduce nose lift and promotes circulation to reduce engine compartment temperature in all conditions.

assist. Upon further investigation, it was determined that though the master cylinder was common to any 1969 Firebird equipped with disc brakes, the Trans Am's vacuum booster (number-5469413) was unique. According to a Delco document, with 100 pounds of input pressure applied through the brake pedal, the typical Firebird booster generated 465 to 545 pounds of output. That same input to the Trans Am's booster generated just 245 to 285 pounds. The result was much greater pedal effort, which translated into predictable braking control at high speed. The difference was accomplished with internal valving and how quickly the vacuum reserve vented to the atmosphere.

The Trans Am exterior included a beautifully styled, stamped-steel hood (number-546016) that featured dual inlet scoops on the leading edge, which routed outside air to the carburetor through a sealed air cleaner. Because of the complexity of the hood's substructure, UB5 Hood-Mounted Tachometer wasn't offered as a factory-installed option on the 1969 Trans Am. Instead, Pontiac developed and released U30 Rally Gauge Cluster with Instrument

As the features and components of the Trans Am were finalized, Pontiac engineer Dan Hardin was tasked with determining the exact angle and height at which the rear spoiler generated maximum downforce. He obtained a section of spoiler from Styling and mounted it to the deck lid of a 1968 PFST. By cleverly connecting it to an electric seat motor mounted under the deck lid, he could change the "angle of attack" while the car was in motion. A passenger then measured the effects from within the car using precision equipment. Hardin snapped this photograph during a testing session.

The blue accent striping of the Trans Am Option ran over the roof and onto the deck lid where it blended into a color-coordinated rear body panel. Original documentation states that the spoiler body was to be free of striping, but that its stanchions were to be painted blue. It's hard to imagine that any original owner wanted to equip his or her new Trans Am with a Cordova top, but at least six were produced with the optional roof covering. Although this particular 1969 Trans Am is certainly not flawless, it's original and in unrestored condition with relatively low mileage. It provided a treasure trove of original details.

Panel Tachometer with Trans Am buyers in mind. About a third added it to their order. A dealer-installed hood-mounted tachometer kit (number-988662) remained available. Although some owners went that route, none were ever factory installed.

Although the fender-mounted louvers found on typical 1969 Firebirds are strictly ornamental, the Trans Am's air extractors are functional. They were among the last components designed for the Trans Am. I have been told that a handful of pre-production samples may have been constructed of cast metal, but those intended for production were constructed of formed fiberglass, and the original component drawing confirms it. The extractor openings coincide with square piercings in the fender skin, giving hot air trapped within the engine compartment an escape path. Although definitely functional, the actual effectiveness of the aerodynamic-appearing side scoops may be negligible.

There are reports of 1969 Trans Am fenders that were not pierced and claims of others with circular openings for extractor venting. It's believed that all original 1969 Trans Am fenders were equipped with rectangular-shaped piercings, and

When equipped with the Trans Am Option, overall body shape didn't vary widely from a typical 1969 Firebird 400 in Cameo White. The accent stripes were painted on during assembly and enhanced the race car theme. Factory documentation reveals that the intended color was Tyrol Blue, a hue last used by Pontiac as a standard exterior color in 1967.

the area around them was painted black. It's possible that Pontiac revised the piercing process when creating service replacement panels as the year progressed and/or removed it entirely, whether purposely or erroneously. It's also quite possible that there may have been a small run of reproductions at one time that may have lacked some details of the originals.

A rear air spoiler (number-9794877) spanning the entire width of the body (designed to provide aerodynamic benefit for the 1969 Trans Am) was among the first features approved for production, and that occurred

Despite the fact that the front end went unchanged, the forward scoops positioned on the leading edge of the hood gave Firebirds equipped with WS4 Trans Am Option a dramatically changed appearance. Developed by former GM designer Harry Bradley for customizer Gene Winfield, who was contracted by Pontiac to propose an appearance package, the positioning increased the scoops' functionality as it placed them in a high-pressure area created by air passing over the nose. (Photo Courtesy Larry Delay)

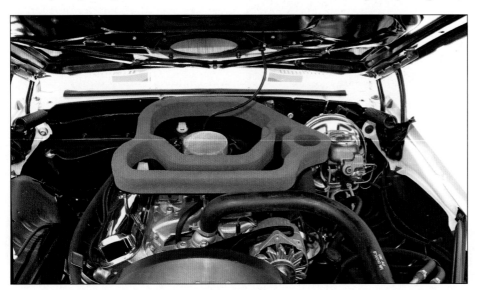

in August 1968. Constructed of rigid urethane foam, its drawing indicates that initial plans called for the entire spoiler to be painted body color. The drawing was revised on February 7, 1969, however, and instructed that the spoiler body now be painted Cameo White with the stanchions in Tyrol Blue. Although some pre-production Trans Ams may have contained blue accent striping on the spoiler body, too, it apparently never actually occurred during regular production.

The Trans Am rear air spoiler was released in October 1968 as a dealer-installed accessory under part number 988708 for regular 1969 Firebirds. At a cost of about $75 plus installation, the kit was comprised of the spoiler, deck lid torsion rods, all associated mounting hardware, and an instructional installation sheet. It's unclear if the spoiler kit was released early or held back until Trans Am production began. Also, there's no telling how many kits were installed onto 1969 Firebirds at the dealer level, but factory installation was limited to Trans Am.

A popular vintage modification that continues today is the addition of the attractive Camaro "ducktail" rear spoiler to first-generation Firebirds. The original drawing for 988708 confirms that it included the Pontiac Trans Am spoiler. To my knowledge, Pontiac never recognized or offered the Chevrolet spoiler through its parts department for Firebird, but any GM dealer could have simply ordered one based on owner request.

Although SCCA rules limited maximum displacement to 305 ci for competition eligibility and Pontiac was actively developing a small-cube race engine for such applications, the division also understood that most buyers would never road-race their Firebird. Its performance image required a brawny base engine that packed plenty of punch on the street. The venerable L74 400 H.O. with Ram Air induction rated at 335 hp was made standard equipment and the 345-hp L67 Ram Air IV was the up-level performance option

The rules of vehicle eligibility for the SCCA Trans-Am series limited engine displacement to a maximum of 305 ci, but Pontiac's Trans Am Option on the Firebird 400 included the 400 H.O. with Ram Air induction rated at 335 hp as standard equipment. The functional Ram Air varied from that of the Firebird 400 in that no manual cable operation was required for fresh-air entry. The 345-hp Ram Air IV was available as an extra-cost option.

Pontiac began detailing the equipment comprising the Trans Am Option, which had been coded with UPC WS4, to dealership sales staffs in early February 1969. This particular bulletin, CDB 69-69, dated March 5, 1969, outlines a series of revisions and/or additions from that issued barely a month earlier and they are noted with an asterisk. It's evident that Pontiac was working feverishly to finalize Trans Am Option content with only the most appropriate equipment aimed at maximum functionality and unique visibility. The Trans Am was introduced to the buying public a few days later.

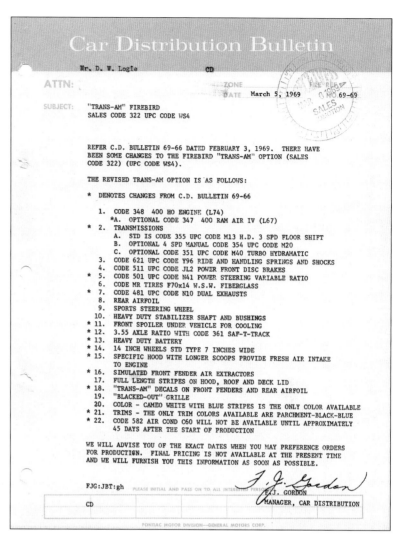

to ensure dragstrip superiority. At least one other engine intended for competition conformity was under development. (You'll learn more about it later in this chapter.)

The M13 heavy-duty 3-speed manual transmission was standard equipment with the Trans Am Option and the M20 Muncie 4-speed manual or M40 Turbo-400 automatic were available at extra cost. The Pontiac-built rear axle with heavy-duty, limited-slip differential and 3.55:1 rear axle ratio was also standard equipment regardless of transmission choice. The rear axle ratio dropped to 3.23:1 whenever C60 Air Conditioning was ordered. It jumped to 3.90:1 (and the M21 Muncie 4-speed was automatically included at extra cost) whenever the L67 Ram Air IV engine was chosen. No other gear ratios or combinations were available.

Trans Am's Formal Introductions

Pontiac introduced the GTO Judge and Firebird Trans Am in midyear 1969. Although they were released months apart, the division took the opportunity to present both in a single media preview. Scores of magazines were invited to view, photograph, and test these performance examples at Riverside International Raceway in Riverside, California, on December 8, 1968. At least two 1969 Trans Ams were present: one painted Paladium Silver (see sidebar "Paladium Silver Prototypes") and a second in the traditional Cameo White with a blue accent scheme.

Pontiac chose the 1969 Chicago Auto Show to formally introduce the new Trans Am to the buying public. Beginning on March 8, 1969, at Chicago's International Amphitheater, a 1969 Trans Am in Cameo White with Tyrol Blue accents was

Magazine writers were introduced to the GTO Judge and Firebird Trans Am at a press preview held at California's Riverside International Raceway in December 1968. The time frame was purposely chosen so that a published editorial reached consumers about the same time that the Trans Am made its public debut. The resultant articles echoed that Trans Am's 400-inch engine was its greatest downfall. It packed plenty of punch, but couldn't compete in the racing series from which it gleaned its name. Pontiac was, however, working to change that. (Photo Courtesy General Motors)

The Chicago Auto Show is considered among the most prestigious and highly attended new-car expositions in the Midwest. Its mid–model year timing makes it an ideal venue for manufacturers that want to introduce new vehicles for the spring selling season. Pontiac chose this venue to introduce its highly successful Firebird line in 1967, and the same event was chosen to host the introduction of the 1969 Firebird Trans Am. The new Trans Am was placed front and center in Pontiac's display, where it generated much traffic when it opened to the public on March 8, 1969. (Photo Courtesy Chicago Auto Show)

displayed for more than a week. The industry buzzed about the newest entry into the sports car market. Not-so-coincidently, magazine coverage from Pontiac's December 1968 media preview in California reached mailboxes and newsstands about the same time. "Trans Am" quickly became a hip word in all consumer media.

Burdette Martin, eventual chief steward of the SCCA Trans-Am racing series, told me that he remembers attending the 1969 Chicago Auto Show and seeing the Firebird Trans Am on display. "I drove Pontiacs and really liked the idea of the car and was excited to see it. I thought it was terrific looking and Pontiac really made sure it wasn't just another Camaro, but I remember being disappointed that a 400 was the only engine available. I thought it was crazy that a car with the Trans Am name wouldn't be able to run in a Trans-Am race!"

Martin felt the publicity of a car named Trans Am was good for the SCCA, but he also remembers the concerns of some SCCA directors when it was first learned that Pontiac was using the organization's Trans-Am name without proper approval. "Other manufacturers were paying the SCCA to use names it held rights to and as I remember, Tracy Bird, who was running Trans-Am series at the time, brought that to Pontiac's attention." The result was a licensing agreement with General Motors that was backdated to an effective date of January 1, 1969. General Motors provided the SCCA with a $5.00 stipend for each Firebird Trans Am that Pontiac sold.

The immense amount of media coverage on the new Trans Am made it an overnight superstar on the performance car scene. Most praised the overall improvement

NEWS FROM PONTIAC

Pontiac Motor Division of General Motors + Public Relations Department + Telephone (313) 332-8111 | Pontiac, Mich. 48053

FOR RELEASE Friday, March 7, 1969

CHICAGO--On the eve of the opening of the 61st annual Chicago Automobile Show, Pontiac Motor Division introduced a new high performance Firebird called the Trans Am.

In the Pontiac tradition of building cars which offer the ultimate in performance while providing excellent everyday driving characteristics, the Trans Am will have outstanding mechanical and styling distinctiveness.

F. James McDonald, Pontiac's new general manager, said the Trans Am will be on display at the Chicago show and will go on sale next month.

As with The Judge, a new super GTO, which was unveiled by Pontiac earlier this year, the Trans Am will "go performance one step better."

The most striking styling feature of the new Trans Am will be a floating 60-inch air foil spanning the rear deck. The car also features a special hood with full length, functional hood scoops and functional air outlets behind the front wheel openings for added engine compartment cooling.

The Trans Am, according to McDonald, will be available as a hardtop and convertible.

Striping will run the full length of the car over the hood, roof, rear deck and air foil. The rear end panel will be painted to match the striping.

(more)

On the eve of the Trans Am's public debut at the Chicago Auto Show, Pontiac issued this press release to explain the features and benefits of its newest Firebird. It was also distributed to media outlets; attached to it was a glossy 8 x 10–inch press photo so that any news stories printed about its release could have an image to accompany it. In vintage newspapers, the 1969 Trans Am was certainly a hot topic.

that WS4 Trans Am Option provided over a typical Firebird 400 for spirited street driving and, recognized its ability to provide Corvette-like performance and handling while carrying four passengers. Some writers shared Martin's sentiment toward its ineligibility with the SCCA and its Trans-Am racing venue, however. "They didn't complain about us using Grand Prix and LeMans on Pontiacs that weren't even close to being able to compete in those forms of racing, but some criticized the Trans Am because of it. I think that's because we had a car right from the factory that had all the necessary equipment, but its engine was too big," remarked Ben Harrison.

Despite the coverage, it took several months for Trans Ams to begin arriving at Pontiac dealerships. The examples on hand for the media preview in California, at the Chicago Auto Show, and in Pontiac's publicity photos were hand-built prototypes assembled in the division's Engineering garage. For reasons presently unknown, actual Trans Am production was delayed several weeks after its formal introduction in early March. That could be related to component procurement and/or issues within the assembly plants preparing to install the new package.

Production Begins

Pontiac knew by February 3, 1969, when it issued CDB 69-66, which explained to dealers WS4 Trans Am Option content and described the order process, that Trans Am production would be limited to the Norwood, Ohio, and Van Nuys, California, assembly plants. April 1 remained the anticipated date for production startup,

and with Firebird production at the Lordstown plant transferred to Norwood by that point, it seems Pontiac had no intentions of ever building a single Trans Am at Lordstown. Some hobbyists believe that a handful of Lordstown-built Trans Ams exist, but a VIN or any documentation to support it has yet to surface.

When Trans Am production finally began in May 1969, the Van Nuys plant had been shut down by a labor strike weeks before. That left Norwood as the only assembly plant producing Firebirds for several weeks during the middle of the model year. The first Trans Am to roll off the Norwood line (VIN 223379N101553) was built on May 21, 1969, and it was placed into service as a company car a few days later. The next three Norwood-built Trans Ams received similar treatment.

June proved to be the most productive month for Trans Am volume with 257 units built. Norwood began filling initial orders and vehicles began hitting dealer lots and reaching customer hands by the month's end. As the pipeline filled, Trans Am production declined in July, and it remained fairly steady for the next several months. The last Trans Am (VIN 223379N119864) was built during the final days of 1969 Firebird production at Norwood, which formally ended on November 10, 1969. In total, the Norwood plant produced 677 Firebirds with WS4 Trans Am Option, and that includes 8 convertibles.

When production resumed at Van Nuys in mid-June 1969, vehicles stopped in progress were finished and only a handful of new Firebird orders were processed. Among them were 20 Trans Ams that were produced, finished, and shipped from Van Nuys on the same day, July

The restyled Firebird for 1969 was quite attractive, but the Trans Am Option added even greater flair and style. The grilles remained trimmed in silver, but the tight mesh texture was painted black. The forward scoops not only added to the Firebird's race-ready aggressiveness, the location and size increased their efficiency when compared to those of the Firebird 400.

To enhance the Trans Am's theme as an aerodynamic sports car, the die-cast "Firebird" badges otherwise found on the leading edge of each front fender were removed. In their place went no-drag "Trans Am" decals that remained flush with the exterior. The decal was color-coordinated to remain consistent with the overall paint scheme.

1969 TRANS AM PRICING

When the Firebird Trans Am made its public debut at the Chicago Auto Show in early March 1969, pricing for WS4 Trans Am Option hadn't been finalized. Consumers left the event with no idea what Pontiac's new supercar would cost. Just days before the car went into production, CDB 69-78 was issued on May 15, 1969, containing the information many potential buyers sought. WS4 package pricing was in addition to the cost of an entry-level Firebird with a basic OHC-6 engine, which was $2,759 for a hardtop and $2,989 for a convertible.

Although a single option representing about 40 percent of a vehicle's selling price could deter passive customers, the pricing of WS4 Trans Am Option also included the cost of W66 Firebird 400 Option, JL2 Power Front Disc Brakes, N41 Variable-Ratio Power Steering, and G83 Safe-T-Track differential. Those options alone were several hundred dollars. In the end, consumers really spent just $441.28 for the special equipment that transformed a Firebird 400 into a Trans Am. Only when viewing it from that perspective does WS4 Trans Am Option seem a real bargain.

Pontiac recognized this too, because Trans Am package pricing on dealer invoices (like that available from PHS Automotive Services) ranges from $1,082.68 to $1,182.74 depending on ancillary equipment. The window sticker, a document most consumers see, simplifies it somewhat, however. It listed and priced W66, JL2, N41, and G83 individually. The remaining components unique to WS4 Trans Am Option are grouped together at a single cost of $441.28. The sum of the components totals exactly what is on the invoices.

The invoice cost of WS4 Trans Am Option was lowered by $26.32 in mid-September 1969. The cost reduction was implemented on September 18, 1968, when Pontiac published 1970 model year pricing, which included fiberglass tires as standard equipment on all models.

Although the 1969 Firebird had been introduced to the public two months prior, pricing of WS4 Trans Am Option hadn't been finalized. The earliest announcement about package pricing was contained in CDB 69-78 issued on May 15, 1969. It varied greatly depending on ancillary equipment, and that made pricing quite confusing.

WS4 Package Pricing

Hardtop with standard M13 3-speed transmission	$1,182.74
Convertible with standard M13 3-speed transmission	$1,166.94
Hardtop with M20/M21 4-speed or M40 automatic, plus transmission	$1,098.48
Convertible with M20/M21 4-speed or M40 automatic, plus transmission	$1,082.68

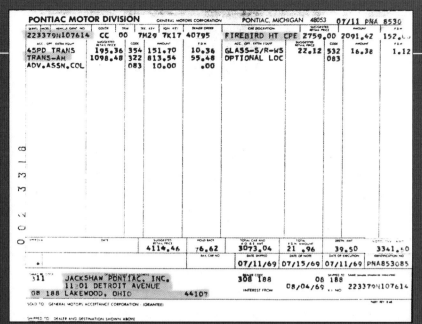

The base price of the carryover 1969 Firebird increased to $2,853 that same day, and a portion of that reflected the upcharge for fiberglass tires. The Trans Am package originally included fiberglass tires in its cost, but the tire option was now wrapped into base pricing of the carryover 1969 Firebird, so the price of WS4 Trans Am Option dropped by the amount that fiberglass tires previously cost, $26.32.

When comparing dealer invoices of 1969 Firebirds, there is an anomaly in the consistency of WS4 Trans Am Option package pricing seemingly unrelated to ancillary options. The most common Trans Am price was $1,098.48 for a hardtop model equipped with an extra-cost 4-speed manual or automatic transmission. The price at that level was reduced toward the end of the 1969 Firebird model year.

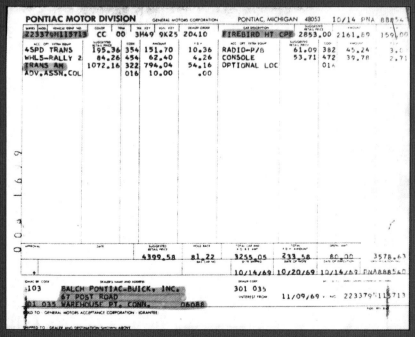

New equipment made standard on 1970 Pontiacs as well as the carryover 1969 Firebird increased the Firebird's base cost. Fiberglass tires were included in the WS4 Trans Am Option package during the 1969 model year and became standard on Firebirds at 1970 model year startup. That allowed a price reduction for the Trans Am package. It started at $1,098.48 and was reduced to $1,072.16 in September 1969.

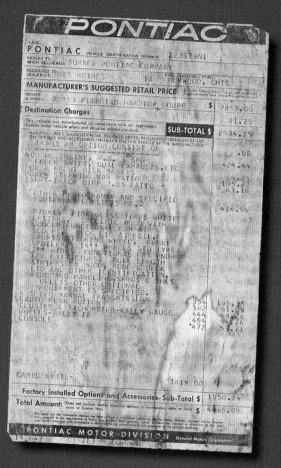

Pontiac enthusiast Richard Forbes was lucky enough to find his Trans Am's original window sticker with the vehicle when he purchased it a few years ago. Legibility is difficult, but Pontiac's vintage window stickers were never intended to survive into posterity. This can only be one of a handful of originals left and provides a detailed look into how Pontiac billed its 1969 Trans Am to consumers.

The epitome of rarity and value is no better exemplified within the Pontiac hobby than with the 1969 Firebird Trans Am convertible. Just eight were produced and availability then seemed to require some sort of connection. All eight have been accounted for. Present value of an example like this is well into the seven-figure range.

7, 1969. Their VINs span less than 400 units. The first was 223379L118850 and the last was 223379L119242. All but one was powered by the standard L74 400 H.O. engine.

Production Facts

It's unclear what delayed Trans Am production from the anticipated start date of April 1 until late-May, but we know that 697 were produced during the 1969 model year. The data in Appendix C was taken directly from monthly Pontiac production records and reflect the number of 1969 Trans Ams produced each month during its production run. This is the first time such information has been published.

Although Chapter 4 included a variety of production totals for all 1969 Firebirds, and Trans Am was included, a detailed equipment breakdown for the 697 Trans Ams produced during the 1969 model year has floated among hobbyists for years. The information was hand-collated by Fred Simmonds, a Pontiac employee who spent hours poring over 1969 Trans Am invoices.

A total of 642 Trans Ams were equipped with the standard L74 400 H.O. engine during the 1969 model year. The standard M13 heavy-duty 3-speed manual transmission was installed into just 15 of them, and only 1 was built at Van Nuys. The M20 Muncie 4-speed was far and away the most popular transmission, installed in

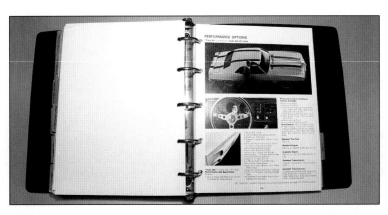

On May 23, 1969, Pontiac distributed an update to its 1969 Sales Manual that outlined the appearance and features of the new WS4 Trans Am Option. The preliminary slick was intended for insertion into the manual's Special Equipment section. Because it was distributed before actual vehicle production began, it's not surprising to find that it contained at least a couple of inaccuracies. The exterior photo depicting the body-length racing stripes showed them extending onto the spoiler while the interior photo included a photo of what we know today was a prototype of the Formula Steering Wheel that was being readied for production.

The interior of Firebirds equipped with the Trans Am Option was typical model line fare without any related enhancements. Basic interior was standard and W54 Custom Interior was available as an extra-cost option. Preliminary sales information states that color availability was limited to Black, Blue, and Parchment. At least a handful of others received Gold, Green, and Red interiors.

A total of 131 Trans Ams were produced during the 1969 model year with the optional M40 Turbo-400 automatic transmission. A column-mounted shifter was standard and a few cars were produced with it, including 3 with the L67 Ram Air IV engine. Most automatic cars were equipped with D55 Front Console, however, and that relocated the shifter to the floor. The Rally Sports Speed Shifter featured dual-gate operation that prevented mistakenly over-shifting into the next gear.

A floor-mounted shifter was standard equipment whenever a Firebird 400 was equipped with a manual transmission, and WS4 Trans Am Option did not deviate from this. Without the optional D55 Front Console, the Hurst shifter protruded from the floor and it was adorned only by a rubber boot and chromed trim plate. A round shift knob was also standard with M09 Custom Gear Shift Knob. Simulated woodgrain texturing was an option. Manual transmission choices included M13 heavy-duty 3-speed, M20 Muncie 4-speed, and M21 Muncie 4-speed.

the option was available throughout the entire production run.

Contrary to what some references claim, C60 Air Conditioning was indeed available on the 1969 Trans Am. It was, however, limited to the L74 400 H.O. Whenever a car was equipped with the $375.99 option, a 3.23:1 rear axle ratio and a two-pinion limited-slip differential accompanied it no matter the transmission choice. An internal memo notes that C60 availability would be delayed for approximately 45 days after production startup, but records I've located reveal that the first one wasn't produced until August 1969.

505 L74-powered cars, while the M40 Turbo-400 went into 122.

Although other performance engines were considered, the L67 Ram Air IV was the Trans Am's only optional mill, priced at $389.68 extra. It was installed into 55 Trans Ams. All were equipped with 3.90:1 rear axle gearing. Nine were backed by the M40 Turbo-400; 46 received the optional M21 Muncie 4-speed. All but 1 of the 55 were assembled at Norwood, and based on the VINs of the first and last Ram Air IV Trans Ams produced,

A total of 31 Trans Ams were equipped with C60 during the 1969 model year, and all were built at the Norwood plant. Including the first, 23 were backed by the M40 Turbo-400 automatic and 8, including the last, were teamed with the M20 Muncie 4-speed. Eleven of the C60-equipped Trans Ams were also equipped with U30 Rally Gauge Cluster with Instrument Panel Tachometer.

At least one 1969 Trans Am equipped with C60 was loaded with additional options. Built at Norwood during

June 4, 1969   P.S.B. 69-66

1969 FIREBIRD TRANS AM OPTION PRICES

Prices have been released for the 1969 Firebird Trans Am Option, Sales Code 322. Included in the Option is the following required equipment:

	M.S.R.P.
400 Cu. In. Ram Air Engine, H.D. 3-Spd Floor Shift, Manual Transmission	$ 508.70
Special High-Effort Power Front Disc Brakes . . .	64.25
Special High-Effort Variable Ratio Power Steering	105.32
H.D. Safe-T-Track Differential, 3.55 Axle Ratio .	63.19

Other performance and specific equipment consists of:

. F70 x 14 White - Lettered Fiberglass Belted Tires
. Special Hood with Longer Functional Air Scoops
. Deck Lid Airfoil
. Sports Steering Wheel
. Front Spoiler
. 14' Wheels with 7" Rims
. Functional Engine Compartment Air Extractors on Front Fenders
. Full Length Stripes on Hood, Roof and Deck Lid Plus other special Trans Am Identification
. Ride & Handling Springs and Shocks . . . . $ 441.28

Total Prices for Coupes and Convertibles are:

2337 without 351, 354 or 358	$1182.74
2337 with 351, 354 or 358	1098.48
2367 without 351, 354 or 358	1166.94
2367 with 351, 354 or 358	1082.68

Performance-minded prospects may be interested in "stepping up" from the Firebird 400 to the elite Trans Am. Sell the price difference -- $750.92 -- by pointing out the many equipment advantages offered by the Trans Am package.

TRANS AM -- newest of the Breakaway cars from PONTIAC!

C. L. Copeland
C. L. Copeland
Sales Promotion Manager

CLC:Rc

PONTIAC MOTOR DIVISION ▼ GENERAL MOTORS CORPORATION

To expand on the overall value of its WS4 Trans Am Option, Pontiac provided dealership sales staffs with a detailed price breakdown when it issued Sales Blueprint 69-66 on June 4, 1969. It may also be the first occurrence where the division actually referenced white-letter tires in place of white-lines to dealership sales staffs.

Although simple warning lights were standard equipment, Trans Am buyers could opt for W63 Rally Gauges with Electric Clock, which included a trio of instruments in the left gauge pod and an electric clock to the right of the 160-mph speedometer. U30 Rally Gauges with Instrument Panel Tachometer was another option, which positioned a tachometer in the left gauge pod and moved a new trio of gauges arranged in a stacked pattern located to the right of the speedometer. A total of 255 buyers selected the U30 option for their Trans Am in 1969.

1969 Trans Am Production

Here are some interesting production numbers. They include breakdowns of Cordova roofs and interior colors as well as interesting optional equipment.

Item	Trans Am Installations	Item	Trans Am Installations
U30 Rally Gauges and Instrument Panel Tachometer	255	C50 Rear Window Defogger	6
		A67 Folding Rear Seat Back	6
W63 Rally Gauges	90	Code-3 Dark Blue Cordova Top	4
207 Parchment Standard Interior	90	Code-2 Black Cordova Top	2
Exported to Canada	31	202 Gold Standard Interior	2
N33 Tilt Steering Wheel	27	206 Green Standard Interior	2
U35 Electric Clock	20	C57 Power Flow Ventilation	2
U69 AM/FM Radio	14	214 Red Custom Interior	1
U57 Stereo Tape Player	10	N95 Wire Wheel Covers (an L67 car)	1
Convertibles	8	Standard equipment only and no extra-cost options appear on its invoice	1
A31 Power Windows	7		
U58 AM/FM Stereo	6		

1969 TRANS AM CONVERTIBLES

It's well documented that Pontiac planned to offer WS4 Trans Am Option on its 1969 Firebird convertible, but whether the division chose to limit its availability to elitists with close company ties or there was simply little consumer demand for the drop-top sports car, only eight were produced that model year. The VINs have appeared in print before and are well known:

- 223679N104808
- 223679N104810
- 223679N105354
- 223679N105380
- 223679N106884
- 223679N107816
- 223679N109938
- 223679N113370

Each Trans Am convertible was built at the Norwood plant and powered by the L74 400 H.O. Four received the M20 4-speed and the remaining four were equipped with the M40 Turbo-400 automatic. Three were originally exported to Canada and five remained stateside. As of late 2015, all cars have been accounted for, documented, and are in private hands. Six of the eight 1969 Trans Am convertibles were on display at the 2011 Muscle Car and Corvette Nationals event in Chicago.

Just eight convertible Trans Ams were produced in 1969. The opportunity of seeing one (let alone two) at a major event is rare. But lucky enthusiasts attending the Muscle Car and Corvette Nationals event in 2011 at Chicago's Stephens Center had the once-in-a-lifetime thrill of seeing six displayed together. It was the first successful attempt of any such occurrence and the show traffic it generated was immense. (Photo Courtesy Don Keefe)

For those who wanted to drive their Trans Am in cool comfort, C60 Air Conditioning was a $376 option. Availability was limited to the L74 400 H.O. engine and it required a 3.23:1 rear axle ratio regardless of transmission choice. Production records indicate that just 31 Trans Ams were equipped with C60 during the 1969 model year.

the last week of August 1969 and shipped on September 17, its invoice reveals it was originally assigned to Pontiac's Zone 24 (Southern California) as a company vehicle. The delay between the build and ship dates likely indicates additional preparation for show service.

Its other options included A39 Deluxe Seat Belts, D55 Front Console, M40 Turbo-400, N98 Rally II Wheels, W54 Custom Interior in blue, D33 remote mirror, and U63 Push-Button Radio. Sticker cost was $4,923.39. Once its tenure as a company vehicle was complete, local area dealers had an opportunity to bid on the Trans Am. Jules Meyers Pontiac in West Los Angeles purchased the car on December 30 for $2,150 and it was likely sold to a private owner not long after.

Production Changes

Trans Ams received the same F70-14 tires with white-line sidewall treatment available on other 1969 Firebirds, sourced from a variety of manufacturers. Shortly after production began, however, Pontiac replaced that tire with an identical size Goodyear Polyglas with raised white

Although the white-line Goodyear tire in size F70-14 was among the many standard features of WS4 Trans Am Option, Pontiac replaced it during the summer months of 1969 with a raised-white-letter Goodyear tire to add racy appeal and to ensure Trans Am's standard content remained on par with its competitors. The very first white-letter tire simply read "Goodyear Polyglas" and included no reference to sizing. "F70-14" was added later and reached the Trans Am toward the end of Firebird's extended production year. (Photo Courtesy The Revs Institute for Automotive Research, Inc.)

Wheel ornamentation ran the gamut of typical Firebird 400 availability. Steel wheels in 14 x 7 sizing adorned with small hubcaps and white-line F70-14 tires were standard on the Trans Am. Full wheel covers were optional at extra cost; one car was equipped with N95 Wire Wheel Covers. Styled-steel N98 Rally II wheels were a popular option with Trans Am buyers. White-letter tires became standard equipment during the summer of 1969.

Although WS4 Trans Am Option didn't contain any up-level seating appointments as part of its option list, internal engineering information reveals that it was to include a genuine leather steering wheel for even greater resemblance to a real race car, particularly with Trans Am's specific high-effort variable-ratio power steering. Delays forced the use of the attractive N34 Custom Sport Steering Wheel with simulated woodgrain rim and brushed spokes at production startup.

letters. This was probably in response to an internal memo dated April 30, 1969, which compared Trans Am's then-standard and optional features to its closest competitors. It clearly noted that raised white-letter tires were standard on others while Trans Am's tires were white-lines.

Not long after the memo's issuance, Pontiac updated the option list of WS4 Trans Am Option to include F70-14 tires with raised white letters. An exact changeover point has yet to be determined, but it appears to have occurred sometime during July or August. The 1969 Firebird tire specification chart was revised June 10, 1969, and the white-letter Goodyear Polyglas tire (number-546650) was a new addition. If that timing is correct, only about half the 697 Trans Ams had been produced when the change-over occurred. It's also worth noting that the sidewall of the first white-letter tires read "Goodyear Polyglas." Lettering changed to read "Goodyear Polyglas F70-14" beginning in September or October 1969.

The attractive N34 Custom Sport Steering Wheel with simulated woodgrain rim and brushed spokes was

The initial plan for WS4 Trans Am Option included a racy steering wheel with a grip that replicated the appearance of genuine leather. Production issues forced its delay and Pontiac issued CDB 70-9 on July 9, 1969, informing dealers of its uncertain status. Note that it had been issued UPC NK1 by this time.

The extended 1969 Firebird model year meant that 1969 Trans Am production continued well into the traditional 1970 model year. On September 5, 1969, Pontiac issued CDB 70-41 announcing the addition of a new steering wheel that replaced N34 Custom Sport Steering Wheel as the Trans Am's standard unit. This bulletin detailed the new Formula Steering Wheel with padded rim that lent the effect of simulated leather. The expected changeover was to occur in mid-September.

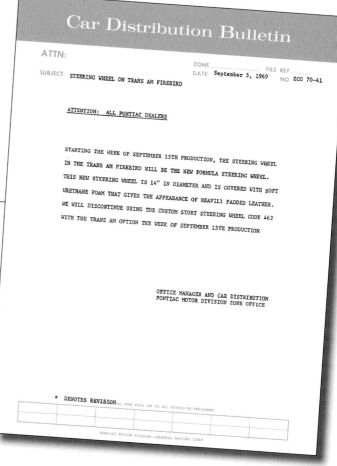

standard issue with WS4 Trans Am Option at production startup, but Pontiac had been actively developing its own racy steering wheel for the 1969 Trans Am based on the leather-wrapped Formula 1–model steering wheel by Momo purportedly first used by product planner Ben Harrison on his own new 1967 Firebird.

"DeLorean wanted a sporty European-type steering wheel for the Trans Am," said Pontiac's assistant interior design chief Bob Luyckz. "He wanted a thick, leather-wrapped grip, not a thin-grip wheel common to American cars at the time. I sketched our Formula Steering Wheel after an aftermarket wheel DeLorean liked. Ours had countersunk Allen-head screws and the Firebird motif on the center horn button really set it off."

Although the new Formula Steering Wheel included a genuine leather wrapping during mockup, Pontiac found that production costs with actual leather were simply too high. In December 1968, Pontiac engineers worked with the Sheller-Globe Corporation to develop a unique process that created a soft, molded grip that replicated the appearance and feel of real leather, complete with texturing and faux stitching.

Measuring 1.1-inch thick and 14.25 inches in diameter, the sporty Formula Steering Wheel finally reached production in September 1969. According to CDB 70-41 dated September 5, 1969, it replaced the Custom Sport

Pontiac pondered using actual leather, but cost was a driving factor in finding a soft-rim substitute that simulated the look and feel of leather. Sheller-Globe pioneered a proprietary process that molded a foam cover onto an aluminum frame. Pontiac used that technology to create the racy Formula Steering Wheel; it was made standard on the Trans Am in September 1969. Many consider it among the most attractive steering wheels ever installed on a production vehicle.

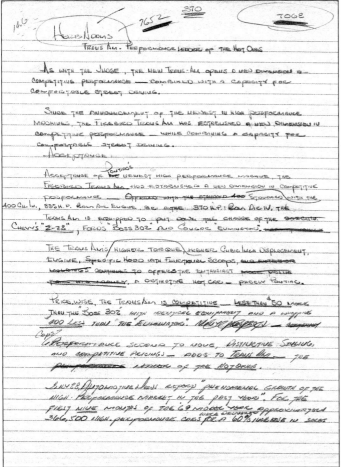

I have a small cache of 1969 Trans Am documents that belonged to C. L. Copeland, Pontiac's sales promotion manager at the time. Among them is this handwritten draft for a bulletin that detailed the advantages of the Trans Am compared to its competitors. Note the reference to Herb Adams in the upper left-hand corner. It's certain that he had input on how to word certain aspects.

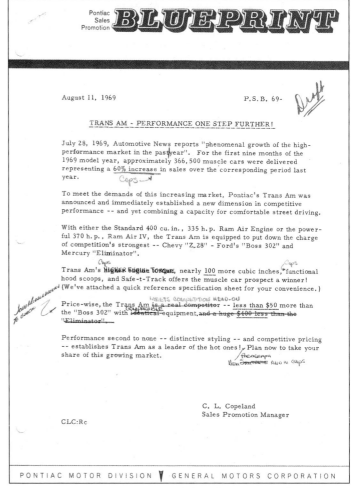

The handwritten draft was typed up on August 11, 1969, into this Sales Blueprint draft, which was further edited by Copeland to ensure its message was absolutely clear to recipients. It's unclear if Pontiac actually distributed the final copy to its dealer network to provide more information about the Trans Am.

The horsepower war of the 1960s brought on technological innovations that were developed covertly but copied by other manufacturers after they were released for production. Pontiac's Ram Air V combined a durable 400-ci base with tunnel-port cylinder heads copied from Ford's racing program. Development began in the mid-1960s. The L85 Ram Air V was a planned Trans Am option for the 1969 model year, but it never reached production. (Photo Courtesy General Motors)

Steering Wheel as the Trans Am's standard unit on the assembly line during the week of September 15. My research based on actual cars seems to agree with the approximate changeover. I estimate that it was installed onto approximately 160 Trans Ams during the 1969 model year.

Pontiac Tunnel-Port V-8s

The new performance-car market was extremely competitive during the mid- to late 1960s and each brand fought to gain an edge in the showroom and on the racetrack. To combat Chrysler's Hemi, Ford developed a high-flow tunnel-port cylinder head for its brawny 427-ci. The casting was released during the 1967 model year and Ford went on to win that year's Daytona 500 with the tunnel-port 427. It also created a variant for its 302-ci V-8 for SCCA's Trans-Am series racing.

The industry was abuzz with "tunnel-port" tech and Pontiac took notice. According to Mac McKellar before his passing, John DeLorean's brother took Ford's new 427-inch tunnel-port head to Pontiac's Engineering garage for all to see. DeLorean was so enamored with its appearance and intrigued by its

PRODUCT ENGINEERING INFORMATION

Bulletin #69-23
January 6, 1969

Ram Air V Engine

Pontiac will have available a new engine for Firebird and Tempest. Target date for initial production is March 1, 1969. The engine differs from the Ram Air IV engine in the following major respects:

1. A revised cylinder head featuring round intake ports, 50% larger in cross-sectional area is used. Valve centers have been repositioned to allow for the larger intake valve and to permit use of a valve seat insert for the exhaust valve.

2. Intake valve size is increased from 2.11" dia. to 2.19" dia., and valve stems are hollow. Sodium cooled exhaust valves are used.

3. A new aluminum intake manifold having larger, round runners to match the cylinder head is employed in this engine. As in the Ram Air IV engine, no exhaust heat is applied to the intake manifold.

4. The separate exhaust crossover has been eliminated and heated air to the carburetor is supplied during warmup from two shrouds or stoves, one on each exhaust manifold.

5. Solid valve lifters replace the hydraulic lifters used in the Ram Air IV. Camshaft is revised for use with these lifters.

6. Cylinder block has been revised to include heavier bulk heads for reduced deflection and increased durability. Cast ribs have been added connecting the two banks of cylinders in the lifter base area for increased block rigidity. Distributor pilot hole is enlarged to accept larger distributor and oil pump drive gear to increase durability of this gear.

ENGINEERING DEPARTMENT
PONTIAC MOTOR DIVISION
GENERAL MOTORS CORPORATION PONTIAC MICHIGAN

On January 6, 1969, Pontiac distributed internal Engineering Bulletin 69-23 that outlined the new Ram Air V for the Firebird and Tempest model lines. The two-page document detailed how the new engine differed from the Ram Air IV and projects availability on March 1, 1969. Although the Ram Air IV was announced at 1969 model year startup, its production was delayed and it hadn't reached vehicle production by the time Pontiac announced the Ram Air V in this bulletin.

Pontiac's tunnel-port cylinder head fit a traditional V-8 block, but its intake and exhaust ports were rearranged so that every port was individual, which promoted improved port-to-port symmetry. About 400 individual cylinder heads were cast and sold through dealership parts departments once the Ram Air V program was canceled. They remain rare and highly valuable.

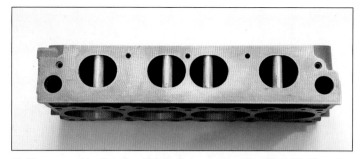

Unlike any other Pontiac V-8 before or after, the Ram Air V casting featured voluminous intake ports with a pronounced round shape that are about 50 percent greater in size than the already-oversized Ram Air IV intake port. The Ram Air V port was so large that the intake valve pushrod ran directly through the center and a tube was pressed into the casting to prevent vacuum leaks. A unique intake manifold was also required.

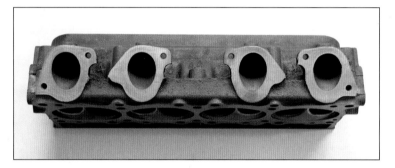

Typical Pontiac V-8 cylinder heads featured siamesed center exhaust ports. In most applications, the outlet's resultant "D" shape lends the name they're most commonly known by (D-port). Select high-performance applications retain the siamesed characteristic, but the outlet shape is truly round and enthusiasts commonly refer to such castings as "round ports." The exhaust port shape and configuration of the Ram Air V cylinder head is unique and requires an exhaust manifold or tubular header unlike any other.

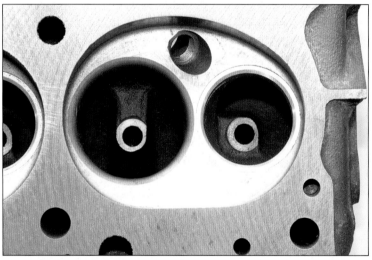

For ease of product packaging and to promote improved propagation, the spark plug within the combustion chamber of the Ram Air V cylinder head is aimed toward the exhaust valve. This feature was never used on any production Pontiac V-8 cylinder heads but is commonplace in today's aftermarket castings. The intake port is capable of providing more than 300 cfm of peak airflow at 28 inches of pressure. Port size is its detriment, however, as poor velocity in the low-lift range limits its effectiveness for street use, where an engine experiences a variety of operating conditions. Combustion chamber volume measures 74 to 75 cc.

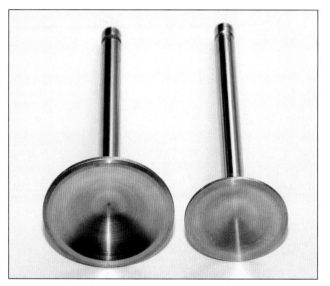

The Ram Air V used specific 2.19-inch-diameter intake and 1.73-inch exhaust valves to seal the ports from the combustion chamber. They were designed specifically for the rigors of high-RPM operation. The exhaust valve features a sodium-filled stem, which not only reduces weight, but improves heat dissipation. As the sodium turns from a solid to a liquid as operating temperature increases, the sloshing action within the stem draws heat out of the head and transfers it to the cylinder head through the valveguide.

A special solid-lifter camshaft was developed for the Ram Air V. The 308/320-degree engine used the same duration and valve timing as the McKellar number-10 from the early-1960s Super Duty 421, but with much greater valve lift. When combined with 1.65:1 rocker arms, gross valve lift measured .520 inch. Lobe placement and a small distributor drive gear made the Ram Air V cam incompatible with any other Pontiac combination.

design that he immediately commissioned McKellar to "make this fit our block." DeLorean envisioned a tunnel-port Pontiac V-8 that would give his division marketability equal to that of the other top brands on the leading edge of performance technology.

McKellar and his team worked feverishly on the directive and churned out two high-performance V-8 packages: L32 303-ci and L85 400-ci. The 303 was intended for racers competing in racing series with maximum displacement limitations; the 400 was intended for the dragstrip. Parts were cast and engines were built, but the projects stalled shortly after DeLorean's departure from Pontiac. Neither tunnel-port engine was ever installed into a production vehicle.

Ram Air V 400

McKellar and his team began working on experimental project number D-18751 in August 1967 with the 1969 model year planned as its introduction. The new cylinder head featured cavernous intake ports that dis-

placed approximately 285 cc, or about 100 cc more than a stock Ram Air IV casting. Fitted with a 2.19-inch valve, peak intake airflow measured more than 300 cfm in stock form. The exhaust featured four individual ports in a unique layout and peak airflow with a 1.73-inch sodium-filled valve measured more than 200 cfm. According to the original drawing, combustion chamber volume displaced 74 to 75 cc with the target compression ratio at an actual 10.75:1.

One of the many revisions occurred on December 8, 1968, when the experimental project was released for production. The casting was officially assigned part number 545064. Some production-type tunnel-port Pontiac cylinder heads were identified with the D-series number noted above, the full casting number, a single "4," a "44," and no casting identification whatsoever.

While in development, Pontiac's tunnel-port cylinder head was reportedly tested on various V-8s including the 400 and 428 as well as with a wide array of experimental single- and dual-carbureted intake manifolds. As the tunnel-port program raced toward production, the

The foundation of the Ram Air V is a specific 400-ci block with four-bolt main caps and reinforcing ribs that solidly tie together each lifter bank, which in total, adds overall rigidity. The enlarged distributor hole accepts an oversize distributor gear that revises the helix angle to reduce the risk of premature wear of the camshaft and distributor gears that drive the oil pump.

Forged aluminum pistons and forged steel connecting rods were among the unique components intended to bolster the durability of the tunnel-port Ram Air V. Regular operation in excess of 6,000 rpm meant imminent failure with the cast component found in regular production engines, but not so with the Ram Air V. It was designed to live in that operating range.

TRW provided Pontiac with a forged aluminum piston for the Ram Air V. Constructed of SAE-328 aluminum alloy, the overall thickness of the material added extreme durability. The crown featured a slight dome to boost compression to its intended ratio of 10.75:1. The off color is a result of the tin plating process, which was commonly used by manufacturers to reduce friction, thereby extending piston and cylinder wall life.

practical decision was made to limit its availability to GTO and Firebird, and corporate rules limited the A- and F-car lines to a maximum displacement of 400 inches. Thus, the Ram Air V (or R/A V) was born.

The Ram Air V was Pontiac's late-1960s attempt at producing a maximum performance engine boasting complete durability. Every component was beefed up or newly designed to endure the added output and extended operating range that the new high-flow tunnel-port heads sustained. Much like the Super Duty 421 of the early 1960s, Pontiac's intent was to create a competition engine capable of taking on the toughest competition, both on the dragstrip and in the media.

A completely new mechanical camshaft complemented the added airflow capacity of the new tunnel-port cylinder head. Number-545713 (further identified by a stamped "V" on the front snout) shared the same advertised duration specs (308/320 degrees) with the famous McKellar number-10 mechanical grind from the Super Duty 421 and the hydraulic number-041 in the Ram Air IV. However, its lobe placement was revised to accommodate the unique intake and exhaust port arrangement of the tunnel-port head.

The Ram Air V's solid lifters were manually lashed and gross valve lift measured about .520 inch with 1.65:1 rocker arms. When factoring the recommended amount of valve lash, however, net valve lift was much closer to .500 inch. One vintage report lists .050-inch duration at 234/246 degrees and with a few degrees consumed by lash, you might consider the number-545713 a manually lashed equivalent of the 041.

McKellar's team beefed up the standard four-bolt 400-ci block to create the number-545686 for the Ram Air V. According to its drawing, dated March 1968, it boasted thicker bulkheads, additional ribbing to solidly connect the lifter bore banks, and a larger distributor hole to accept an oversize gear with a 45-degree helix angle (as opposed to 35 degrees) intended to more evenly spread the operational load of the high-pressure oil pump. Its 4.12-inch bores were filled with forged aluminum pistons (number-545856) from TRW. The pistons had a slight dome to attain the intended compression ratio of 10.75:1.

Engineers were aware that most Ram Air V buyers would replace its factory-issued cast-iron exhaust manifolds with tubular headers to maximize performance, but the production manifold developed for the 1969 Trans Am equipped with the tunnel-port engine shares an appearance to the long-branch units found on other Firebirds, which proved to be very efficient. Only a few examples of this tunnel-port 303 manifold exist today.

Pontiac began development of a new crankshaft constructed of forged 4640-alloy steel in September 1967. The number-545671 crankshaft with 3.75-inch stroke and 3-inch main journals was complemented by a unique forged steel connecting rod. Number-545855 was quite heavy and that may have contributed to reliability issues in extreme applications. That girth negatively affected rod concentricity at very high RPM leading to spun bearing shells. A larger-than-normal harmonic dampener (number-545072) and forged (rather than cast) flywheel were also unique to Pontiac's tunnel-port engine.

Feeding the beast was a high-flow cast-aluminum intake manifold (number-545288) with large tunnel-port runners and no exhaust heat. It was topped with an 800-cfm Holley 4-barrel carburetor with vacuum-actuated secondary barrels and an electric choke for operation in inclement weather. High-flow exhaust manifolds with individual runners constructed of cast iron were created for both A- and F-car chassis fitment. A high-intensity Capacitive Discharge (or CD) ignition system with a number-1111972 distributor was used.

At least two vintage magazines' articles reported that Pontiac planned to build 1,500 engines for production 1969 Firebirds and GTOs to satisfy the homologation requirements of various racing bodies. A Pontiac document stating rated output has yet to surface, but at least two other vintage articles claim the division planned for a factory rating of 380 hp, or 14 more than the Ram Air IV's 366 hp rating in the GTO. Knowing all too well just how conservative Pontiac was when rating its top performance engines, there's no telling how capable the Ram Air V really was.

An internal engineering bulletin dated January 6, 1969, states that the Ram Air V's target production date was March 1, 1969. Given UPC L85, the tunnel-port Pontiac was so close to production that engine codes were assigned for A- and F-car applications with automatic and manual transmissions. They even appear in at least one midyear engine chart. Another internal document outlining preliminary GTO Judge and Firebird Trans Am material also listed the Ram Air V as an

Repco was an Australian automotive engineering company that designed aftermarket components during the 1960s. Australian racer Jack Brabham used Repco to produce the engine components he competed with on the Formula One circuit. In 1968, John DeLorean commissioned Brabham to build an experimental 303-ci Pontiac V-8 using the overhead cam technology of his Formula One engines. Brabham had Repco manufacture the one-off components. The goal was to provide the Firebird with an exotic race engine to successfully compete in the SCCA Trans-Am racing series. Although the Repco-Brabham 303-ci never lived up to Pontiac's performance expectations, Repco shared information about its build later. This press photo taken at Repco's facility was distributed by the company in response to a specific inquiry about it.

The block casting of the tunnel-port 303 was similar to a typical Pontiac V-8 block with four-bolt main caps. However, its main journals measured 2.5 inches and approximately 1 inch was removed from its deck surface to shed weight and shorten rod length. The lifter gallery was cast solid for added rigidity. About 25 blocks were cast, but when engine output didn't meet expectations and the SCCA was reluctant to accept its production status, the tunnel-port 303 program was scrapped. Reportedly all of the short-deck blocks ended up in the hands of professional racers when the program was canceled. (Photo Courtesy General Motors)

Pontiac's engineers were aware that the amount of horsepower needed to remain competitive in the displacement-limited Trans-Am series meant an engine capable of operating reliably at very high RPM. To ensure that the 303-ci V-8 could efficiently operate above 7,000 rpm, it was fitted with a variation of Pontiac's tunnel-port cylinder head. The engine wasn't overly successful, but a total of 25 complete units were assembled in an attempt to display to the SCCA that it was truly a production engine for homologation purposes. This press photo is among the many that Pontiac provided to the SCCA, but the engine was never approved. (Photo Courtesy General Motors)

How close was the tunnel-port 303 to becoming a production reality? Pontiac Engineering had at least one fully functional prototype Trans Am fitted with the experimental 303-ci that it made available to media outlets for test drives. Some complained of its poor idle quality and low-speed street manners, but many praised its ability to rev past 7,000 rpm. The complete package looks right at home in this vintage Pontiac press photo. (Photo Courtesy General Motors)

available option in both those specialty vehicles.

For reasons unknown, however, its availability was delayed. That may have been due to emissions and/or warranty concerns. Another possibility is the fact that Pontiac contracted an outside supplier to provide the number-545855 connecting rods and the company defaulted on production. The Ram Air V was nearly ready for installation into production vehicles but sat idle as the 1969 model year came to a close.

Some early 1970 Pontiac information reveals that manufacturing was ramping up for Ram Air V availability that year. Some components were even revised to accommodate the redesigned Firebird chassis with new part numbers assigned accordingly, but it was ultimately canceled before any official release. A handful of completed Ram Air V engines and a host of individual components were sold to savvy customers through dealership parts departments.

Tunnel-Port 303

During the SCCA Trans-Am series 1968 season, Jerry Titus competed with a Firebird. Because Pontiac didn't have a high-performance small-cube engine, he persuaded the racing body to allow him the use of a small-block Chevy V-8, arguing that Canadian Pontiacs sold new were Chevy-powered at the time. Along with Titus' continued requests for a small-cube Pontiac V-8, media coverage of the SCCA events often made mention of Titus' Chevy-powered Firebird. Divisional brass took notice.

After going to great lengths to separate its F-car from Chevrolet's, Pontiac wasn't about to let the Firebird and Camaro conjoin on the racetrack, so the decision was made to create a high-output V-8 compliant with the SCCA rules. Although the corporation reaffirmed its stance on the development of race-oriented packages in 1963, Pontiac's rebellious general manager, John DeLorean, once again bucked corporate's directive, giving his engineering team specific instructions to develop its own competition engine, and to do it on the fast track. He even sought input from Repco-Brabham, an outside source that provided Pontiac with a fuel-injected, overhead-cam 303-ci V-8 for testing, but it ultimately underperformed and was deemed too costly.

Pontiac's assistant chief engineer Bill Collins tasked Herb Adams and his Special Projects group with developing the division's newest V-8. With the rulebook limiting maximum displacement to 5 liters (305 ci), Special Projects found that the 4.12-inch bore diameter of the 400 block offered the least amount of valve shrouding with the available valve architecture. By combining a typical 400 block with a new 2.84-inch-stroke crankshaft, it could easily create a high-winding 303-ci engine that, at least on paper, would be capable of producing the type of high-RPM horsepower required to be competitive with other makes on the SCCA circuit. The 303 was born.

The 303 program was initiated around August 1968 with plans to have the new engine ready for the 1969 SCCA season. Concurrently, McKellar's engine group experimented with a Pontiac V-8 block whose deck was 1 inch shorter to shed weight and had reduced packaging for typical passenger car applications. "The 303 program initially used a standard block in developmental testing, but when we learned of McKellar's short-deck block and that it saved 60 pounds over the standard casting and that we could run a much shorter connecting rod, we quickly incorporated it into the 303-ci," recalls Adams.

The original drawing for the short-deck 303-ci block (number-546313) is dated November 1, 1968. It reveals several interesting features, including a target deck height of 9.1 inches compared to 10.2 for the standard block. Bore sizing measured 4.12 inches and the main bearing journals were sized to accommodate a crankshaft with 2.5-inch-diameter main journals. Pontiac outsourced the low-volume, forged steel crankshaft with 2.84-

inch stroke to aftermarket specialty companies such as Moldex and Reath. Only a handful are known to exist.

Development of the 303's number-546184 tunnel-port cylinder head began early December 1968. Its high-flow intake ports seemed a natural fit for the high-winding V-8 deemed to make big horsepower numbers, and the 303-ci casting was virtually identical to the Ram Air V casting in all respects. However, its combustion chamber volume was reduced, subsequently displacing 53 cc.

Reportedly 25 short-deck blocks were cast and used to produce the same number of complete tunnel-port engines in an effort to gain SCCA homologation. "We had a photographer come in and take photos of all the 303-ci engines together and we sent that to the SCCA hoping to convince them that our 303-ci was actually a production engine that we installed on racer request, but they knew better. It was never approved for competition during the 1969 season," said Jeff Young, a former Pontiac engineer who joined the Special Projects group about that time.

Prior to Young's arrival, Herb Adams, Tom Nell, and Leo Hilke were the Pontiac engineers directly involved with developing the 303-ci. "Those three really got the project going and the engine was producing about 375 hp when I replaced Leo Hilke," Young said before his passing. "We played around with it some more and got peak power up to about 400 hp, but that just wasn't

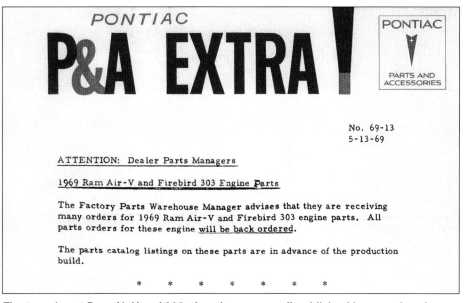

The tunnel-port Ram Air V and 303-ci engines were well-publicized in magazines in 1969 and part numbers began appearing in parts manuals by May 1969. Racers and performance enthusiasts inundated dealership parts departments with so many purchase requests that Pontiac specifically clarified in P&A Extra 69-13 issued on May, 13, 1969, that regular production hadn't yet begun and that all components were officially backordered.

enough to be competitive. I felt that the tunnel-port head just wasn't right for the engine. Its intake ports were too big and the pushrod tube running in the center was a disruption."

Young theorized that the available airflow capacity of a typical round-port Ram Air IV cylinder head would allow for an equal amount of horsepower while the reduced intake port volume would significantly improve low-speed torque, which was ideal for accelerating from a turn. "I shared my thoughts with Herb, and he told me

he and Tom had the same idea. It was at that moment that tunnel-port 303 development ceased and we moved forward with the Ram Air IV–headed 303-ci, or the 303 II as we sometimes referred to it. The engine really started to come alive at that point."

An airflow expert, Young helped develop Pontiac's in-house flow bench for further testing. It was comprised of a 100 hp electric motor connected to a GM 6-71 supercharger that created the air feed. He and the others used the bench to measure and improve on the flow capacity of the Ram Air IV casting for the 303 II. Young found gains by focusing his attention on the valve bowl area. The group then sent typical as-cast Ram Air IV cylinder heads to a handful of well-known aftermarket head-porting services with instructions to simply improve them.

"I wanted to cross-check our efforts with what the professionals were doing at the time to make sure we were on the leading edge of airflow technology," Young explained. "We then tested each set of ported heads on the dyno and at least two performed no better than our own modified Ram Air IV castings. Those by Warren Brownfield's Air Flow Research did, however, pick up some and we closely studied where he applied his efforts, which was in the short turn area and widening the port at the pushrod bugle. We applied those techniques to our modified Ram Air IV castings to further improve our 303 II."

Young stated that, to the best of his recollection, the short-deck 303 block was abandoned about the same time as the tunnel-port heads. "Despite our exhaustive efforts, the tunnel-port 303 never ran in an SCCA race during the 1969 season. And then when we found it wasn't going to make the power level we sought with a short-deck block, there was no reason to further develop the block or heads, especially when we learned that the SCCA was changing its rules for 1970 to allow larger

MAKE: Pontiac   MODEL: Firebird Trans-Am   YEAR: 1969

BOX 791
WESTPORT, CONN. 06880
203-227-1266

1969 SCCA SEDAN CATEGORY RECOGNITION FORM

SCCA Sedan Category automobiles shall normally be those which are series-produced with normal road touring equipment in quantities of at least 1,000 within a 12-month period.

Statement of Quantity Produced:

This is to certify that:
Pontiac Motor Division

has produced a minimum of 1,000 identical
Pontiac - Firebird - Trans-Am
(Make, Model, and Designation)

automobiles to the specifications listed herein during period beginning
__3-1-69__ and ending __12-31-69__.

Date: 2-4-70   Pontiac Motor Division - GMC
(Manufacturer)

(Authorized signature)

Prod. Planning Monitor
(Title)

Trans-Am series racing was so hot in the late 1960s that many manufacturers embellished production figures just to gain homologation status. Pontiac was no exception, as evidenced by this document in which a division official certified to the SCCA that it produced at least 1,000 Firebird Trans Ams during the 1969 model year. We know today that number was not-so-coincidentally overstated by more than 300 units!

engines so long as the size could be reduced to 5 liters. We began utilizing our typical 400 block as its basis."

Although at least one tunnel-port 303 was installed into a developmental 1969 Trans Am for media demonstrator service, race teams competing with Firebirds in SCCA events were forced to revert to 1968 rules, running 1968-spec Chevy engines and modifying the 1969 Firebird body to accept 1968 hardware. That put excellent racers, including Titus, at a great disadvantage. Although others used the most current equipment approved for 1969, the Pontiac teams were making only as much horsepower as the 1968 combinations allowed. The division wasn't exactly proud to fall short of its goal.

Pontiac sent its cache of short-deck 303-ci blocks to professional racers campaigning Pontiac V-8s on other circuits and refocused its attention on producing a standard-deck 303-ci, putting power on par with other makes for the 1970 season. One internal report reveals that in GM20 Maximum Power conditions, the 303 II made 454 at 6,800 rpm and 387 ft-lbs at 5,800 rpm. It goes on to say that although that number makes the 303 competitive with Chevrolet, Ford's 302 was generating closer to 500 hp, suggesting further development was needed.

As developmental efforts during the early 1970s were refocused toward a 366-inch engine and eventually the Super Duty 455, continued development of the 303 II waned, but as Young recalled, not before gross horsepower peaked at 476 at 8,200 rpm in its final configuration. This last 303 iteration was campaigned in SCCA events by professional racers for the next few years, and even by Herb Adams who installed one into his own 1964 Tempest that he privately raced on the SCCA circuit. Although the engine was plagued with oiling issues and its success was limited, only now can we appreciate this race-bred small-cube Pontiac V-8 that has spent much of its life in obscurity.

Ultimately, the 1969 Trans Am wasn't immediately approved by SCCA for the racing series from which it took its name for a number of reasons. At the start of the 1969 race season, drivers seeking to compete with a Firebird were forced to modify its body appearance to replicate Pontiac's 1968 treatment and use Chevy power. Once the 1969 Firebird received approval, it proved to be an uphill battle that very few teams were willing to accept. Limited racing success and small-cube engines had little effect on its perception with average consumers. The Firebird Trans Am went on to define the 1970s and remained a staple of American culture throughout the 1980s.

Although the concept was somewhat radical for the times, Pontiac envisioned the 1969 Trans Am as a better seller than the 697 units it produced that model year. Don't forget that it was a very late-year addition to the model lineup and the fact that the package wasn't eligible for competition directly from the factory certainly didn't help. The redesigned 1970 Firebird was also a hot topic in the media and many buyers held out to see what the new model year would bring. The 1969 Trans Am became an iconic part of Pontiac history that's highly coveted by performance enthusiasts and collectors alike. (Photo Courtesy Larry Delay)

APPENDIX A: 1967 FIREBIRD

1967 Firebird Exterior Colors (All Series)

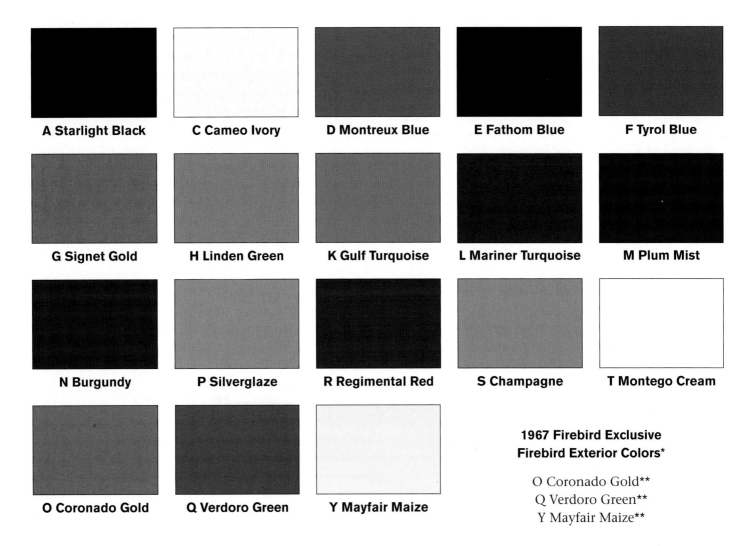

A Starlight Black C Cameo Ivory D Montreux Blue E Fathom Blue F Tyrol Blue

G Signet Gold H Linden Green K Gulf Turquoise L Mariner Turquoise M Plum Mist

N Burgundy P Silverglaze R Regimental Red S Champagne T Montego Cream

O Coronado Gold Q Verdoro Green Y Mayfair Maize

**1967 Firebird Exclusive
Firebird Exterior Colors***

O Coronado Gold**
Q Verdoro Green**
Y Mayfair Maize**

* Starlight Black, Plum Mist, and Montego Cream exterior colors are available only on a Special Order (extra cost) basis for Firebird models, and have been replaced by the following standard Firebird colors.

** Available in two-tone combination with this upper area color: Cameo Ivory (Code C)

1967 Firebird Cordova Top Colors

Code	Color
291	Ivory
292	Black
297	Cream

1967 Firebird Convertible Top Colors

Code	Color
1	Ivory
2	Black
4	Blue
5	Turquoise
7	Cream

1967 Firebird Interior Color Codes

Code	Color	Level	Seating
250	Dark Blue	Standard	Bucket
251	Gold	Standard	Bucket
252	Red	Standard	Bucket
253	Black	Standard	Bucket
254	Parchment	Standard	Bucket
255	Medium Blue	Custom	Bucket
256	Turquoise	Custom	Bucket
257	Gold	Custom	Bucket
258	Red	Custom	Bucket
259	Black	Custom	Bucket
260	Parchment	Custom	Bucket
265	Medium Blue	Custom	Bench
267	Gold	Custom	Bench
269	Black	Custom	Bench
270	Dark Blue	Standard	Bench
271	Gold	Standard	Bench
272	Black	Standard	Bench

1967 Firebird Known Engine and Transmission Production Totals

	M12/M13 3-Speed Manual	M20 4-Speed Manual	M30 2-Speed Auto	M31 2-Speed Auto	M40 Turbo-400	Total Manual	Total Automatic	Total All
OHC-6	Unknown*	720	7,549	N/A**	N/A**	2,905	7,549	10,454
Sprint-6	3,695	1,621	1,894	N/A**	N/A**	5,316	1,894	7,210
326 2-barrel	Unknown*	Unknown*	N/A**	32,401	N/A**	7,719	32,401	40,210
326 H.O.	Unknown*	Unknown*	N/A**	2,843	N/A**	3,235	2,843	6,078
400	1,274	7,522	N/A**	N/A**	9,902	8,796	9,902	18,698
Total	13,198	14,773	9,443	35,244	9,902	27,971	54,589	82,650

* No data available

** Not available

1967 Firebird Production Totals

Series	Engine	Level	Manual Trans	Auto Trans	Total
2337	6-cylinder	Standard Coupe	4,640	4,734	9,374
2367	6-cylinder	Standard Convertible	618	863	1,481
2537	6-cylinder	Deluxe Coupe	2,488	3,161	5,649
2567	6-cylinder	Deluxe Convertible	475	685	1,160
2437	V-8	Standard Coupe	6,798	12,320	19,118
2467	V-8	Standard Convertible	1,426	2,981	4,407
2637	V-8	Deluxe Coupe	9,206	23,685	32,891
2667	V-8	Deluxe Convertible	2,320	6,160	8,480
Total			27,971	54,589	82,560

1967 Firebird Sprint Production Totals

Series	Engine	Model	Total
2337	6-cylinder	Standard Coupe	3,080
2367	6-cylinder	Standard Convertible	557
2537	6-cylinder	Deluxe Coupe	2,956
2567	6-cylinder	Deluxe Convertible	617
			7,210

1967 Firebird H.O. Production Totals

Series	Engine	Model	Total
2437	326 H.O.	Standard Coupe	1,645
2467	326 H.O.	Standard Convertible	388
2637	326 H.O.	Deluxe Coupe	3,179
2667	326 H.O.	Deluxe Convertible	866
			6,078

1967 Firebird 400 Ram Air Production

Body Style	Manual	Auto	Total
Coupe	39	18	57
Convertible	6	2	8
Total	45	20	65

1967 Firebird Installed Options

Code	UPC	Description	Total Production
531	A01	Soft Ray Glass	14,447
532	A02	Soft Ray Windshield	30,707
551	A31	Power Windows	2,283
431	A39	Deluxe Seat Belts	24,962
572	A52	Head Rests	1,051
654	A67	Folding Rear Seat	9,884
568	AL4	Bench Seat	3,834
434	AS1	Shoulder Harness, standard belts	354
631	B32	Front Floor Mats	16,478
632	B33	Rear Floor Mats	9,553
362	B42	Luggage Mat	3,274
382	B93	Door Edge Guards	9,544
544	C06	Power Convertible Top	10,331
29-	C08	Cordova Top	21,275
584	C48	Heater Delete	Unknown
374	C50	Defogger	2,155
582	C60	Air Conditioning	14,850
384	D28	Delete Outside Review Mirror, export only	Unknown
394	D33	Remote Outside Mirror	14,821
391	D34	Visor Vanity Mirror, right only	1,603
392	D42	Visor Vanity Mirror, right and left	6,902
472	D55	Console	53,650
491	D98	Sprint Stripe	4,704

Code	UPC	Description	Total Production
N/A	D99	Two-Tone Paint	Unknown
634	FG1	Adjustable Shock Absorbers	154
731	G80	Safe-T-Track Differential	13,274
738	G92	Performance Axle Ratio	Unknown
732	G94	Special Order Axle	Unknown
734	G95	Economy Axle Ratio	Unknown
502	J50	Power Brakes	21,853
521	J52	Front Disc Brakes	6,074
414	JL1	Pedal Trim Package	22,630
514	K02	Heavy-Duty Fan and Clutch	Unknown
684	K08	Heavy-Duty Engine Fan	Unknown
612	K19	Air Injector Exhaust Control, California	Unknown
614	K24	Closed Circuit Crank Case	Unknown
441	K30	Cruise Control	347
361	K45	Heavy-Duty Air Cleaner, possibly W66 only	10,307
674	K82	Heavy-Duty Alternator, 55-amp	Unknown
333	L30	326 2-Barrel	40,121
	L67	400 Ram Air 4-Barrel	65
334	L76	326 H.O. 4-Barrel	4,515
524	M09	Custom Shift Knob	1,784
786	M12	3-Speed Manual, floor shift	9,785
784	M20	4-Speed Manual	14,773
782	M30	Automatic Trans, 6-cylinder	Unknown
	M30/M31	Automatic Trans	44,687
782	M31	Automatic Trans, V-8	Unknown
781	M40	Turbo 400 (400 engine only)	9,902
481	N10	Dual Exhaust	25,535
482	N25	Exhaust Extensions	803
462	N30	Deluxe Steering Wheel	23,674
504	N33	Tilt Steering Wheel	3,043
471	N34	Custom Sport Steering Wheel	4,895
501	N40	Power Steering	54,072
622	N64	Conventional Spare Tire	29,380
452	N95	Wire Wheel Discs	3,505
453	N98	Sprint Wheels (Rally II)	8,107
461	P01	Deluxe Wheel Discs	23,271
458	P02	Custom Wheel Discs	4,427
454	P05	Rally I Wheels	Unknown
372	P17	Spare Tire Cover	23
HD	P26	E70 x 14 White-Lined Tires	52,945
604	P32	Delete Space Saver Tire, export only	Unknown
KM	P33	185R x 14 Radial-Ply White-Lined Tires	1,050

Code	UPC	Description	Total Production
HC	PX3	E70 x 14 Red-Line Tires	20,754
331	STD	230-ci 1-Barrel 6-Cylinder	10,454
783	STD	3-Speed Manual (Column Shift)	3,413
HE	STD	Black Wall Tires	7,763
678	T60	Heavy-Duty Battery	1,928
494	U05	Dual Horns (2300 and 2400)	7,878
442	U15	Speed Guard Speedometer	642
704	U16	Hood-Mounted Tach	6,872
602	U18	Export Speedometer (KPH)	Unknown
402	U23	Ignition Switch Lamp	Unknown
401	U25	Luggage Compartment Lamp	6,647
421	U26	Underhood Lamp	4,560
444	U30	Rally Gauges	8,667
474	U35	Electric Clock	17,337
354	U57	Stereo 8-Track Tape Player	1,863
342	U63	AM Radio, with manual front antenna	7,6233
344	U69	AM/FM Radio, with manual front antenna	3,731
341	U73	Manual Antenna Rear	Unknown
351	U80	Rear Seat Speaker	9,638
681	V01	Heavy-Duty Radiator	Unknown
601	V48	Canadian Anti Freeze	Unknown
332	W53	230-ci 4-Barrel 6-Cylinder	7,210
554	W54	Custom Interior	48,180
594	W58	Export Preparation	Unknown
335	W66	400 4-Barrel	18,698
621	Y96	Ride and Handling Package	7,627
Unknown		Shoulder Harness, deluxe belts	240

1967 Options

Standard Firebird
230-ci OHC-6 engine with 1-barrel carburetor
3-speed manual transmission, column shifted
E70-14 Wide Oval tires with black sidewall

L30 Firebird 326 Option
326-ci V-8 with 2-barrel carburetor
M12 3-speed manual transmission, column shifted
E70-14 Wide Oval tires with black sidewall

W53 Firebird Sprint Option
L72 Sprint-6 engine with 4-barrel carburetor
Chromed air cleaner lid
Low-restriction single exhaust (same as V-8)
M12 3-speed manual transmission, floor shifted
Heavy-duty clutch
Heavy-rated front and rear springs
E70-14 Wide Oval tires with black sidewall
Special "Sprint" identification

L76 Firebird H.O. Option
L76 326 H.O. V-8 with 4-barrel carburetor
N10 dual exhaust
M12 3-speed manual transmission, column shifted
T60 heavy-duty battery
Heavy-duty starter
D98 Rally side stripes
Heavy-rated front and rear springs
E70-14 Wide Oval tires with black sidewall

W66 Firebird 400 Option

400-inch V-8 with 4-barrel carburetor
Chrome-plated engine appointments
N10 dual exhaust
T60 heavy-duty battery
Heavy-duty starter

Heavy-duty radiator
Dual-scooped hood
M13 3-speed manual transmission, floor shifted
Heavy-rated front and rear springs
E70-14 Wide Oval tires with red sidewall
Special "400" identification

1967 Option Package Groups

061 Basic Group

K45 Heavy-Duty Air Cleaner
U35 Electric Clock
U63 Push Button Radio (with manual antenna front)

062 Protection Group

A39 Custom Seat Belts, front and rear
B32 Floor Mats, front
B33 Floor Mats, rear
B93 Door Edge Guards
C50 Rear Window Defogger (coupe only)

064 Décor Group

JL1 Pedal Trim Package
N30 Deluxe Steering Wheel
P01 Deluxe Wheel Discs

071 Mirror Group

D33 Remote-Control Outside Mirror
D42 Visor Vanity Mirrors, right and left

074 Lamp Group

U25 Luggage Lamp
U26 Underhood Lamp
W65 Interior Courtesy Lamps

1967 Firebird Springs and Shocks

Level	Front Shocks	Rear Shocks	Front Coil Springs	Rear Leaf Springs	Front Stabilizer Bar Diameter	Rear Stabilizer Bar Diameter
Firebird 6-cylinder or V-8	Standard	Standard	Standard	Standard	.625 inch	None
Custom Option Firebird 6-cylinder or V-8	Standard	Standard	Standard	Special	.625 inch	None
W53 Sprint Option	High Rate	High Rate	High Rate	High Rate	.625 inch	None
L76 Firebird H.O. Option	High Rate	High Rate	High Rate	High Rate	.625 inch	None
W66 Firebird 400 Option	High Rate	High Rate	Heavy Duty	Heavy Duty	.625 inch	None
Y96 Ride and Handling Option (available all)	Heavy Duty	Heavy Duty	Heavy Duty	Heavy Duty	.625 inch	None

Note: FG1 Koni Adjustable Shocks optional all levels

1967 Engine Codes

UPC	STD	STD	STD	STD	L72	L72
Displacement	230	230	230	230	230	230
ID Code	ZN	ZM	ZK	ZS	ZE	ZL
Transmission	Auto	Auto	Manual	Manual	Auto	Auto
Bore x Stroke	3.88 x 3.25	3.88 x 3.25	3.88 x 3.25	3.88 x 3.25	3.88 x 3.25	3.88 x 3.25
Cylinder Head	9778692	9778692	9778692	9778692	9778693	9778693
Advertised Compression	9:1	9:1	9:1	9:1	10.5:1	10.5:1
Camshaft	9782012	9782012	9782012	9782012	9782218	9782218
Carburetor	1-barrel	1-barrel	1-barrel	1-barrel	4-barrel	4-barrel
Gross HP	165 hp at 4,700 rpm	165 hp at 4,700 rpm	165 hp at 4,700 rpm	165 hp at 4,700 rpm	215 hp at 5,200 rpm	215 hp at 5,200 rpm
Gross Torque	216 ft-lbs at 2,600 rpm	216 ft-lbs at 2,600 rpm	216 ft-lbs at 2,600 rpm	216 ft-lbs at 2,600 rpm	240 ft-lbs at 3,800 rpm	240 ft-lbs at 3,800 rpm
Notes		California Emissions		California Emissions	Sprint 6	Sprint 6 California Emissions

UPC	L72	L72	L30	L30	L30	L30
Displacement	230	230	326	326	326	326
ID Code	ZD	ZR	YJ	XI	WC	WH
Transmission	Manual	Manual	Auto	Auto	Manual	Manual
Bore x Stroke	3.88 x 3.25	3.88 x 3.25	3.72 x 3.75	3.72 x 3.75	3.72 x 3.75	3.72 x 3.75
Cylinder Head	9778693	9778693	140	140	140	140
Advertised Compression	10.5:1	10.5:1	9.2:1	9.2:1	9.2:1	9.2:1
Camshaft	9782218	9782218	9777254	9777254	9777254	9777254
Carburetor	4-barrel	4-barrel	2-barrel	2-barrel	2-barrel	2-barrel
Gross HP	215 hp at 5,200 rpm	215 hp at 5,200 rpm	250 hp at 4,600 rpm	250 hp at 4,600 rpm	250 hp at 4,600 rpm	250 hp at 4,600 rpm
Gross Torque	240 ft-lbs at 3,800 rpm	240 ft-lbs at 3,800 rpm	333 ft-lbs at 2,800 rpm	333 ft-lbs at 2,800 rpm	333 ft-lbs at 2,800 rpm	333 ft-lbs at 2,800 rpm
Notes	Sprint 6	Sprint 6 California Emissions		California Emissions		California Emissions

1967 Engine Codes CONTINUED

UPC	L76	L76	L76	L76	L78	L78
Displacement	326	326	326	326	400	400
ID Code	YM	XO	WK	WO	YT	WZ
Transmission	Auto	Auto	Manual	Manual	Auto	Manual
Bore x Stroke	3.72 x 3.75	3.72 x 3.75	3.72 x 3.75	3.72 x 3.75	4.12 x 3.75	4.12 x 3.75
Cylinder Head	141	141	141	141	670	670
Advertised Compression	10.5:1	10.5:1	10.5:1	10.5:1	10.75:1	10.75:1
Camshaft	9777254	9777254	9777254	9777254	9779066	9779067
Carburetor	4-barrel	4-barrel	4-barrel	4-barrel	4-barrel	4-barrel
Gross HP	285 hp at 5,000 rpm	285 hp at 5,000 rpm	285 hp at 5,000 rpm	285 hp at 5,000 rpm	325 hp at 4,800 rpm	325 hp at 4,800 rpm
Gross Torque	359 ft-lbs at 3,200 rpm	359 ft-lbs at 3,200 rpm	359 ft-lbs at 3,200 rpm	359 ft-lbs at 3,200 rpm	410 ft-lbs at 3,400 rpm	410 ft-lbs at 3,400 rpm
Notes	326 H.O.	326 H.O. California Emissions	326 H.O.	326 H.O. California Emissions		

UPC	L78	L67	L67	L67
Displacement	400	400	400	400
ID Code	WU	XN	WI	WQ
Transmission	Manual	Auto	Manual	Manual
Bore x Stroke	4.12 x 3.75	4.12 x 3.75	4.12 x 3.75	4.12 x 3.75
Cylinder Head	670	670	670	670
Advertised Compression	10.75:1	10.75:1	10.75:1	10.75:1
Camshaft	9779067	9785744	9785744	9785744
Carburetor	4-barrel	4-barrel	4-barrel	4-barrel
Gross HP	325 hp at 4,800 rpm	325 hp at 5,200 rpm	325 hp at 5,200 rpm	325 hp at 5,200 rpm
Gross Torque	410 ft-lbs at 3,400 rpm	410 ft-lbs at 3,600 rpm	410 ft-lbs at 3,600 rpm	410 ft-lbs at 3,600 rpm
Notes	California Emissions	400 Ram Air	400 Ram Air	400 Ram Air California Emissions

1967 V-8 Cylinder Heads

Casting Number	140	141	670	997
Application	326 2-barrel	326 H.O.	400 4-barrel	400 Ram Air
Valve Sizes (interior/exterior)	1.92/1.66	1.92/1.66	2.11/1.77	2.11/1.77
Rocker Arm Studs	Pressed	Pressed	Threaded	Threaded
Advertised Compression Ratio	9.2:1	10.5:1	10.75:1	10.75:1
Actual Chamber Volume	67 cc	58 cc	72 cc	72 cc
Actual Compression Ratio	8.2:1	10.0:1	10.0:1	10.0:1

APPENDIX B: 1968 FIREBIRD

1968 Firebird Exterior Colors (All Models)

Codes are unknown for Carnival Red, Marigold Yellow, Pink Mist, and Windward Blue

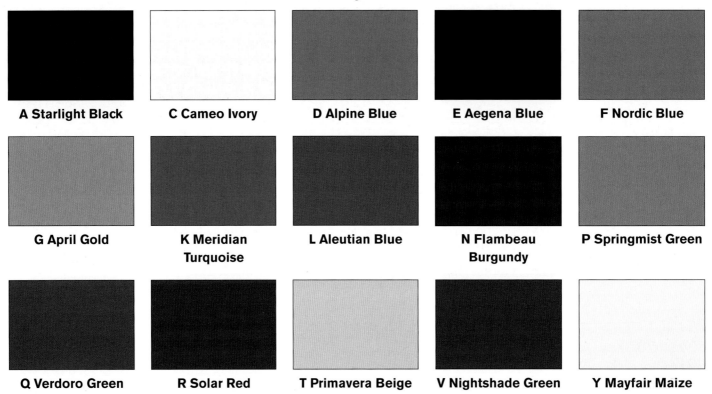

A Starlight Black	C Cameo Ivory	D Alpine Blue	E Aegena Blue	F Nordic Blue
G April Gold	K Meridian Turquoise	L Aleutian Blue	N Flambeau Burgundy	P Springmist Green
Q Verdoro Green	R Solar Red	T Primavera Beige	V Nightshade Green	Y Mayfair Maize

New Exterior Color for 1968

I Autumn Bronze

Standard for all 1968 Firebirds. This new color replaces Starlight Black (Code A), which is available only on Special Order and at extra cost for Firebird models. Autumn Bronze is also available as a Special Paint Option at extra cost on all other 1968 Pontiac models except GTO.

Cameo Ivory (Code C) is recommended as the upper area color with Autumn Bronze when a two-tone paint combination is desired.

Stripe Application

Exterior Color	Code	Stripe Color	Interior Trim Combination
Autumn Bronze	I	Cameo Ivory	260, 262, 273, 275
		Starlight Black	253, 259, 269, 272

Two-Tone Availability

Lower Body	Code	Upper Body	Code	Interior Trim Combination
Autumn Bronze	I	Cameo Ivory	C	253, 259, 260, 262, 269, 272, 273, 275

Convertible/Cordova Top Colors

1 Ivory-White
2 Black

1968 Pontiac Special Order Exterior Colors

| 868-99466 | 868-99539 | 927-99576 | L67YD003 |
| Pink Mist | Carnival Red | Windward Blue | Marigold Yellow |

To help satisfy those customers who request special exterior paint, Pontiac made available four distinctive new colors for 1968: Pink Mist, Carnival Red, Windward Blue, Marigold Yellow. These special exterior colors are available for all 1968 series except GTO with Endura bumper.

1968 Firebird Cordova and Convertible Top Colors

Code	Color
1	Ivory
2	Black

Code	Color
5	Dark Teal
8	Medium Gold

1968 Interior Color Codes

Code	Color	Level	Seating
250	Teal	Standard	Bucket
251	Gold	Standard	Bucket
252	Red	Standard	Bucket
253	Black	Standard	Bucket
261	Turquoise	Standard	Bucket
262	Parchment	Standard	Bucket
255	Teal	Custom	Bucket
256	Turquoise	Custom	Bucket
257	Gold	Custom	Bucket
258	Red	Custom	Bucket
259	Black	Custom	Bucket
260	Parchment	Custom	Bucket
281	Saddle Leather	Custom	Bucket
269	Black	Custom	Bench
275	Parchment	Custom	Bench

1968 Firebird Known Engine and Trans Production

	M12 3-Speed Manual-Column	M12 3-Speed Manual-Floor	M13 HD 3-Speed Manual	M20 4-Speed Manual	M31 2-Speed Automatic	M40 Turbo 400	Total
OHC-6	Unknown*	3,298	N/A**	1,997	8,725	N/A**	13,832
Sprint-6	N/A**	2,544	N/A**	1,093	1,025	N/A**	4,662
350 2bbl	Unknown*	N/A**	Unknown*	Unknown*	49,879	N/A**	60,879
350 H.O.	Unknown*	N/A**	Unknown*	Unknown*	2,640	N/A**	6,423
400	N/A**	N/A**	754	8,629	N/A**	11,933	21,316
Total	2,002	5,842	6,841	18,225	62,269	11,933	107,112

* No data available
** Not available

1968 Firebird Total Production

Series	Engine	Level	Van Nuys	Lordstown	CKD	Total
2337	6-cylinder	Standard Coupe	1,215	12,785	0	14,000
2367	6-cylinder	Standard Convertible	69	1,900	0	1,969
2537	6-cylinder	Deluxe Coupe	122	1,884	72	2,078
2567	6-cylinder	Deluxe Convertible	20	427	0	447
2437	V-8	Standard Coupe	5,919	41,383	0	47,302
2467	V-8	Standard Convertible	604	7,976	0	8,580
2637	V-8	Deluxe Coupe	3,741	23,031	0	26,772
2667	V-8	Deluxe Convertible	458	5,506	0	5,964
			12,148	94,892	72	107,112

1968 Firebird Sprint

Series	Engine	Model	Total
2337	6-cylinder	Standard Coupe	3,045
2367	6-cylinder	Standard Convertible	458
2537	6-cylinder	Deluxe Coupe	960
2567	6-cylinder	Deluxe Convertible	199
			4,662

1968 Firebird H.O.

Series	Engine	Model	Total
2437	350 H.O.	Standard Coupe	3,261
2467	350 H.O.	Standard Convertible	596
2637	350 H.O.	Deluxe Coupe	2,107
2667	350 H.O.	Deluxe Convertible	459
			6,423

1968 Firebird 400 Production

Series	Model	Manual	Auto	Total
2437	Standard Coupe	4,779	4,159	8,938
2467	Standard Convertible	738	729	1,467
2637	Deluxe Coupe	3,161	5,787	8,948
2667	Deluxe Convertible	705	1,258	1,963
		9,383	11,933	21,316

1968 Firebird 400 with C60 Air Conditioning

Series	Model	Total
2437	Standard Coupe	2,042
2467	Standard Convertible	202
2637	Deluxe Coupe	3,401
2667	Deluxe Convertible	482
		6,127

1968 Firebird with C60 Air Conditioning

Series	Engine	Level	Total
2337	6-cylinder	Standard Coupe	553
2367	6-cylinder	Standard Convertible	42
2537	6-cylinder	Deluxe Coupe	135
2567	6-cylinder	Deluxe Convertible	14
2437	V-8	Standard Coupe	12,196
2467	V-8	Standard Convertible	989
2637	V-8	Deluxe Coupe	9,749
2667	V-8	Deluxe Convertible	1,148
			24,826

1968 Firebird Installed Options

Code	UPC	Description	Total Installed
531	A01	Soft Ray Glass (all)	24,356
532	A02	Soft Ray Glass (windshield)	39,479
551	A31	Power Windows	3,256
564	A46	Power Bucket Seat	278
772	A48	Delete Standard Seat Belts (front and rear), export	Unknown
771	A49	Custom Front Seat Belts, export	Unknown
604	A67	Folding Rear Seat	5,150
754	A85	Deluxe Front Shoulder (convertible only)	113
492	A90	Deck Lid Release	698

1968 Firebird Installed Options *CONTINUED*

Code	UPC	Description	Total Installed
568	AL4	Contoured Bench	3,721
754	AS1	Standard Front Shoulder (convertible only)	30
571	AS2	Head Rest Bench	1,711
432	AS4	Deluxe Rear Shoulder	147
631	B32	Front Floor Mats	20,270
632	B33	Rear Floor Mats	9,036
732	B36	Fitted Trunk Mat	3,003
412	B93	Door Edge Guards	12,639
544	C06	Power Convertible Top	Unknown
295	C24	Cordova Top	39,037
802	C48	Heater Delete, export	Unknown
404	C50	Electric Rear Window Defogger	3,808
582	C60	Air Condition	24,826
424	D33	Outside Remote Mirror	19,860
421	D34	Visor Vanity Mirror, right	4,068
422	D42	Visor Vanity Mirror, right and left	6,652
472	D55	Front Console	76,776
494	D98	Rally Stripes	Unknown
634	FG1	Adjustable Shocks, front and rear	695
502	J50	Power Brakes	33,093
521	J52	Front Disc Brakes	6,766
534	JL1	Pedal Trim	30,282
441	K30	Cruise Control (V-8 with Auto Trans only)	698
731	K45	Heavy-Duty Air Cleaner	16,046
692	K82	Heavy-Duty Alternator	71
343	L30	350 2-Barrel V-8	60,879
347	L67	400 4-Barrel V-8 Ram Air	523
348	L74	400 H.O. 4-Barrel V-8	2,087
344	L76	350 H.O. 4-Barrel V-8	6,423
524	M09	Custom Gear Shift Knob	Unknown
356	M12	3-speed Manual, floor shift, 6-cylinder only	5,842
355	M13	Heavy-Duty 3-Speed Manual (floor shift)	6,841
354	M20	4-Speed Manual, floor shift	18,225
352	M31	Automatic Trans, except W66	62,269
351	M40	Turbo-400	11,933
481	N10	Dual Exhaust (V-8 only)	28,945
482	N25	Exhaust Extensions	1,733
462	N30	Delux Steering Wheel	47,532
504	N33	Tilt Steering Wheel	6,025
471	N34	Custom Sport Steering Wheel	3,655
501	N40	Power Steering	84,594

Code	UPC	Description	Total Installed
702	N64	Conventional Spare Tire	22,602
452	N95	Wire Wheel Discs	2,932
453	N98	Rally II Wheels	26,563
461	P01	Deluxe Wheel Discs	40,887
554	W54	Custom Trim	35,260
458	P02	Custom Wheel Discs	4,300
402	P17	Spare Tire Cover	520
N/A	PW7	Wide Oval White Wall Tires	66,386
N/A	PW8	Wide Oval Red-Line Tires	27,324
782	T64	Battery Delete, export	Unknown
764	T70	Export Headlamps	Unknown
442	U15	Safe-Guard Speedometer	742
804	U18	Kilo Speedometer, export	Unknown
672	U23	Ignition Switch Lamp	6,005
652	U25	Luggage Compartment Lamp	8,317
671	U26	Utility Lamp	2,068
444	U30	Auxiliary Guage Cluster	9,895
474	U35	Electric Clock	18,792
382	U63	AM Radio	96,310
384	U69	AM/FM Radio	6,194
381	U73	Manual Antenna	32,315
391	U84	Stereo Tape	2,870
701	UA1	Heavy-Duty Battery	2,236
434	UB5	Hood-Mounted Tachometer	6,780
414	UC5	Dual Horns	12,161
681	V01	Heavy-Duty Radiator	Unknown
752	V48	Canadian Car Engine Coolant	Unknown
804	V60	Foot Tire Pump, export	50
774	V78	Export Body Plate	Unknown
742	VK1	Delete Front License Plate Mounting	Unknown
342	W53	OHC 6-Cylinder 4-Barrel	4,662
761	W58	Export Preparation	Unknown
762	W59	Hawaii Export Prep	Unknown
345	W66	400 Sport Option	21,316
N/A	WS1	Deluxe Belts and Shoulder Harness	26,616
621	Y96	Ride and Handling Package	Unknown
353	M12	3-Speed Manual (column shift)	2,002
491	N/A	Delete Paint Stripe	Unknown
N/A	N/A	White-Wall Tires	70,120
N/A	N/A	Fiberglass Tires	77
STD	STD	OHC 6-Cylinder 1-Barrel	13,832

1968 Options

Standard Firebird
250-ci OHC-6 engine with 1-barrel carburetor
3-speed manual transmission, column shifted
E70-14 Wide Oval tires with black sidewall

W53 Firebird Sprint Option
L72 Sprint-6 engine with 4-barrel carburetor
Chromed air cleaner lid
Low-restriction single exhaust (same as V-8)
M12 3-speed manual transmission, floor shifted
Heavy-duty clutch
High-rated front and rear springs
F70-14 Wide Oval tires with black sidewall
Special "Sprint" identification

L30 Firebird 350 Option
350-ci V-8 with 2-barrel carburetor
M12 3-speed manual transmission, column shifted
F70-14 Wide Oval tires with black sidewall

L76 Firebird H.O. Option
L76 350 H.O. V-8 with 4-barrel carburetor

N10 dual exhaust
M12 3-speed manual transmission, column shifted
UA1 heavy-duty battery
Heavy-duty starter
D98 Rally side stripes
High-rated front and rear springs
F70-14 Wide Oval tires with black sidewall

W66 Firebird 400 Option
400-inch V-8 with 4-barrel carburetor
Chrome-plated engine appointments
N10 dual exhaust
UA1 heavy-duty battery
Heavy-duty starter
Heavy-duty radiator
Dual-scooped hood
M13 heavy-duty 3-speed manual transmission, floor shifted
High-rated front and rear springs
Heavy-duty shock absorbers
F70-14 Wide Oval tires with red sidewall
Special "400" identification

1968 Option Package Groups

321 Basic Group
K45 Heavy-Duty Air Cleaner
U35 Electric Clock
U63 Push Button Radio (with front manual antenna)

322 Protection Group
A39 Custom Seat Belts, front and rear
B32 Floor Mats, front
B33 Floor Mats, rear
B93 Door Edge Guards
C50 Rear Window Defogger (coupe only)
P17 Spare Tire Cover

324 Décor Group
JL1 Pedal Trim Package
N30 Deluxe Steering Wheel
P01 Deluxe Wheel Discs

331 Mirror Group
D33 Remote-Control Outside Mirror
D42 Visor Vanity Mirrors, right and left

332 Lamp Group
U23 Ignition Switch Lamp
U25 Luggage Lamp

1968 Firebird Springs and Shocks

Level	Front Shocks	Rear Shocks	Front Coil Springs	Rear Leaf Springs	Front Stabilizer Bar Diameter	Rear Stabilizer Bar Diameter
Firebird	Standard	Standard	Standard	Standard	.625 inch	None
W53 Sprint Option	High Rate	High Rate	High Rate	High Rate	.625 inch	None
L76 Firebird H.O. Option	High Rate	High Rate	High Rate	High Rate	.625 inch	None
W66 Firebird 400 Option	High Rate	High Rate	High Rate	High Rate	.625 inch	None
Y96 Ride and Handling Option (available all)	Heavy Duty	Heavy Duty	Heavy Duty	Heavy Duty	.625 inch	None

Note: FG1 Koni Adjustable Shocks optional all levels

1968 Engine Codes

UPC	STD	STD	L72	L72	L30	L30
Displacement	250	250	250	250	350	350
ID Code	ZN	ZK	ZE	ZD	YJ	WC
Transmission	Auto	Manual	Auto	Manual	Auto	Manual
Bore x Stroke	3.88 x 3.65	3.88 x 3.65	3.88 x 3.65	3.88 x 3.65	3.88 x 3.75	3.88 x 3.75
Cylinder Head	9791194	9791194	9791195	9791195	17	17
Advertised Compression	9:1	9:1	10.5:1	10.5:1	9.2:1	9.2:1
Camshaft	9790826	9790826	9792539	9792539	9777254	9777254
Carburetor	1-barrel	1-barrel	4-barrel	4-barrel	2-barrel	2-barrel
Gross HP	175 hp at 4,800 rpm	175 hp at 4,800 rpm	215 hp at 5,200 rpm	215 hp at 5,200 rpm	265 hp at 4,600 rpm	265 hp at 4,600 rpm
Gross Torque	240 ft-lbs at 2,600 rpm	240 ft-lbs at 2,600 rpm	255 ft-lbs at 3,800 rpm	255 ft-lbs at 3,800 rpm	355 ft-lbs at 2,800 rpm	355 ft-lbs at 2,800 rpm
Notes			Sprint 6	Sprint 6		

UPC	L76	L76	L78	L78	L74	L74
Displacement	350	350	400	400	400	400
ID Code	YM	WK	YT	WZ	YW	WQ
Transmission	Auto	Manual	Auto	Manual	Auto	Manual
Bore x Stroke	3.88 x 3.75	3.88 x 3.75	4.12 x 3.75	4.12 x 3.75	4.12 x 3.75	4.12 x 3.75
Cylinder Head	18	18	16	16	16	16
Advertised Compression	10.5:1	10.5:1	10.75:1	10.75:1	10.75:1	10.75:1
Camshaft	9779066	9779067	9779066	9779067	9779067	9779068
Carburetor	4-barrel	4-barrel	4-barrel	4-barrel	4-barrel	4-barrel
Gross HP	320 hp at 5,100 rpm	320 hp at 5,100 rpm	330 hp at 4,800 rpm	330 hp at 4,800 rpm	335 hp at 5,000 rpm	335 hp at 5,000 rpm
Gross Torque	380 ft-lbs at 3,200 rpm	380 ft-lbs at 3,200 rpm	430 ft-lbs at 3,300 rpm	430 ft-lbs at 3,300 rpm	430 ft-lbs at 3,400 rpm	430 ft-lbs at 3,400 rpm
Notes	350 H.O.	350 H.O.			400 H.O.	400 H.O.

UPC	L67	L67	L67	L67
Displacement	400	400	400	400
ID Code	XN	WI	XT	WU
Transmission	Auto	Manual	Auto	Manual
Bore x Stroke	4.12 x 3.75	4.12 x 3.75	4.12 x 3.75	4.12 x 3.75
Cylinder Head	31	31	96	96
Advertised Compression	10.75:1	10.75:1	10.75:1	10.75:1

1968 Engine Codes *CONTINUED*

Camshaft	9779068	9785744	9779068	9794041
Carburetor	4-barrel	4-barrel	4-barrel	4-barrel
Gross HP	335 hp at 5,300 rpm	335 hp at 5,300 rpm	340 hp at 5,300 rpm	340 hp at 5,300 rpm
Gross Torque	430 ft-lbs at 3,600 rpm	430 ft-lbs at 3,600 rpm	430 ft-lbs at 3,600 rpm	430 ft-lbs at 3,600 rpm
Notes	Ram Air I	Ram Air I	Ram Air II	Ram Air II

1968 V-8 Cylinder Heads

Casting Number	17	18	16	31	96
Application	350 2-barrel	350 H.O.	400 4-barrel	Ram Air I	Ram Air II
Valve Sizes (interior/exterior)	1.96/1.66	1.96/1.66	2.11/1.77	2.11/1.77	2.11/1.77
Rocker Arm Studs	Pressed	Pressed	Threaded	Threaded	Threaded
Advertised Compression Ratio	9.2:1	10.5:1	10.75:1	10.75:1	10.75:1
Actual Chamber Volume	83 cc	66 cc	74 cc	72 cc	71 cc
Actual Compression Ratio	8.2:1	10.0:1	9.8:1	9.9:1	10.0:1

APPENDIX C: 1969 FIREBIRD

1969 Firebird Exterior Colors (All Series)

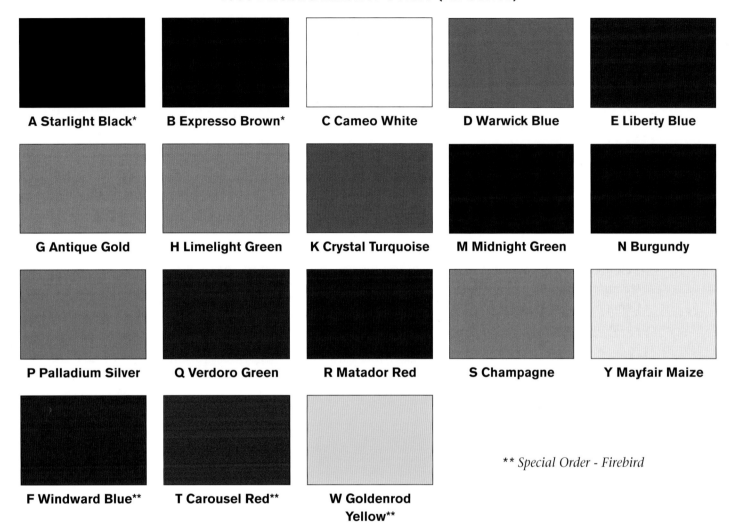

A Starlight Black*	B Expresso Brown*	C Cameo White
D Warwick Blue	E Liberty Blue	
G Antique Gold	H Limelight Green	K Crystal Turquoise
M Midnight Green	N Burgundy	
P Palladium Silver	Q Verdoro Green	R Matador Red
S Champagne	Y Mayfair Maize	
F Windward Blue**	T Carousel Red**	W Goldenrod Yellow**

** Special Order - Firebird

1969 Firebird Cordova Top Colors

Code	Color	Code	Color
1	White	5	Parchment
2	Black	8	Dark Brown
3	Dark Blue	9	Dark Green

1969 Firebird Convertible Top Colors

Code	Color	Code	Color
1	Ivory	3	Dark Blue
2	Black	9	Dark Green

1969 Firebird Interior Color Codes

Code	Color	Level	Seating
200	Blue	Standard	Bucket
202	Gold	Standard	Bucket
206	Green	Standard	Bucket
207	Parchment	Standard	Bucket
208	Black	Standard	Bucket
210	Blue	Custom	Bucket
212	Gold	Custom	Bucket

Code	Color	Level	Seating
214	Red	Custom	Bucket
216	Green	Custom	Bucket
217	Parchment	Custom	Bucket
218	Black	Custom	Bucket
227	Parchment	Custom	Bench
228	Black	Custom	Bench
238	Gold Leather	Custom	Bucket

1969 Firebird Known Engine and Transmission Production Numbers (includes Trans Am)

	M12 3-Speed Manual-Column	M12 3-Speed Manual-Floor	M13 HD 3-Speed Manual	M20 4-Speed Manual	M21 4-Speed Manual	M31 2-Speed Auto	M38 Trubo 350	M40 Turbo 400	Total
OHC-6	Unknown*	2,644	N/A**	Unknown*	N/A**	4,368	1,792	N/A**	9,052
Sprint-6	N/A	1,098	N/A**	399	N/A**	N/A**	482	N/A**	1,979
350 2-barrel	Unknown*	N/A**	3,915	3,883	N/A**	10,692	29,000	Unknown*	59,280
350 H.O.	10	N/A**	465	1,569	Unknown*	N/A**	N/A**	2,422	4,466
400 4-barrel	N/A**	N/A**	296	Unknown*	Unknown*	N/A**	N/A**	Unknown*	11,302
400 H.O.	N/A**	N/A**	35	939	113	N/A**	N/A**	422	1,509
Ram Air IV	N/A**	N/A**	N/A**	N/A**	116	N/A**	N/A**	41	157
Total	1,276	3,742	4,711	10,576	535	15,060	31,274	20,534	87,745***

* No data available

** Not available

*** *Pontiac production records indicated 87,708 Firebirds produced.*

1969 Firebird Monthly Production

September 1968	6,571
October 1968	11,361
November 1968	11,734
December 1968	9,019
January 1969	9,444
February 1969	8,560
March 1969	6,739

April 1969	1,307
May 1969	2,733
June 1969	4,680
July 1969	1,653
August 1969	3,007
September–October 1969	9,599
November 1969	1,301
Total	87,708

1969 Firebird 400 H.O. Monthly Production*

September 1968	40	April 1969	34
October 1968	146	May 1969	57
November 1968	180	June 1969	312
December 1968	114	July 1969	156
January 1969	77	August 1969	89
February 1969	103	September–October 1969	58
March 1969	119	November 1969	24
		Total	1,509

Includes Trans Am

1969 Firebird Ram Air IV Monthly Production*

February 1969	15	July 1969	12
March 1969	53	August 1969	9
April 1969	7	September–October 1969	20
May 1969	15	November 1969	1
June 1969	25	Total	157

Includes Trans Am

1969 Firebird 400 Monthly Production

September 1968	1,188	April 1969	197
October 1968	1,856	May 1969	291
November 1968	2,084	June 1969	215
December 1968	1,538	July 1969	145
January 1969	1,210	August 1969	206
Februry 1969	1,092	September–October 1969	458
March 1969	772	November 1969	50
		Total	11,302

1969 Trans Am Monthly Production

May 1969	5	August 1969	80
June 1969	257	September–October 1969	189
July 1969	146	November 1969	20
		Total	697

1969 Firebird Installed Options

UPC	Code	Description	Total Installed
AS1	438	Standard Front Shoulder Strap	49
A01	531	Soft Ray Glass (all)	367
A02	532	Soft Ray Windshield	586
A31	551	Power Windows	2,784
A39	434	Deluxe Seat Belts, front and rear	1,469
A46	564	Power Bucket	949
A67	604	Folding Rear Seat	2,527
A90	492	Deck Lid Release	7,015
B32	631	Front Floor Mats	18,900
B33	632	Rear Floor Mats	8,969
B42	732	Fitted Trunk Mat	17,896
B93	412	Door Edge Guards	10,362
CD1	591	Arctic Wiper Blades	523
C06	544	Power Convertible Top	8,795
C08		Cordova Top	37,819
C50	404	Rear Window Defogger	3,523
C57	588	Power Flow Ventilation	54
C60	582	Air Conditioning	28,091
DH5	422	Visor Mirror, left-hand	1,554
D33	424	Remote-Control Driver's Mirror	20,630
D34	421	Visor Mirror, right-hand	10,416
D55	472	Front Console	68,284
FG1	634	Adjustable Shock Absorbers, front and rear	232
G80	361	Safe-T-Track Differential	10,439
G90/G92	368	Performance Axle Ratio	958
G95/G97	364	Economy Axle Ratio	382
JL1	514	Brake Pedal Trim Package	55,854
JL2	511	Power Front Disc Brakes	21,080
J50	502	Power Brakes	18,500
KB2	692	Heavy-Duty Variable-Pitch Fan	134
K02	691	Heavy-Duty 7-Blade Fan	219
K30	441	Cruise Control	490
K45	731	Heavy-Duty Air Cleaner	9,537
K82	682	55-Amp Alternator	12
K96	688	55-Amp Alternator, self-regulated	70
L30	343	350 2-Barrel	59,280
L67	347	Ram Air IV	157
L74	348	400 H.O.	1,509
L76	344	350 H.O.	4,466
M09	534	Custom Gearshift Knob	1,673
M12	356	3-Speed Manual, floor shift	3,742

UPC	Code	Description	Total Installed
M13	355	Heavy-Duty 3-Speed Manual	4,711
M20	354	4-Speed Manual	10,576
M21	358	Close-Ratio 4-Speed Manual	535
M31	352	2-Speed Automatic	15,060
M38	359	3-Speed Automatic	31,274
M40	351	Turbo-400	20,534
N10	481	Dual Exhaust	17,248
N25	482	Exhaust Extensions	11
N30	461	Deluxe Steering Wheel	62,155
N33	504	Tilt Steering Wheel	5,025
N34	462	Custom Sport Steering Wheel (wood)	5,191
N41	601	Power Steering	75,773
N64	704	Conventional Spare Tire	NOW STD
N95	453	Wire Wheel Disc	1,334
N98	454	Rally II Wheels	27,329
P01	451	Deluxe Wheel Discs	49,145
P02	452	Custom Wheel Discs	1,379
P17	402	Spare Tire Cover	N/A
T42	611	Hood-Ram Air Inlet	877
UA1	672	Heavy-Duty Battery	1,770
UB5	471	Hood-Mounted Tachometer	3,486
U05	414	Dual Horns	44,957
U15	442	Safeguard Speedometer	285
U25	652	Luggage Lamp	6,409
U26	671	Underhood Lamp	2,262
U30	444	Rally Gauge Cluster and Instrument Panel Tach	881
U35	474	Electric Clock	19,166
U57	394	Stereo Tape Player	3,070
U58	388	Stereo AM/FM Radio	1,191
U63	382	AM Radio	78,235
U69	384	AM/FM Radio	5,244
U75	381	Power Antenna	4,233
U80	391	Rear Speaker	11,209
V01	701	Heavy-Duty Radiator	542
V64	694	Vacuum Operated Tire Pump	585
WS1	431	Deluxe Seat Belts and Front Shoulder Harness	11,824
WS2	432	Deluxe Seat Belts and Front/Rear Shoulder Harness	233
WS4	627	Trans Am Package	697
WT5	754	Mountain Performance Package	147
W50	554	Custom Trim Group, bench seat	1,570
W53	342	Sprint Sport Option	1,979

1969 Firebird Installed Options CONTINUED

UPC	Code	Description	Total Installed
W54	554	Custom Trim Group, bucket seat	15,616
W63	484	Rally Gauge Cluster and Electric Clock	6,313
W66	345	400 Sport Option	11,302
Y81	464	Décor Moldings	45,609
Y96	261	Ride and Handling Package	12,664
N/A	N/A	White-Line Tires	59,575
N/A	N/A	Fiberglass Tires	14,678
N/A	N/A	Red-Line Tires	16,068

1969 Options

Standard Firebird
250-ci OHC-6 engine with 1-barrel carburetor
3-speed manual transmission-column shifted
E70-14 Wide Oval tires with black sidewall

W53 Firebird Sprint Option
L72 Sprint-6 engine with 4-barrel carburetor
Chromed air cleaner lid
Low-restriction single exhaust (same as V-8)
M12 3-speed manual transmission, floor shifted
Heavy-duty clutch
High-rated front and rear springs
F70-14 Wide Oval tires with black sidewall
Special "Sprint" identification

L30 Firebird 350 Option
350-ci V-8 with 2-barrel carburetor
M12 3-speed manual transmission, column shifted
F70-14 Wide Oval tires with black sidewall

L76 Firebird H.O. Option
L76 350 H.O. V-8 with 4-barrel carburetor
N10 dual exhaust
M12 3-speed manual transmission, column shifted
UA1 heavy-duty battery
Heavy-duty starter
D98 Rally side stripes
High-rated front and rear springs
F70-14 Wide Oval tires with black sidewall

W66 Firebird 400 Option
400-inch V-8 with 4-barrel carburetor
Chrome-plated engine appointments
N10 dual exhaust
UA1 heavy-duty battery
Heavy-duty starter
Heavy-duty radiator
Dual-scooped hood
M13 heavy-duty 3-speed manual transmission, floor shifted
High-rated Front and Rear Springs
Heavy-duty shock absorbers
F70-14 Wide Oval tires with red sidewall
Special "400" identification

WS4 Trans Am Option
L74 400-inch V-8 with functional Ram Air
M13 heavy-duty 3-speed manual transmission, floor shifted
Special high-effort power front disc brakes
Special high-effort power steering
Heavy-duty Safe-T-Track differential with 3.55:1 gears
F70-14 fiberglass belted tires
7-inch-wide rims
Heavy-duty ride and handling
Specific Ram Air hood
Special deck-lid air foil
Functional fender-mounted air extractors
Special striping and ornamentation
Special steering wheel

1969 Option Package Groups

321 Basic Group
A90 Deck Lid Release
D33 Remote-Controlled Outside Mirror
D42 Visor Vanity Mirror, right
K45 Heavy-Duty Air Cleaner
U35 Electric Clock
U63 Push Button Radio (with front manual antenna)

322 Protection Group
A39 Custom Seat Belts, front and rear
B32 Floor Mats, front
B33 Floor Mats, rear
B93 Door Edge Guards
C50 Rear Window Defogger (coupe only)
P17 Spare Tire Cover

324 Décor Group
JL1 Pedal Trim Package
N30 Deluxe Steering Wheel

P01 Deluxe Wheel Covers
U05 Dual Horns
464 Bright Wheel-Opening and Roof-Drip-Rail Moldings

331 Power Assist Group
JL2 Power Disc Brakes, front
M38 or M40 Automatic Transmission
N41 Variable-Ratio Power Steering

332 Turnpike Cruise Group
A46 Power Seat, driver's bucket
K30 Cruise Control
N33 Tilt Steering Wheel

334 Rally Group
N34 Custom Sport Steering Wheel
N98 Rally II Wheels
W63 Rally Gauge Cluster with Electric Clock
Y96 Ride and Handling Package

1969 Firebird Springs and Shocks

Level	Front Shocks	Rear Shocks	Front Coil Springs	Rear Leaf Springs	Front Stabilizer Bar Diameter	Rear Stabilizer Bar Diameter
Firebird 6-cylinder	Standard	Standard	Standard	Standard	.625 inch	None
Firebird V-8	Standard	Standard	High Rate	High Rate	.625 inch	None
W53 Sprint Option	Standard	Standard	High Rate	High Rate	.625 inch	None
L76 Firebird H.O. Option	Heavy Duty	Heavy Duty	Heavy Duty	Heavy Duty	.625 inch	None
W66 Firebird 400 Option	Standard	Standard	High Rate	High Rate	.625 inch	None
W66 Firebird 400 with L74 400 H.O.	Heavy Duty	Heavy Duty	Heavy Duty	Heavy Duty	.625 inch	None
WS4 Trans Am Option	Heavy Duty	Heavy Duty	Heavy Duty	Heavy Duty	1.00 inch	None
Y96 Ride and Handling Option (where available)	Heavy Duty	Heavy Duty	Heavy Duty	Heavy Duty	.625 inch	None

1969 Engine Codes

UPC	STD	STD	STD	STD	L72	L72
Displacement	250	250	250	250	250	250
ID Code	ZN	ZK	ZF	ZC	ZE	ZL
Transmission	Auto	Manual	Auto	Manual	Auto	Auto
Bore x Stroke	3.88 x 3.65	3.88 x 3.65	3.88 x 3.65	3.88 x 3.65	3.88 x 3.65	3.88 x 3.65
Cylinder Head	9795458	9795458	9795458	9795458	9795457	9795457
Advertised Compression	9:1	9:1	9:1	9:1	10.5:1	10.5:1
Camshaft	9790826	9790826	9790826	9790826	9792539	9792539
Carburetor	1-barrel	1-barrel	1-barrel	1-barrel	4-barrel	4-barrel
Gross HP	175 hp at 4,800 rpm	175 hp at 4,800 rpm	175 hp at 4,800 rpm	175 hp at 4,800 rpm	215 hp at 5,200 rpm	215 hp at 5,200 rpm
Gross Torque	240 ft-lbs at 2,600 rpm	240 ft-lbs at 2,600 rpm	240 ft-lbs at 2,600 rpm	240 ft-lbs at 2,600 rpm	255 ft-lbs at 3,800 rpm	255 ft-lbs at 3,800 rpm
Notes					Sprint 6	Sprint 6

UPC	L72	L72	L30	L30	L30	L30
Displacement	250	250	350	350	350	350
ID Code	ZD	ZH	XL	YU	XB	YE
Transmission	Manual	Manual	Auto	Auto	Auto	Auto
Bore x Stroke	3.88 x 3.65	3.88 x 3.65	3.88 x 3.75	3.88 x 3.75	3.88 x 3.75	3.88 x 3.75
Cylinder Head	9795457	9795457	17	17	47	47
Advertised Compression	10.5:1	10.5:1	9.2:1	9.2:1	9.2:1	9.2:1
Camshaft	9796327	9796327	9777254	9777254	9777254	9777254
Carburetor	4-barrel	4-barrel	2-barrel	2-barrel	2-barrel	2-barrel
Gross HP	230 hp at 5,400 rpm	230 hp at 5,400 rpm	265 hp at 4,600 rpm	265 hp at 4,600 rpm	265 hp at 4,600 rpm	265 hp at 4,600 rpm
Gross Torque	260 ft-lbs at 3,600 rpm	260 ft-lbs at 3,600 rpm	355 ft-lbs at 2,800 rpm	355 ft-lbs at 2,800 rpm	355 ft-lbs at 2,800 rpm	355 ft-lbs at 2,800 rpm
Notes	Sprint 6	Sprint 6		California Emissions		California Emissions

UPC	L30	L30	L76	L76	L78	L78
Displacement	350	350	350	350	400	400
ID Code	WC	WM	XC	WN	YT	WZ
Transmission	Manual	Manual	Auto	Manual	Auto	Manual
Bore x Stroke	3.88 x 3.75	3.88 x 3.75	3.88 x 3.75	3.88 x 3.75	4.12 x 3.75	4.12 x 3.75
Cylinder Head	17	47	48	48	62	48

Advertised Compression	9.2:1	9.2:1	10.5:1	10.5:1	10.75:1	10.75:1
Camshaft	9777254	9777254	9779067	9779068	9779066	9779067
Carburetor	2-barrel	2-barrel	4-barrel	4-barrel	4-barrel	4-barrel
Gross HP	265 hp at 4,600 rpm	265 hp at 4,600 rpm	325 hp at 5,100 rpm	325 hp at 5,100 rpm	330 hp at 4,800 rpm	330 hp at 4,800 rpm
Gross Torque	355 ft-lbs at 2,800 rpm	355 ft-lbs at 2,800 rpm	380 ft-lbs at 3,200 rpm	380 ft-lbs at 3,200 rpm	430 ft-lbs at 3,300 rpm	430 ft-lbs at 3,300 rpm
Notes			350 H.O.	350 H.O.		

UPC	L74	L74	L67	L67
Displacement	400	400	400	400
ID Code	YW	WQ	XN	WH
Transmission	Auto	Manual	Auto	Manual
Bore x Stroke	4.12 x 3.75	4.12 x 3.75	4.12 x 3.75	4.12 x 3.75
Cylinder Head	62	48	722	722
Advertised Compression	10.75:1	10.75:1	10.75:1	10.75:1
Camshaft	9779067	9779068	9794041	9794041
Carburetor	4-barrel	4-barrel	4-barrel	4-barrel
Gross HP	335 hp at 5,000 rpm	335 hp at 5,000 rpm	340 hp at 5,400 rpm	340 hp at 5,400 rpm
Gross Torque	430 ft-lbs at 3,400 rpm	430 ft-lbs at 3,400 rpm	430 ft-lbs at 3,700 rpm	430 ft-lbs at 3,700 rpm
Notes	400 H.O.	400 H.O.	Ram Air IV	Ram Air IV

1969 V-8 Cylinder Heads

Casting Number	17	47	48	62	48	722
Application	350 2-barrel	350 2-barrel	350 H.O.	400 Auto	400 Manual	Ram Air IV
Valve Sizes (interior/exterior)	1.96/1.66	1.96/1.66	2.11/1.77	2.11/1.77	2.11/1.77	2.11/1.77
Rocker Arm Studs	Pressed	Pressed	Threaded	Threaded	Threaded	Threaded
Advertised Compression Ratio	9.2:1	9.2:1	10.5:1	10.75:1	10.75:1	10.75:1
Actual Chamber Volume	83 cc	83 cc	66 cc	77 cc	66 cc	71 cc
Actual Compression Ratio	8.2:1	8.2:1	10.0:1	9.8:1	10.3:1	10.0:1

APPENDIX D: 1967–1969 CAM SPECS

Part Number	Stamped Code	Advertised Intake Duration	Advertised Exhaust Duration	.050-inch Intake Duration	.050-inch Exhaust Duration	Intake Centerline
9782012	D	228	228	172	172	107
9782218	E	244	244	193	193	108
9790826	C	240	240	180	180	106
9792539	E	244	244	193	193	108
9796327	H	260	260	209	209	108
9777254	U	269	277	190	201	113
9779066	N	273	282	198	210	106
9779067	P	273	289	198	213	113
9779068	S	288	302	212	225	113
9785744	H	301	313	225	236	113
9794041	T	308	320	230	240	112

Part Number	Lobe Separation Angle	Valve Overlap	Intake Lobe Lift (inches)	Exhaust Lobe Lift (inches)	Gross Intake Valve Lift at 1.5	Gross Exhaust Valve Lift at 1.5
9782012	107.0	14	.266	.266	.399	.399
9782218	109.0	26	.289	.289	.434	.434
9790826	106.0	28	.266	.266	.399	.399
9792539	109.0	26	.289	.289	.434	.434
9796327	109.0	42	.289	.289	.434	.434
9777254	113.5	47	.249	.271	.374	.407
9779066	111.0	55	.272	.270	.408	.405
9779067	113.0	54	.269	.271	.404	.407
9779068	115.5	63	.272	.271	.408	.407
9785744	115.5	76	.271	.271	.407	.407
9794041	113.5	87	.313	.313	.470*	.470*

* .516-inch lift with 1.65:1 rocker arm

INDEX

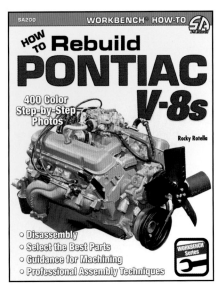
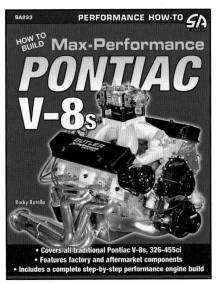
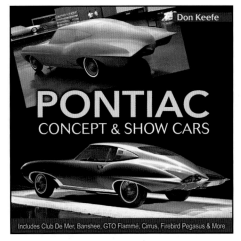
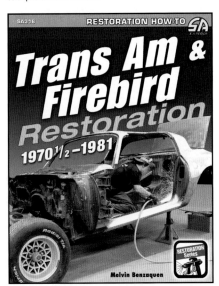